BOY
MEETS
BOY

Other Books by Lawrence Schimel

The Drag Queen of Elfland: Short Stories

Two Hearts Desire:
Gay Couples on Their Love
(*with Michael Lassell*)

The Mammoth Book of Gay Erotica

PoMoSexuals:
Challenging Assumptions About Gender and Sexuality
(*with Carol Queen*)

Switch Hitters:
Lesbians Write Gay Male Erotica and
Gay Men Write Lesbian Erotica
(*with Carol Queen*)

Food for Life and Other Dish

Things Invisible to See:
Gay and Lesbian Tales of Magic Realism

Kosher Meat

The Erotic Writer's Market Guide

BOY
MEETS
BOY

Edited by
Lawrence Schimel

St. Martin's Griffin
NEW YORK

The editor is grateful for permission to print copyrighted material.
These permissions appear on pages 193-94, which constitutes a
continuation of this copyright page.

DESIGN BY JAMES SINCLAIR

ISBN 0-312-20636-4

First St. Martin's Griffin Edition: October 1999

10   9   8   7   6   5   4   3   2   1

To all the boys I have yet to meet . . .

Contents

Introduction

Dating.

Seldom has one word been so confusing, but in that it is sort of like the act itself, which often can seem like an alien, desert terrain where the ground(rules) shift suddenly with the wind.

Dating can mean so many contradictory things:

AVAILABILITY/PROMISCUITY
i.e., "I'm newly single and am dating again, playing the field until I find someone to settle down with."

GETTING TO KNOW SOMEONE
i.e., "We've gone on two dates so far. He's sweet. I think I like him. Tonight he's cooking me dinner. This will be the clincher. Of *course* I'll call you and tell you how it goes. *Tomorrow!*" (wink, wink)

PASSING THE TIME
i.e., "We're just dating, it's not like we're married or anything."

EXCLUSIVITY (OR AT LEAST SOME DEGREE OF
COMMITMENT)
i.e., "He and I had a little 'talk' last night and we're
officially 'dating' now, and not simply regularly sharing spit."

There is confusion, as well, as to what exactly constitutes a "date." Dating can often seem to be the com-
pulsory stuff one does to pass the time before jumping
into the sack, so as not to seem base animals engaging
their (hopefully mutual) lust. Does a meal or some
other nonhorizontal activity have to take place, like going rollerblading in the park or to the movies?

What is the part of dating that is not sexual? Because
men can certainly meet and have sex—even regularly—
without anyone confusing their activity with dating. For
many of us, it is some element of romance that is
necessary—although not all gay men ape the heterosexual "tradition" of going on at least three dates before
having sex. In the gay world it is possible to go on your
first "date" after already having had sex with someone,
depending on where and how two men met. In fact, it
is not uncommon for gay men to sleep together first and
then decide, if they had enough of a good time, whether
to continue seeing each other and begin to get to know
each other better. At which point, one man might show
up on the other's doorstep with flowers—something
bright and cheery like daisies or tulips, but not yet so

serious as a dozen red roses (let's not get ahead of ourselves now; however, a single red rose is acceptable).

There are so many unwritten rules and codes of dating behavior, like the bit about what flowers mean or
imply above. But as gay men, we are quite familiar with
all sorts of elaborately coded gestures and language,
manners of dress and speech. These are by no means
an exhaustive or fail-proof system, but they offer some
clues that we have developed over the years to help men
who may be interested in other men find one another.
As gay men, we have already overthrown many of so-
ciety's imperatives on how we are to behave sexually,
and while we do sometimes use those heterosexual dating "rules" as a sort of crib sheet for how we should act
in a given situation, we have our own traditions and
customs as well. Given the lengths to which we will
sometimes go to fall in love, pursue someone we think
we are in love with, or simply to get laid, there is no
rule too arcane to follow—or so writ in stone it cannot
be broken.

As confusing as all of this dating activity can be, it is
one of the things which drives most gay men. The
search for Mr. Right—or Mr. Right Now—preoccupies
much of our social time. Most gay events or locales are
designed to facilitate meeting one another—that is often a (if not *the*) primary reason for many of the men
who show up there. Even when in a relationship, many
gay men still keep their options open, or are allowed by

their partners to indulge a wandering eye. It all depends on the men involved; an open relationship has saved many a couple I know, while at the same time it has ruined its share of once-happy partners.

Boy Meets Boy tells the stories of some memorable dating moments in the lives of an array of different gay men—some of whom write habitually and others for whom this is their first publication. These are anecdotes by men who are aware that they are dating, or trying to date, or at least thinking about dating and the absurdity it can sometimes take on. Because sometimes, in the heat of the moment—as you'll read shortly—we can say or do things which in hindsight seem risible, incredible, or even beyond the pale.

PART ONE

LOOKING FOR
MR. RIGHT

Sometimes, when we meet someone, there is some sub-liminal signal that goes off that makes us think, "This one has potential." When this happens, we are often more nervous than if we are just tricking without the intention of connecting in some deeper manner—some-times for life, sometimes for a not-insignificant relation-ship that lasts months or years.

I know that I personally find it easier to trick when I am traveling, because I can lose myself in the romance of the moment, really ham it up if I wish, while all the time knowing that I will be leaving in a few days or weeks. There is emotional safety in not needing to com-mit to a relationship, since relationships are something that I—like so many of us—am often gun-shy about. When I meet someone while at home, even what seems a heat-of-the-moment pickup on the streets of Chelsea is overshadowed by the potential of its turning into something more—if there is chemistry between us that lasts beyond the physical.

This first section of *Boy Meets Boy* contains essays about men who are looking for something more than just sex, and some of their various misadventures while stumbling down the often rocky road toward love.

Missing Paul

Marc J. Heft

When I signed on to the Internet, back in 1994—way before it was the mass medium it is today, when it was still controlled largely by propeller heads and a few of us cool people who had slipped under the radar—I had only one purpose in mind: I was going to find me a man on this thing!

And I did. I met all sorts of boys. I met boys who were funny, boys who were weird, boys who were smart, and boys who were dumb as a bag of dirt. Each encounter was carefully orchestrated to insure that it could easily be prolonged if we were enjoying ourselves, or easily be ended if I found my eyes rolling to the back of my head as I slipped into a coma trying to force continued interest in the screen.

Paul and I first talked on-line in the nycm4m (New York City Men for Men) chat room, a place I found myself spending more time in than I cared to admit. In our first chat, we talked about all the things that boys talk about on-line: what movies we had seen, where we worked and lived—your basic run-of-the-airwaves cyberchat. Of course, I looked up Paul's on-line profile to gather as much information as possible to keep the conversation going.

I did ask him my standard icebreaker: "You are not an ax-wielding psycho killer are you?—not that you would tell me anyway" (meaning it as a joke of course, but not entirely). I followed it up with a little smiley face :-) just to let him know that I was kidding and to show him how incredibly clever I could be.

Just when I was beginning to feel fairly comfortable chatting away in relative anonymity, Paul popped the first big question in the predate cyber ritual.

"So, Marc, do you have a gif?"

Oh, no, I thought, *the dreaded gif exchange!*

Now, this is a critical moment in the cyber process. This either catapults you to the next level or stops you dead in your tracks. *What do I say?* I thought. *If I say yes, then I have to send it; if I say no, then he won't know what I look like and may lose interest. What if he is way better looking than me and I feel inferior; what if I am way better looking than him and he stalks me on-line for the rest of my cyber life?*

"Yes, Paul, I do have a gif. Do you?"

"Yes. Wanna swap?"

"Sure," I said with another of those smiley faces to give some levity to the situation and to communicate that I know this is all in good fun. Heeheeheehee . . . no ego damage possible here. Ha! (We both know, of course, that we will be scrutinizing these photos for the slightest imperfection. We'll be on those images like a jeweler looking for flaws in a five-carat ice-blue dia-mond.)

I checked my mailbox and found his E-mail: it was given the acceptably unobnoxious title *mypic*. A lot of boys go for damage control at this point by using file names for their gifs like *badpic.gif*, *cuterinperson.gif*, or *ilookbetternow.gif*.

I began the download. First the black box appeared on my computer screen, and I knew that within seconds my anticipation would be over and I would get to see him for the first time. *Will he be beautiful? Will he be sexy? Will he be hideous, fat, thin, short, tall, blond, dark? Hurry!—I can't wait anymore.* Then the unthink-able happened: I lost my modem connection, and my program shut down. (This, as all Internet users know, is an all-too-common occurrence.)

"Noooooooooo!" A bloodcurdling scream pierced the silence of my apartment. It seemed to be coming out of my mouth. Naturally, I panicked. *Oh, no! What do I do? He will think I saw his picture and was so horrified that I ran screaming into the night. I will have damaged the boy forever. Quick! Sign back on!*

The first try was busy. I double-panicked, then tried again. Success! I heard that glorious modem sound and knew that within seconds my connection would be rees-tablished. I found him again and offered a phrase that I had had occasion to utter many times before (and have

had since): "Sorry, got bumped." I followed it with another smiley face, hoping he was not upset.

His response popped up on my screen: "No prob. Did you get my pic?"

"Yes. I'll download it now. Did you get mine?"

"Yes."

Oh, no, I thought. *That's not good. He didn't comment. He is trying to spare my feelings. He thinks I'm hideous. I am never leaving the house again.*

Then a second line—equally as short but much more fulfilling: "Cute." Followed with a little smiley face of his own. My heart resumed beating.

I downloaded his picture and thought the same thing. *Cute,* I said to myself, and then to him. It was not a good-quality picture but was good enough for me to want to proceed. We had survived the hair-raising picture exchange and were both still here and interested, a miracle.

"So," I asked him as casually as possible, "do you want to talk on the phone?"

Now this is also a critical hurdle, because you are asking the person to get off the computer, where it is entirely possible that he is simultaneously having six conversations identical to—or even better than—the one he's having with you. You are asking him to dismiss all the other contestants—*Thank you for playing. We have some lovely parting gifts for you. Jay, tell them what they've won!*—and choose you as the winner, at least for now.

"Sure," Paul answered. "Give me a few minutes."

Now, I always try at this point to get them to give me their phone number, instead of the other way around. This ensures that if, after the phone conversation, I decide they don't get to participate in the swimsuit competition, we won't ever have to speak again. Remember, I have done this before. I am a professional. Unfortunately, while I was thinking how smart I was about to be, Paul beat me to it.

"Give me your number and I will call you," he said.

Not wanting to sound paranoid or like I had anything to hide, I gave him my number.

The phone rang a mere five minutes later. A good sign, indeed.

"Hello," I said, wanting to sound mysterious, sexy, funny, intelligent, warm, and well-adjusted in just a single word—not an easy task, mind you.

"Hi, Marc. It's Paul."

I thought to myself, *No kidding? I was expecting it to be Brad Pitt at two-thirty in the morning, calling to invite me over for a pajama party!*

I said something dorky like, "I know. I recognize your voice from the computer," which I followed with even dorkier nervous laughter. We talked for a few minutes. *Hey, this doesn't suck,* I found myself thinking, which is always a surprise.

It turned out Paul lives in the East Village and is a writer. At the very moment he revealed this information to me, I began planning our lives together.

"So," I blurted out, taking control of the situation, "wanna meet?"

"It's almost three in the morning."

"Not *now*." (I am trying not to appear shocked that he would think I might actually leave my house at this hour to meet a complete and total stranger—something I would never do, no matter how tempting it might be.)

We agreed to meet the next afternoon for coffee.

Now, Paul may have beaten me to the phone number thing, but I was certainly not going to make the same mistake twice. I quickly suggested a location that was my standard meeting place for all Internet encounters: it's close to my house, and they don't serve anything that takes more than five minutes to eat. At least I don't have to travel to be disappointed, and I don't have to suffer through a multiple-course dinner.

I told him to sit on the outdoor bench to the right of the entrance and that I would meet him at *exactly* five o'clock.

I managed to get his phone number *just in case something comes up*.

At four o'clock the next afternoon I had to run home and drop off the Bed, Bath & Beyond bags before my date. It would be way too stereotypical to bring them. I mean, I might as well have had a Judy Garland album in one hand and a bouquet of calla lilies in the other! By the time I got back to my apartment, I realized I had a scant twenty minutes to make myself gorgeous—not enough time. I decided to just go for nonrepulsive.

Of course, my head was giving me the usual instructions: *Don't talk too much. Let him say something once in a while. Look interested and intelligent, warm and caring, funny and . . . Yeah, yeah, yeah. Shut up. I know the drill.*

As I crossed Christopher Street, I glanced over to the coffee bar. There on the bench was Paul, right on time. I looked over and thought, *He doesn't look exactly like his picture,* but then again they never do. He wasn't bad, though. I didn't have that nauseous feeling when I saw him, and my Flee Now instinct was nowhere to be found.

"Hi, Paul," I said in my cheery, emotionally available voice.

"Hi," he replied in a slightly flat, lifeless tone.

"How are you?"

"Good," he responded somewhat uncomfortably. "How are you?"

"Fine, thanks. Great day, isn't it? Beautiful weather."

Oh no, I remember thinking, *fifteen seconds into the date and we're already talking about the weather. This is not a good sign. Not to worry, I reassured myself, I am the professional. I will take control.*

And so I did. I started talking a mile a minute. At one point I almost passed out from lack of oxygen—*Breathe, Marc. Breathe!* I decided I needed to give him a chance to speak.

After a few minutes of painful silence, it was obvious that this strategy was not going to work. I started to ask him direct questions in the hopes of stimulating some semblance of conversation.

Apparently seeing through my strategy, Paul responded to each question with a one-word answer.

Now, I have seen this many times before. It is known as MIPP, or Meeting-in-Person Paralysis, and it happens to approximately one in five boys on Internet dates, according to my extensive data. It can pass, and you move forward—or it doesn't, and you remember why you picked this coffee bar in the first place.

After about five minutes with Paul, I noticed that this was not just MIPP, but that he evidently had a serious personality disorder or perhaps he hadn't quite got his lithium/Prozac combination down right. As I said, it has happened before, but I decided to give him a bit more time, since he had such potential on-line and on the phone. I stood up to go inside and asked Paul if he would like something.

"No," he responded. "I'm fine, thanks."

What I wanted to say was: "I can see that, you inconsiderate freak. You obviously did not feel it was necessary to wait for me to order coffee."

I decided, however, that this might have sounded rude, and besides, he could still stab me from behind.

Once inside, I ordered a cup of tea, nothing to eat, being fairly certain that I would need to pull the rip cord any minute and bail. Food would just hinder my getaway. Finally, the nose-ringed, attitude-ridden, tip-expecting serving shrew handed me my tea, but it was way too hot. It needed some cooling-down time. Hhmmmm, this could be a problem. I asked the charming young lady to give me an ice cube. You would have thought I'd asked her to paint my apartment from the annoyed look she gave me. I scanned the room while waiting for the morsel of ice that would help quicken my escape.

I looked around the crowd and wondered how these people had met and if any of them were here doing the same two-step of death as Prozac Patty and me. I took my tea with ice, not to be mistaken for ice tea, and rejoined Paul on our bench.

We had a few more minutes of excruciatingly dull conversation while I tried to finish my tea without burning the skin off my tongue. There was another thing that I noticed after a few more minutes of sitting and talking with Paul: he is one of those people who avoids direct eye contact at all costs. This is a most annoying character trait as far as I am concerned. I was really getting the signal loud and clear: this child was s-t-r-a-n-g-e.

We were at Defcon Four, and I needed to get out of this situation immediately, if not sooner. This boy was giving me the heebies. This is the kind of person who keeps a shoe box full of beheaded Barbie dolls under his bed and refers to them as his "girls."

Too bad— he was kinda normal and funny on the phone. I made my move. I stood up, said it was nice meeting him but that I needed to be on my way. I informed him that I had dinner plans. I shook his soggy, moist, fishlike hand and was gone before he knew what hit him.

I was indeed a professional at this. But my timing, like my intuition, was off a bit. The date had lasted twenty-five minutes, five minutes longer than usual when they are that much fun. I blamed it on the temperature of the tea.

All in all I had managed to depart relatively emotionally unharmed. I was not rude or unpleasant, which I would never be (unless absolutely necessary), but I did not lead Paul to believe that we would *ever* see each other again. I proceeded to meet my friend for dinner, a friend I had met on-line, and regaled him with my tale of the latest Internet debacle.

When I got home, I found three messages on my answering machine. The first was from my mother, asking how my weekend was and asking me to call her when I had a moment in my busy schedule, which half made me smile and half made me want to delete the message immediately. The second was from a friend asking if I wanted to see a movie the following evening. (*Absolutely.*) The third message, much to my dismay, was from Paul. It went something like this:

"Hi, Marc, this is Paul. I waited for you at the coffee bar this afternoon, but you never showed up. Oh, well, maybe something happened. Call me if you want to re-schedule. Bye."

I stared blankly at the answering machine until it hit me like a ton of bricks, like one of those flashback sequences in a movie when all the pieces suddenly fit together. Paul never actually said my name the entire time we were sitting there together, he'd avoided making eye contact with me, and he was nothing like the guy I had spoken to the night before on the phone. There was, of course, a good reason for these things: the horror of this encounter was that the guy on the bench that afternoon was not Paul. I dialed his number.

"Hi, Paul. It's Marc."

"Oh. Hi, Marc," he replied in a tone that was perfectly acceptable from someone who thought he had been blown off by a stranger. I then started to tell him what happened. At one point he interrupted me and said, "Did you ask the girl behind the counter for ice for your tea?"

"Yes, yes, that was me," I answered with complete

relief, realizing now that he would know I was telling the truth and had not callously failed to show up for our date.

"Well, who the hell was that guy you were talking to?"

"I have absolutely no idea."

"Then why were you talking to him?"

"Because he was sitting on our bench, and I mistook him for you."

I asked Paul why, if he had recognized me from my photo, he didn't say hello or ask if it was me.

He said that he thought it was me, but he wasn't sure. When he saw that I was with someone else, he assumed it wasn't me. He said that he could not sit at our prearranged bench because when he arrived, the fake Paul was already sitting on it, so he sat inside instead.

The hilarious absurdity of the situation hit me, and I started to laugh. I laughed really, really hard—until tears were streaming down my face. All of a sudden it dawned on me that there was only silence on the other end of the phone.

"Paul," I asked, "are you still there?"

"Yup."

"Don't you think that this is absolutely hilarious?"

"No, not really."

"You don't?" I said in disbelief.

"No."

16

Well, that one simple statement probably saved me weeks of dating before I found out that he was not the boy for me. If something like that just didn't hit him right smack in the funny bone, then I am pretty certain that there was no future for us.

I apologized to him for the mix-up, and he said that it was okay. I wished him well, and he did the same. We said our good-nights, both knowing that our meeting was just not meant to be.

I walked upstairs and looked into the den at my computer. We glared at each other for a moment. I smiled and thought, *What if he is on there tonight and I miss him?*

I sat down, signed on, and waited impatiently. Finally came that oh-so-familiar automated voice: "Welcome. You've got mail."

I'll read it later, I thought to myself. *I've got a chat room to get to.*

17

Skin Deep

Patrick Barnes

"You have a face I could wake up to for the rest of my life."

Which was something I had never heard before. Particularly not at a bar like the Spike, populated by rough-talking, tough-looking guys in leather vests who rested their bottles of Bud Light on their guts and called everyone "boy" as they discussed Deborah Voigt as Isolde or Ann Reinking as Roxie Hart. Not that I mind any of those things, but having just escaped a conversation on how to dress one's slave when one takes him to the Whitney Biennial, hearing someone softly tell me that I had a face he could wake up to, etc., turned me instantly to butter.

Butter that congealed the moment I turned and saw him who told me.

I want to make clear to you, right now, before you evaluate my ego, that *I am not a model*. I am no beauty. Men don't rave about my captivating visage. I have launched no ships. I *do*, when tipping my face down and looking up from under my eyebrows, possess an understated cuteness, but that's as far as it goes. And I have a good butt. The guys who go for me are the ones who go for the dorky-sweet type—you know what I mean?

But this guy was ugly. Gasp ugly. Choke ugly. Have you ever turned, on the street or in a store, and seen a face that looked like it had been taken apart and then put back together by something that just didn't get the concept of what a face is? I did that night. I saw a prospect of angles and curves and bumps and ridges, none of which made any sense. I admit it, I stared. It was all wrong. Why was that nose so much bigger on the left than on the right? Why was that right nostril so much larger than the left? Why was that left eye a full inch higher than the right? Were those ears? Which direction was the chin pointing? Was a dermabrasion really anything more than an existential suggestion?

"Hi," he said, smiling, and I heard the mirrors of my mind crack. How many teeth? Pointing in how many compass bearings?

"Hi," I managed, "that's a very good line."

"I mean it, too. You're so handsome. Do you know that?"

I leaned away. "That's a nice thought, but stop it. Does that work for you often?"

He leaned in. "You're the first person I've ever said it to." I thought, *Oh my God, he's going to touch me. He's going to try to kiss me.* I was in a panicked quandary; my rules of conduct forbid outright rudeness to anyone in a bar scene, but I'd never been in this sort of pinch

19

before. What should I do? Exhale forcefully and pray that my breath was bad? Try to fart? Throw up?

Salvation strolled along in the form of my best friend, Rob. "Oh!" I chirped in a kind of Lily Pons imitation. "Here comes my best friend, Rob! *Rob!* How *nice* to see you!" "How *nice* to see you" was the cunningly devised code Rob and I had worked out to mean *"Help get me out of this at once."*

Rob belted out "Hi!" in his Appalachian twang while he picked me up and squeezed me. "Who's the stud? Hi! I'm his best friend in the *whole wide world,* and I'm taking him for a walk round the bar. See you later, stud!" He grabbed my wrist and pulled. Over my shoulder, I called, "See you later," then turned back, whispering, "I can *not* thank you enough for that."

Rob pulled me into a dark corner. "That one," he muttered, "could tree a ghost. What was going on there?"

"Oh, another man devastated by my beauty. Wanted to buy me a drink. I thought he was going to try to kiss me for a second there."

"Don't *even* . . ." Rob gagged. "Come on, let's go have fun. I don't have to be home to Greg for hours."

It was a dry night. Nothing, to quote Wilde, to be had even for ready money. Rob left at one-thirty; I, as a single man, stayed to closing, then went to collect my jacket at the coat check.

20

"Ticket," grunted Coat Check Daddy. I searched my pockets. I searched again.

"I think I lost it. But I remember the number. It was fifty-three, and it's a black leather bomber jacket."

"Ohhhhhhh? A black leather bomber jacket? Well," sniffed Pissy Pierced Garment Goddess, "*that* shouldn't be hard to find." He withdrew into the recesses of his hole, emerging smugly a few moments later. "I guess someone found your little ticket, number fifty-three, because it's right here, and your jacket has already been claimed. Sorry! Next." He reached out to the man in cop drag behind me. I'd had little enough to drink to realize that a confrontation would get me nowhere. But it wasn't until I exited the bar that I realized that my keys were in the pocket of that jacket.

"Oh, nooooooooooooooooooo!" I wailed, collapsing to the sidewalk.

This may sound a bit extreme or overly dramatic, but I live in a building with no doorman, no live-in super, and no friendly neighbors. Even if I could have gotten buzzed in at the downstairs door, I had no way of getting into my own apartment until the next day, when I could call the landlord's office to get a duplicate key. And calling a friend to crash, at 4 A.M., although not impossible, isn't something that occurs readily to someone well brought up. Like me.

"Are you okay?" I heard. I looked up, hoping against

hope for an endless two seconds before being dashed to an even lower, colder circle of hell than the one I'd just occupied.

It was Ugly Face.

All right, I went back to his place. He was nice and lived only three blocks away and said that we could just sleep, that I could have the couch if I wanted. It was a really nice place, and I'm not the couch type, and the bed was king-sized, so I figured that I could take care of myself. He came out of his bathroom in white briefs and a T-shirt, suddenly shy and hesitant.

"I like to listen to music while I fall asleep, do you mind?"

I yawned. "Not at all. Whatever."

"Do you know Piazzolla?"

"Is he related to Émile Zola?"

"Ummmm . . . no. The whole last name is Piazzolla. Astor Piazzolla. Tangos."

"Whatever, like I said."

Do you know Piazzolla? I listen to it all the time now. It has a way of getting into your head for life. The first piece that he put on that night began with soft piano, floating, floating, then was joined by a single violin, quietly sad. The two instruments were separate, floating and sad, until they suddenly seemed to be floating and sad together, dancing with one another. He turned out the light and stood across the room for a minute, then slowly pulled off his T-shirt and slid his briefs down to the floor and walked over to the bed, lying down on top of the covers. In the vague light that squeezed between the blinds, his skin looked so white. As if it never saw the light of day. Like the tangos, his body had unexpected curves and upheavals, whorls and eddies, crescendos and decrescendos. He lay still beside me; I was under the covers in my shirt and boxers. I was captivated by the hour and the music and the way his body seemed a part of both. I put my hand on the lowest part of his back that wasn't yet his butt, one of my favorite parts of a man's body. His skin was the softness of the piano, his sigh was the sadness of the violin. I closed my eyes and thought of Spain. The rest of the night was a long, long, soft, thick, hot dance.

And in the morning, there was still that *face*.

He had a house in a quiet suburb of New Jersey. I went out a few times, helped him in the garden. Cooked. We both read *D.V.*, the memoirs of Diana Vreeland, one weekend, and gave one another book reports, with visual aids. He made some good sock puppets for his.

We went to the opera, *Billy Budd*, which we enjoyed, but I was nervous we might run into someone I knew, who would make fun of my ugly date the next time we spoke. I tried to keep our time together private, or, if

23

we did go out, I chose remote movie theaters or restaurants.

One night, as we strolled among the spindly trees and puffy boys of Chelsea's Eighth Avenue, I spotted my friends Buddy and Bart coming toward us, about a block away. Buddy and Bart, successful and handsome lovers, are a less cartoony Rod Jackson and Bob Paris. Or is it Bob Jackson and Rod Paris? Whichever. My beautiful friends.

"Let's go down this street." I pulled him to the right suddenly. "I want to have a drink at that bar, Sturgeon. My friend Rob says it's fun."

"Well, okay." He laughed. "If that's what you want. But you could just have a drink at dinner, you know."

Wait, I thought. Maybe Buddy and Bart are going to Sturgeon. They're fabulous, it's fabulous . . .

I pulled him in another direction. "You're right," I declared. "I could have a drink at dinner, but, you know what, we're so close to A Different Light, let's go browse there for a few minutes."

"You want to go to a bookstore now? But I'm hungry —aw, okay."

But, I considered, Buddy is in publishing. Maybe they're going there, not Sturgeon. Wait! Buddy's in recovery, he wouldn't go to Sturgeon anyway!

I wheeled us around again. "No, I don't need any

24

books, I need a drink, let's go to Sturgeon. Always follow the first impulse, right?"

He stared at me, then blew up with laughter. Some people, when they laugh, get cuter. But not him. His laughter made one eye open much wider than the other, and his mouth went all to one side and his teeth seemed to protrude even more, and . . . well, he laughed. "You are truly spontaneous, I can say that. And fun to be with. I'll go anywhere with you."

I thought, for a brief moment, that he was going to add, "And I love you." But he didn't.

Guess what? He dumped me. That's right. Maybe someone else would've seen it coming. I didn't. I enjoyed spending time with him, dreaded having my friends meet him, and expected I'd have to say, sometime, probably just before Halloween, "I think this isn't working out as well as it should be." And then one night in the second week of September, over dinner at a basement bistro on the Lower East Side, he said suddenly and softly, "This isn't working out as well as it should be."

He didn't even have the grace to blame himself. He felt I was too distant and withholding. That I was fun, but unreliable, that he felt he couldn't depend on me. He wanted someone duller and more predictable, someone to be comfortable with.

I didn't put up a fight. I knew that I would've dumped

25

him eventually anyway. But I missed him something terrible for the next few months. Him and that Piazzolla music.

And I suppose no one will ever again say, "You have a face that I could wake up to for the rest of my life."

The Right Man

by Jameson Currier

In the last three months I have had over thirty dates—more, I think, than perhaps the total I have had in the previous eleven years I have been gay. In this short period I have dated men younger, older, and the same age as I. I have dated blonds, brunets, a redhead, and a few who have been balding. One, I remember, wore his hair in a ponytail. Another had a body so astounding it made me nervous to sit near him. And for the most part I have met these men on neutral territory, neither his place nor mine, our rendezvous occurring outside restaurants, theaters, bars, bookstores, and once, a grocery store.

And these dates have been simple activities: a drink, maybe dinner, sometimes something athletic—bowling, biking, just walking around town, or hiking through a park. I have met these men through a variety of methods: a friend's introduction, a personal ad, a dating service, a social organization, and yes, even at a bar. As one of my friends says, I am on the prowl. But as I carefully explain, these dates are not arranged or intended as sexual encounters. These days, I am more interested in a permanent relationship. In fact, these

Jameson Currier

dates have served other purposes for me as well: a way
of getting over a prior unfulfilling relationship, a way of
meeting new friends, a way of discovering and exploring
the area around my new home, and yes, possibly, a way
of finding that special someone, the right man for me.

Who is the right man? Does he exist? In the last three
months I have had a brief affair with a younger man in
Philadelphia, a slightly longer one with an older gentleman who owned a farm near the Delaware River, and a
much shorter one with a man whose biggest passion was
belonging to a gay water polo team. Each man was intelligent and attractive; each possessed a personality
that both interested and intrigued me enough to want
to see him again. And each possessed the right sexual
chemistry. But with each, something was also wrong or
missing. On some level there wasn't a connection or
need or spark between us. Each presented me with a
major problem for which I could find neither a solution,
an adjustment, nor an arrangement. And each one I let
end in its own way, drifting politely apart through either
neglect or avoidance. Each one hurt when it was over.
And every time, I managed to pick myself up, go out,
and find another date.

One friend of mine thinks I'm too particular. I tell
him I don't think I'm particular at all, I only expect the
same qualities in my dates that I enjoy in my friends.
Another friend thinks I place too much emphasis on
looks. He thinks I'm shallow and insincere when I tell

28

him that the chemistry wasn't right with someone I just met. And I tell him that I expect that attraction to be a part of any relationship I undertake, though I am quick to add I have no particular type or demand for any certain physical requirements. For me he can be tall or short, blond or brunet. He can be muscular or lean or smooth or hairy or even overweight. I know this as a fact; I have fallen for a variety of men. So, physically, I know the right man for me exists; I see him all the time—at the beach, at the bar, at the gym, on the street. I'm not talking about a man so beautiful and handsome and flawless that he approaches and becomes a fantasy or ideal or god. Even if I were to meet such a man, he might still not be the right one for me. All I ask is that the package be right. And the right package includes the right attraction, in both directions, for both me and him.

And as I tell my friend, chemistry implies much more than just physical aspects. It includes a combination of other qualities and traits—background, education, personality, intelligence—and encompasses not just similarities but a mixture of differences as well. And as I explain further, I don't expect to find someone perfect; the right relationship, I believe, includes a certain amount of give-and-take, complements and compromises. Finding the right man means a lot more than being at the right place at the right time with the right attitude. Theoretically, I cannot describe the right man for me. I can't really supply a list of right or wrong, or good or bad qualities.

This realization slapped me in the face one day last week when my friend Jon called me at work. Jon, a man my age and height with a similar educational background and professional and avocational interests, had recently ended a seven-year monogamous gay relationship. His ex-lover had moved out of the apartment, and now Jon was ready to start dating again. But he did not feel comfortable in a gay bar and was unaware of what he should do to meet the right man. So he turned to many resources I had also used: friends of friends, personal ads, a gay religious organization. But each had left him unsatisfied. Now he was ready to try a dating service. His frantic call that day was for help in filling out the application form.

Here, in black and white, in words, phrases, sentences, and questions, he was asked to list the qualities of the men he would like to meet as well as to rate his own characteristics, both in temperament and looks. As he read the questions to me over the phone and we discussed each of his decisions and answers, I was struck by the absurdity of it all. How could you choose between a man who acts more from his thoughts than one who acts from his feelings? What if you wanted someone who was both imaginative and realistic, which this questionnaire didn't allow. What if, as in my case, you didn't care if he was clean shaven or had a mustache or a beard. What if the man who is perfect for you, according to this questionnaire, prefers someone who is taller? What if the only man you're right for is a deaf and dumb, hunchbacked midget? I understood my friend's dismay when I told him I thought he was a man who is ruled more by his head than by his heart; but that's what friends are for, they keep you honest and grounded. Before hanging up, I gave him some advice, the same advice, in fact, he had given me shortly after a relationship I had been both serious about and committed to had faltered. "It takes time," I said. "You just have to keep trying."

So who is the right man for my friend? Who is the right one for me? What is it I want or expect or need? A therapist once told me I'm searching for a father figure. But for her, that was an easy concept to grasp. Yes, in many ways I am initially drawn to men who seem to be the fatherly type. But that's not the type of relationship I want. What I want in life is what most people are searching for: a nice home, self-satisfaction from career, and a chance to share my time with someone. And that someone I expect to be attentive and caring, loving and loyal, masculine, and well-grounded with morals and ethics: a man who brings out those qualities in me and who regards me as an equal in all aspects of the relationship. Someone preferably close to my age, someone within the same generation. I am looking for someone honest and communicative and committed, not someone who'll "give it a try and see how it turns out." As for dating, it's not so much the activity but the person I'm sharing time with that matters.

So what exactly was wrong with all these dates? Nothing specific; they were all sincere and genuinely nice guys. My friend Martin thinks I put too much emphasis on first impressions. He constantly reassures me that it took him six months of dating his lover, Larry, before he fell in love. In many ways I know there is something right in what he says. And I keep reminding him that the last man I fell in love with certainly fit into that pattern. So I'm realistic enough not to expect a white knight to sweep me off my feet. Yet perhaps I'm sometimes too rational in following my instincts, never allowing a second date to happen with someone who is interested in me.

There's nothing more I want right now in my life than to be in a relationship. But it's not a crime to be single. As I tell one friend, I would rather spend my life alone than spend it with the wrong person. But I go out on dates and keep looking for Mr. Right. I don't know what it will be that will make me fall in love. All I can answer is that I keep trying and looking and I'll know what it is when it happens. And all I can hope is that I, too, am the right man for him.

The Art of Shining Boots

Aubrey Hart Sparks

"I hate dating," I said, but Tom wasn't listening. His eyes weren't following a big blond who was making the rounds of the bar, flirting with everyone. Suddenly, Tom dismissed the blond as a possibility, saying something derogatory about his promiscuous manner. Tom's attention transferred to another man, a lone wolf, standing against the wall with a bottle of beer in his hand. Their eyes met and the guy almost smiled.

"You're a cynic," Tom said to me.

"And you're a romantic."

Tom smiled, still watching the man against the wall. He took hunting seriously and seldom went home with anyone. Tom preferred to talk, and if his criteria for the perfect man were met, he would make a date to meet for dinner or a movie or in some other neutral territory. Tom was looking for love and I was after something else.

"See the man against the wall?" he asked, trying to look as if he weren't looking, pointing to him without pointing.

"Married," I replied, having had prior experience. "He's here looking for a date because his husband will

33

not piss on him." As expected, Tom's attention shifted to someone else.

Watching Tom and knowing the eventual outcome, I thought the whole thing seemed far too complex and too unrealistic for anything to come of it, even a storybook ending. In ten years, I had seen only one marathon man make it to a second date with Tom, the others swept away like ash.

I had hoped that if nothing else, the rituals of dating and then marriage would help me through, and I was angry when these illusions were proved false. Perhaps I am a cynic, but I long ago lost my faith in love, along with the Easter Bunny, Santa Claus, Jesus, patriotism, and other childhood toys. With each new illusion shattered, there was a deeper abyss into which I had to fall. Letting go of the fantasy of love and my belief that it could make me happy was the most painful. Sometimes I envy Tom, for whom everything is so clear, and I know that likewise there are situations where Tom wishes he were me.

Tom was saying something, but I wasn't listening. I could feel a speech coming on, and I hate ranting about love, especially on a Friday night. I usually end up feeling foolish. What good is philosophy when you are drinking your third beer and the men who are looking for a good time are just starting to arrive? It's just that I wish Tom could realize that my choices are as important to me and just as well thought-out as his are to him. This is the painful point of our relationship.

My goal is to be ready and awake for the moments so unique that they defy and yet define the fantasy that I will be masturbating to later. It's a circle: fantasy, its destruction, the realization of reality, then finally the memory of the fantasy. It drives me crazy, which is why I don't date. Sadly, when I express this out loud, it usually makes me laugh. Perhaps this is among the things that need to remain silent and can only be expressed by action or deed. What good is a theory about relationships if that's all it remains, never sees the light of day?

As if to prove my point, a boy appeared out of nowhere, armed with the best pickup line of my life. There was a lull in the conversation with Tom, and I had not noticed the boy standing next to me, waiting for my attention. In the boy's simple question, all the pain that comes from the destruction of fantasy became worth it as I was able to hear him without the usual filters and expectations that would have made it impossible to recognize his request. He never told me his name and I never told him mine. The formality of names was irrelevant.

"Sir!" he said in perfect military style. "I believe that I have scuffed your boot, sir! Is there anything I can do to rectify the situation? Sir!"

Of course I had to say no. Anything less would have taken the wind out of his sails and would have made us both seem slightly foolish in our leathers and attitudes.

He dropped to his knees, knowing that I had actually meant yes.

"Please, sir, let me try." The crotch of his tight jeans was almost touching the toe of my boot. His hands were behind his back and his pleading eyes were staring up at me. My cock was filling the crotch of my jeans, inches in front of the boy's face.

I stretched out my hand and ran the end of my index finger across the pout of his lip, slipping into his mouth until I found the tip of his tongue.

He wanted to shine my boots. I finished my beer and made a date for lunch with Tom while the boy sucked on my fingers, showing off his abilities to suck cock for those who cared to watch. I enjoyed making the boy wonder if I was going to give him a chance or abandon him to the bar. Tom was becoming uncomfortable. His eyes avoided the boy on the floor and could not look at the bulge in my pants. I finished the conversation with Tom, who went to get another beer and disappeared into the crowd, and turned my attention back to the boy on the floor. To my surprise, there actually was a scuff on my boot.

Romantic/Sexual Agenda

D. Travers Scott

6:17 P.M. FRIDAY

I. MYSELF
  A. GAY
  B. SINGLE, UNINVOLVED

II. EVENT: Eighteenth birthday party for my roommate, Collin. The party is being held down on the third floor of the dorm, as the jocks down there are willing to devote their entire hall space to a party—any party (unlike our science compatriots here on Hermann King Center Residence Hall, 5th floor). Given the designation of the jocks' environment as ground zero, the evening's primary prospect is:
  A. JAY: downstairs neighbor.
    1. GAY
      a) Thinks his floormates and teammates don't know, presenting one obstacle—he may be less willing to openly flirt. Closetedness may make him too subtle; I may miss any signs or flirtatious overtures. It may become necessary

to get him away from the crowd (e.g., into the inner stairwell or up into Collin's and my room [necessitating removal/absence of Collin]).

b) Since Jay's homosexuality is not acknowledged between him and his peers, in all likelihood those who may be aware of my sexual orientation (such as his roommate, who sucked me off in the third-floor PolySci men's room during orientation) have not mentioned it to him. If he does not yet know I'm gay, the whole problem of discreetly broaching the general subject arises.

2. **SINGLE:** may be seeing someone.
   a) Works at eastside bar I happen to know is Lobo, a gay bar. Must meet tons of cute guys and get asked out constantly.
   b) Roommate suspects he had a date last Sunday night.

3. **RELATIONSHIP:** friendly and neighborly thus far.
   a) Helped Collin and me move our computers up the inner stairwell when the elevator was inactive.
   b) Gave me directions to financial-aid office

using Commons' men's room as a directional landmark.

c) Invited Collin and me downstairs to dinner last Sunday night.

   (1) Very hospitable; provided lots of microwave Velveeta Shells 'n' Cheese and beer.

   (2) However, he had to "go to work" soon after we got there, said he had to pick up his check. He took some beer with him, which is why his roommate suspected he really had a date. I was disappointed, specifically having hoped to connect with him that night.

d) Brief visit down on their floor this afternoon.

   (1) Very outgoing, anxious to let us know he would be at this evening's party.

   (2) Mentioned his floor's huge maintenance room and took me to see it. Made lots of small talk. Nice time alone with the brooms and air filters, getting familiar with each other, but nothing happened.

4. QUALITIES

a) Attractive but not International Male gorgeous (thereby increasing my chances).

b) Fairly well built, but his friendliness overrides my intimidation by such.

c) Not stupid, but we haven't had a chance to really talk in depth about anything.

d) Highly recommended as a nice guy by roommate (they've had no sexual contact or even discussion).

5. PLANS

a) Establish I am gay through casual conversation topics such as sarcastic comments toward Mel Gibson "male-bonding" films, recent Lesbian Avenger demonstration on campus, compare and contrast *Priscilla* . . . v. *To Wong Foo* . . . , etc. (99% probability).

b) Get him to admit he is gay, again through casual conversation, e.g., "Are you reading any E. M. Forster in British Lit?" (75% probability).

c) Make innocuous physical contact under the guise of drunk affection: punching, slapping, arm around neck, etc. (90% probability).

d) Increase intimacy by talking alone in stairwell, bedroom, or leaving party to go out for coffee (50% probability).

e) Kiss—contingent upon all of the above and general atmosphere (15% probability).

f) Sex—contingent upon all of the above as well as careful consumption of alcohol and/or

other mood-enhancing substances (stimula-
tion without impairment—5% probability).

B. MITCH: friend from Calc. class.

1. GAY

2. APPEARS UNATTACHED

3. RELATIONSHIP THUS FAR

a) Seen at LesBiGay Student Union meeting.

b) Introduction and very amiable conversation
at Alicia's party last week.

4. QUALITIES

a) Knockout appearance, which is why I didn't
originally try to speak with him. I assume he's
hit on constantly (he arrived at Alicia's with a
whole group of gays) and I didn't want to appear predatory.

b) Shy but very friendly, up-front, unaffected,
very promising. Architecture student. Not
flamey, but why did he arrive with all those
gays?

5. PLANS: Don't know if he'll be here tonight.
I haven't seen him since Alicia's party, but I
invited several of the gays he was with that
night. If he shows up, follow same procedure
as with Jay (minus the gay-establishment
conversation). Open sexuality may facilitate
flirtation, or embarrass and inhibit, requiring
greater finesse.

41

C. GENE: friend of Alicia's.

1. GAY

2. SINGLE, UNINVOLVED

3. RELATIONSHIP THUS FAR

a) We are described by Alicia and Collin as "a perfect match."

b) The four of us met for coffee last week. Fun time, but no major connection occurred.

c) Alicia's party:

(1) He looked around for me immediately upon his arrival.

(2) We were both prodded by friends to hang out together.

(3) We hung out together and talked a great deal about a variety of subjects.

(4) He became irritable and left without saying good-bye to me.

(5) Alicia said that he really does like me and is interested but was just in a bad mood so I should keep in pursuit.

4. QUALITIES

a) Funny, positive personality, semi-established professionally, older (27) and unfortunately has kind of a hang-up about that.

b) Pleasant appearance, although not knock-out.

D. TIM: friend from old job doing environmental canvassing. Attraction vibes in past, but nothing major for a long time. I haven't called him about the party yet, but possibly will later.

E. ROB: ex-boyfriend from high school. Broke up over four months ago, and although sexual tension does arise on occasion, I'm not interested in reviving anything.

F. BRIAN: another jock downstairs. He's straight but totally hot and I could easily see myself doing something drunk and stupid.

LIVE UPDATES FROM PARTY, TRANSCRIBED FROM NOTES MADE ON PORTABLE TAPE RECORDER

1. I haven't really talked to Jay much because I've been, like, walking around doing the party thing and seeing everyone here. He's holding a baby right now that some woman brought with her, so that's sweet and kind of interesting—a topic of conversation or something. . . . There's nothing else really to report other than I'm sad because a section of the inner stairwell railing just collapsed from all the people standing on it with the keg, and now the downstairs jocks probably won't be

able to throw any more parties down here. Shit. Anyway, that's all that's really going on, on the sex/ romance front. Nothing really. No sign of Mitch or Gene.

2. Okay, so it's about 11:53; it's not that late. Mitch is nowhere to be found and Alicia just told me Gene had to leave town this weekend, but he's still interested in me, but that doesn't help me to-night. *Anyway,* the good news is I finally had a talk alone with Jay, but I don't remember what we talked about. Oh, somehow he was talking about his job and I said, "Oh, yeah, that's not one of my favorite places," and he got real secretive and, like, you know, "How'd you find out where I work?" And I said from his roommate and he said something like "Don't worry" or "Don't. . ."—I don't know, something weird. He asked me if I was into blow and I thought he meant jobs, but he was referring to cocaine, which I'm not, really, and I've never done before 'cause I figured it was a good place to draw the line but . . . He invited me to hang around after the party and do some, which I don't really want to do, but it would be a way to hang with him, which I would be more than happy to do. So we at least had kind of a connection and that's nice, but I don't know about this cocaine thing. . . .

44

3. Okay, it's—12:49. . . . Quite a while ago Jay invited me down to his dorm room to meet some people and it was basically this coke party going on. He introduced me, then kind of wandered off into a group at the back of the room. The coke was all laid out on a mirror on one of the beds, but no one offered me any and I didn't want to be rude and just take some, so I didn't do any. Nothing really happened, but it was nice of Jay to invite me down. . . . Oh, it turns out the baby is the daughter of the dealer who's supplying all the coke tonight, which is kinda gross, bringing his kid and all. Anyway, when I left, Jay was all kind of like "Come down again later" and we kinda, like, you know, squeezed arms and were kind of physically affectionate, so that seems . . . faintly hopeful. His roommate was glaring at me from across the room.

4. I don't want to say too much right now. Flirting with Brian a lot, which is weird and surprising because he's kind of flirting back. Rob thought I slept with him, and when he found out I hadn't, he bet me like twenty bucks he could sleep with him before I could. But Rob had some trauma earlier tonight with that girl he's dating now, and he was telling me about it at the same time he's betting money on bagging Brian. I don't know, for some

reason I felt really upset and sad about Rob all of a sudden and had to leave, so I walked in here, the bathroom on my floor, and locked the outer door with a doorstop I snagged from the maintenance room on Jay's floor. I'm waiting for everything to die down and mellow so I can go back downstairs and see what Jay's up to. I don't want to say anything else.

5. Rob is gone. Collin is passed out. Brian is in bed with Alicia. Mitch never showed and I never called Tim. Almost everyone's left the party. It's 2:37. Went downstairs a little while ago and Jay said he was just getting ready to come up here to my and Collin's room, so, you know, maybe he will later on when things mellow out. There's still a few people downstairs.

CONTINUATION: AGENDA FOR FOLLOWING WEDNESDAY

I. Update on relationship with Jay: After everyone left the party, Jay and friend Cheryl came upstairs and had a long talk with me. Jay brought out coke; he and Cheryl did some; I did a line. Cheryl left; Jay and I continued talking for quite a while. He told me about the foster homes he grew up in, one of his brothers being sexually abused, and his being blackmailed by another guy on his high school football team. We bonded. We went downstairs to his room. Talked more there after locking out roommate. Jay showed me his photo scrapbook. Knees touched. Knees remained touching. Leaned in closer under auspices of peering at photographs. Hair brushed, foreheads touched. Pressed face against his. Jay kissed my forehead, eyebrow, nose, mouth. Extensive, forceful tongue-probing on both our parts. Scrapbook fell to floor and he pushed me down onto bed. Tight fit on foldout dormitory twin mattress. Bumped heads and shoulders repeatedly against cement-block walls. His mouth tasted like beer and sweat. He pulled my shirt off, sucked my nipples, licked my armpits. I followed suit. We rolled around a long time, tight in mutual armlock, kissing shoulders, chests, faces. Minimal biting. He seemed to be waiting for me to orchestrate things, so I unbuttoned his cutoff jeans and he had his jock on. I chewed and spit through it; he dug his fingers into my hair and came before I could even get his cock out. He fell down beside me and we huddled under the sheet, squeezed against the white cement wall. I was feeling slightly sick, the black room spinning as I listened to his snoring. Fell asleep clutching his sticky jock. Woke up next morning to pounding on door. Roommate had to get to class. Jay signaled me to be quiet and we waited for him to leave, Jay's dick growing hard against my ass. He thrust in and out between my legs and held his hand over my mouth. I bit and sucked on his fingers. He spit and got his dick and my legs slippery. His dick slipped in my ass (so that's what it feels like). I shouted out but luckily roommate had already given up and walked away. I pulled off Jay and asked him where his condoms were. He didn't have any so I fished one out of my wallet. He fucked me on the bed and across his roommate's desk and leaning against the cement wall. He pulled out and we sat on the bed, jacking off facing each other with legs wrapped around legs. We kissed deep and silently with cum dripping down chests. Wiped off on T-shirt, fell back asleep. I left around eleven to avoid his roommate's return. Ambiguous parting. I couldn't say "When can I see you again?" since we already live in the same dorm. However, he wasn't blasé or cold by any means. Sunday night Collin and I got stoned and watched TV in the lounge on Jay's floor. Jay came home from work around 12:30 P.M. and mentioned he was going to call in sick to work Tuesday. The TV lounge emptied out. Collin made moves to leave Jay and me alone, but it was late and I didn't feel up to dealing with it. Went upstairs with him.

II. MYSELF: feelings of friendship and affection forming. Excellent sex. Interested in further pursuit.

III. JAY: feelings unknown.

IV. EVENT: Jay's staying home from work Tuesday.

V. PLANS

A. Dis-obligate myself from other activities.

1. Cancel appointment with Rob (99% probability).

2. Catch up on homework (245% probability).

B. Hang out with Jay in group situations to reinforce comfortableness with each other.

1. Eye contact (80% probability).

2. Time alone together.

    a) Intimate conversation (73% probability).

    b) Physical affection (60% probability).

    c) Acknowledgment of events of last Friday night (30% probability).

3. Sex (20% probability).

C. Via progress of above-mentioned events, attempt to determine future direction of relationship: i.e., friend, occasional lover, romantic partner, etc.

FINAL TAPE-RECORDED NOTE, THURSDAY A.M.

Just finished hanging downstairs with Collin, Alicia, Jay, and the jocks. Went pretty smooth, a little tension when Jay and I were alone together, but we dealt with it through small talk. Collin and Alicia went for coffee, and Jay said he was going to crash. He seemed to kinda, like, motion for me to follow him and didn't seem surprised when I knocked on his door a few minutes later. He'd gotten rid of his roommate. We started talking and it was pretty stilted until we got into coming out. Then he got excited. I told him to go ahead and tell his friends, that most of them knew already so why sneak around, especially with where he works and all. He got real encouraged, excited, and decided to go and find his roommate and talk to him about it right that minute. So he hugged me good-bye and said, "I'll talk to you soon," and left me downstairs. I went up here to bed, kinda bummed but happy he was all psyched about coming out.

ASSESSMENT AS OF FOLLOWING TUESDAY

Remaining neighbors and friends on good terms, possibility of friendship increasing. Faint possibility of occasional sex in future, but doubtful and not anything I'm actively pursuing. Experience viewed, at this point in time, as overall positive and mutually beneficial.

Don, the Pizza

Sam Sommer

My therapist insists we size people up—potential lovers, that is—and know everything we need to know about them in the first few minutes—the psychosexual components, at least. Perhaps that's true. He's the one with all the degrees. I've always believed it's chemical. I can feel something begin to percolate deep down inside almost immediately. Something akin to the reaction some animals have to pheromones. Once they kick in, that's that. I'm hooked.

It was definitely chemical the day I met Don. He walked through the door of my local watering hole and—*pow!* Chemistry. The fact that we had nothing in common—that I wrote copy for a living, and Don had a problem putting together a simple sentence; that he was looking for someone to take care of him, and I was already supporting a son and an ex-wife; that he lived in Brooklyn, and I in Queens—didn't seem to bother either of us. Well, not at the beginning, anyway. What we had, seemed at the time far more important. We had chemistry. *Wow! Pow! Holy hormones, Batman!*

In the beginning we tried dating in the traditional sense, but it proved to be a disaster. For us, communication on any level other than the physical seemed hopeless. Dancing proved to be safe territory. It was like having sex standing up. No need for conversation. Our bodies did all the talking. Movies were nonparticipatory and therefore okay as well—when we could agree on one we both wanted to see (our tastes, of course, were mutually exclusive) and promised not to discuss it afterwards. You see, the more we talked, the less likely it was we'd end up in bed—the one place we did get along. The truth was, we didn't really like each other very much. A fact we both tried to overlook for the sake of our raging hormones and overactive libidos. In time the two of us learned to negotiate a minefield of dating do's and don't's, just so we could end up naked together in bed. Once there, all hostility was set aside, and that unbelievable chemistry took over. We were amazing in bed. Utterly amazing! We could go for hours without uttering a single word, aside from certain sexual directions and the occasional groan of pleasure. In this one way, we were so compatible, so in tune, our sex seemed almost choreographed.

As long as we were naked, we were just fine. Even after sex, we could lie for hours together, hardly saying a word, inhaling each other's odors, caressing, finding new positions that allowed us access to the other's most sensual, erogenous zones. We'd often fall asleep head to foot, a tangle of arms and legs. In the morning we'd have sex again. We'd shower, have coffee and juice, without saying two words to each other. As long as we could fondle, kiss, suck, touch, grope, or caress, there was no need for superfluous conversation. We knew better. Once we were dressed, the date was over. We said good-bye and went our separate ways. It was bizarre, to say the least.

As the weeks went by, we began to see less and less of each other. Who knows why? After all, we didn't talk. Our dates, if you could call them that, now consisted of dinner and sex. Sometimes we'd forgo the dinner part. Don could be in the door and I'd have him undressed and in bed in under five minutes.

I can't remember now who stopped calling whom. I guess it doesn't matter. It was inevitable under the circumstances, even with our kind of chemistry. Once the habit of getting together had ended, the need to get together seemed less and less important. Perhaps it was the fact that we never liked each other to begin with. Had I met Don on the street, something told me we'd end up in bed together again; but we never did.

A few weeks ago my friend Alan called. "How's the pizza?" he asked.

"What are you talking about?" I said.

"Don. Don, the pizza? You still dating him?"

"No," I said, still confused as to his obscure reference.

"Too bad. He was as close as they come to the perfect date."

"How's that?"

Alan didn't believe in relationships, although he was a good friend. "Great sex, no entanglements . . . the only thing missing was his ability to turn himself into a pizza."

"Excuse me?" I inquired.

"You know, the way you're always hungry after really good sex?"

"Yes?"

"Well, the perfect date," he said with all candor, "fucks your brains out and then turns into a pizza. That way you don't have to sleep with him or make him breakfast in the morning, and he's solved the problem of what to do with the 'nibbly fits' after sex. I've been searching for this guy my whole adult life. You came pretty close to finding him."

"Alan, you're a sick, sick boy."

"I know, but you love me anyway, don't you?"

"I'll have to think about it."

"Don't think too long, I have a date in a few minutes."

Rhymes with Waiting

John McFarland

I am sitting in my apartment reading a book about compassion and how to develop it. I am waiting for a call from somebody I met on the street earlier this day. The somebody—let's call him David, because that's his name and he should be held accountable—is working late but is supposed to let me know when he's through so that we can meet for a drink and whatever follows. I'm excited. I'm waiting.

It's getting really late. How late can David be working, I ask myself. The book is making me furious. Fuck compassion, I think, I want the phone to ring.

So, I go downstairs to get my laundry out of the dryer. I know that once I leave the apartment David will call, and then *he* will have to wait for a change. I have learned this much, although I have yet to learn compassion.

When I come back upstairs, there's a message and I think of David's cute little butt in his black slacks as he walked away from me and how it'll probably look out of those same slacks. I hit the PLAY MESSAGE button. It's not David. It's zany old Frank telling me about his latest job disaster. He ends with, "So I took my apron off and walked. Don't cry for me, John, they just didn't get me there. By the way, I got a better job starting tonight. And I'm in love. Don't you fucking laugh. This time it's the real thing. Kisses. Ciao, baby."

That's the only message. I am in a rage at David, him with no pager for times like this. I decide that I'm not sticking around anymore. I call a cab, planning to go out to a club and be surrounded by mindless diversions and some cute guys. The cabbie shows up and I tell him the address.

As I'm settling into the backseat, the cabbie starts relating a story about the glamorous fare he had earlier. He says that she took his breath away so bad that he didn't know if he was going to be able to talk. Once she had folded her swell self into the cab, he managed to clear his throat, make eye contact with her in the rear-view mirror, and ask, "Where to?" Out of the fare's mouth came this deep bass voice and the no-nonsense order, "Take me to Buddy's." (That happens to be the same place I'm going.)

"So," I ask, "are you going to see her again?"

The cabbie just gives me a look.

Inside Buddy's, I'm standing next to a hot man. Various people on the dance floor come to a complete stop, not knowing what to do, when some audio relic by the Bee Gees blasts out of the speakers. Others boo. The man next to me breathes out an extremely sexy, "God!" and rolls his eyes at me. I roll mine right back and say, "You can't fight this." He gives me the once-over and says, "Oh, yes, you can. Usually I bring my friends and we take over the place." I say to him, "Until your friends show up, let's be brave," and we hit the floor. Later, in a cozier environment, we also hit the floor. Things work out fine. No thanks to David, that asshole.

The next morning, looking pretty good considering what I've been through, I'm at the bus stop on my way to work and one of my neighbors, whom I know on a nodding basis, bounds up to me. "Hi," I say, "how are you?" He smiles and says, "Fine, now that it's decided. You know, four years here is more than enough." I say, "You guys are moving?" He grows distinctly cheerier and says, "I am. We just broke up, and I'm on the loose. Enough already." I guess that he thinks we're closer than I realized, and I counter with, "Good for you! Action is always better than suffering and waiting."

He gives me his new telephone number. He writes down his name: Charles. "Maybe we can go out for a drink sometime," he says.

I give him my number, too. I don't ask if he works late and expects people to wait all night, although I am tempted.

A couple of days later, a Friday, there's a message

from Charles. He says he's working late that night but is wondering if I wanted to meet for a drink at eleven-fifteen. I begin to shake. I wonder if I'm being psychic and having a full-body premonition that this will end badly, or whether I'm just still raw from that unreliable tramp David. I try to decide which, but can't. I call Charles to say I'm going to a play but will meet him at eleven-fifteen at Buddy's, since it's on my way home from the theater. Then I hang up and check out the paper to pick out a play. I decide on one by Molière that shouldn't contain any unsettling references to voice-mail torture or waiting in general.

I'm at the theater by seven, ready for the doors to open. The setting sun is blazing hot, and all of us waiting in line are dying to get inside where it has to be cooler. As I feel sweat beading up on my back, I'm imagining the people behind me eventually being splattered by my copious sweat. I tune in to their conversation, which is being carried on in a discreet whisper and requires real effort on my part, to see if they are concerned about the swamp spreading and spreading on my back.

One is saying, "Tomorrow isn't supposed to be as hot. We could go paddleboating." The other doesn't say anything as far as I can hear. The first one asks, "Was that a yes?"

"Either way," says the other one, but blankly.

"If you don't want to go, say so," the first one says.

"You always say we never *do* anything and this is a chance to *do* something. Do you, or don't you?" The first one is starting to lose it by the time he demands, "Yes or no?"

"Yes," the second one says.

But this answer isn't good enough for the first one, who starts in, "You don't say that with much enthusiasm. And if you can't be enthusiastic about it, maybe we should forget it."

At this point I wish I hadn't started to listen in, but at least I know that they couldn't care less about being splashed by the sweat now pouring off my back in buckets. I can't control my curiosity any longer. Pretending to look for friends in line, I turn around to check out the two lovebirds. The nag is one dried-up prune and the laconic one is very, very cute. This relationship is doomed if the nag doesn't lighten up. I actually feel something like compassion for them—I've been on this date once or twice myself.

I get to Buddy's at exactly eleven-fifteen to find Charles with a beer in his hand. He says, "You're on time!" and smiles.

I say, "I'm a fanatic about it."

"Good. You can't imagine what a mess I become when I have to wait. I think the other person isn't coming. Ever."

I laugh, but I don't tell him the whole story. Not yet.
I save it for the third date when we're in a paddleboat
and it feels more serious than having a simple beer at
Buddy's.

Giving It Up

Matthew Rettenmund

I didn't go out on what I would consider a true date until after I'd slept with at least two men. Well, two *males*; how can you really consider your eighteen-year-old friends "men"? My first date came after my first kiss, which had been given to me in my senior year of high school by a bi-curious best friend who took pleasure in stealing innocence no matter its gender. He loved women too much to ever be gay, but his confident kiss, forceful and hot, slapped onto me in his apartment with a clueless straight comrade just out of sight around a corner, made me finally feel 100 percent gay. It was like he'd shown me with his mouth what I'd been looking for all those years ago, when I'd been waiting for the eyelashed kid to drop his pants.

(Actually, this was my second kiss. His first attempt had been aborted by my extreme preoccupation with whether or not it would work, voiced at the exact right moment to have caused it to fail; the sound of four lips banging dryly for an instant. But I don't count that, because there was no tongue involved and as anyone knows—anyone who doesn't take old movies too literally—kissing isn't kissing unless both tongues are present and accounted for.)

Compared to the elation of my first kiss, my first date is too boring to record. In fact, I have to say I'm not sure which one counts as a first date.

I was once asked to go to Denny's by an extremely clever Irish exchange student who everyone knew was queer, and who shared with me an ill-advised true love for a grumpy soccer player who kept us on a string and at arm's length. The Irish guy wasn't very good-looking. At all. But he charmed me and I think we enjoyed the thrill of amateurish hand-jobbing mostly to spite our jealous hetero love object, who was beside himself when he found out we'd passed him over in favor of each other. But that wasn't a true date because I'd had no idea that the Irish wit had designs on me until he'd reached over on the drive home and placed his dead-white hand on my thigh; it was a date only in retrospect. No doubt I might have behaved quite differently had I been informed in advance.

The next date, also at Denny's (this was Michigan, after all), was more obvious: a meeting with an adorably tiny future Gap employee whom I'd heard about through a friend. We both knew the score as we downed our cheap milk shakes—and were tragic boyfriends within the month. On the date, we'd spilled our hearts out to each other, confided a mutual passion for Depeche Mode, and then gone to see *Mystic Pizza*, a movie

I will forever hold responsible for our eventual disinte-
gration, his flight into the arms of a sexier closet case,
and his general flakiness. It was no great loss. Short
men are nice to look at, but the proportions are a drag.

After that was a blurry stream of date-mates ranging
from the sweet but stupid to the utterly repulsive, both
physically and spiritually, though rarely both. As wildly
diverse as they were, from the selfless Christian Korean
academic to the sincere and perceptive Mexican janitor
to the two-dimensional Missouri stripper with a truly
unique take on HIV transmission ("I always ask if
they're positive before I do it without a condom"), my
involvements with them were marked by three similarities; they were insubstantial; they were extremely short-
lived, with three months standing as a record; and there
were virtually no true "dates" involved. I met them the
same way most gay guys meet—at bars. I met the stripper at a record store and seduced one or two—okay,
one—repressed college student in my dorm, but for the
most part, it was outside my realm of experience to see
someone I liked, get a phone number, call him up, pop
the question, then do dinner and a movie.

I don't think it's just me. Do gay men "date" in the
same way straight men do? Or straight women? I've always found it hilarious to listen to a straight female
friend narrating the events of a date she's been on, cul-
minating with her thoughts on how he was a nice boy
but she thinks they'll just go out for a while, no sex

involved. It seems that queers don't really date unless the sex is a given. Dating becomes the stuff you do to pass the time before you take off your clothes and laugh at the hetero world. Dating is sometimes understood to be synonymous with fucking (I think I'm plagiarizing this sentence from my own novel!).

The one time I recall going out on a getting-to-know-you date during my early twenties, I returned to find that a treacherous friend of mine from home had lost his virginity to my horrifying roommate, the very one I'd complained to him about so loudly for months, the very one who'd nearly vetoed my friend's visit in the first place. I wasn't informed that they'd coupled until days later, but somehow I knew. As a joke, when I'd entered the apartment and had seen them so immersed in, so undistractible from, their individual pursuits, I had asked loudly, "What did you two guys do while I was gone? *Have sex?*" I'm better at recognizing guilt now. Then, I had interpreted their brittle stares as simple embarrassment or even distaste.

As I hit my mid-twenties and beyond, barhopping had lost its appeal. I'm aware that many gay men still feel a sort of euphoric redemption when they snag a dish at a club, whether or not the connection is intended to last indefinitely or for twenty minutes. For me it's a thing of the past, like vinyl records or my attraction to collecting sports cards. Bar boredom mandated that I find men some other way, a dire challenge for even the most bold and outgoing and imaginative queer. With dry spells extending as long as a year or more, I knew I needed to socialize more or I'd never get any. Love, sex, *or* conversation.

The first time I had a truly adult date that was a date from start to finish—that started with my seeing him, him seeing me, numbers being obtained, and an invitation extended—it didn't happen at Denny's and didn't end in three weeks. It was with a nice guy whom I still see frequently. I see him every single day when I open my eyes and he's out cold next to me, hoping I won't make him wake up and go to work. (When my boyfriend first read this, after uncomfortably skimming the preceding revelations about my dating history ["You dated a *stripper*?"], he demanded to know who this guy was, this guy I still see so frequently. Then he reread the paragraph and cooed.)

Dating is not easy, nor is it fun. At the time it's happening, it's usually queasy and vaguely mind-boggling. You're never sure you're connecting, even when he tells you he feels it, too. He could be lying. Nobody knows why men lie in these situations, when it would be so much easier to tell the truth, but they have been known to do it.

Dating is a hardship, an organized stressfest: "Would you like to meet me at a café somewhere and spend an hour or so extremely ill at ease?"

But even though it's as evil as a publicist, dating is a

necessity if you have any hope of finding a man to spend more than three months with.

The best thing about dating is that the more you do it, the better you get, until you finally find someone with whom to give it up forever.

PART TWO

STRANGE LOVERS
AND
LOVING STRANGERS

It does sometimes happen: You spot someone in a bar or on the street or anywhere two men might meet, your body says, "We want this one," you exchange glances, and lo and behold, he's interested back! It seems too good to be true, and sometimes—when you've gone to his place or he to yours or both of you to some temporary locale—you find out that it *was* too good to be true. Oh, it may be bliss for a short while, but something is missing, and after that brief idyll, it begins to fall apart as you realize it was not how you expected it would be.

If there is something more mysterious than why and how we fall in love, it is why and how we fall out of love. Or lust.

In this middle part of *Boy Meets Boy* are some of these stories, from men who found someone and then lost him, for reasons known or mysterious, mundane or ineffable. They're tales of those handsome strangers who enter our lives, and then somehow become estranged once again.

Past Perfect

Michael Lassell

APOLLO SEEKS ZEUS
Tall, blond, uninhibited, 28. I have a
body of Epic proportions and genuinely prefer older men, any race, any
size, for soulful service.
I'm a nonsmoker, D/D free. UB2.

"It's too good to be true," Marvin said, dribbling skim milk from his oatmeal down his scraggly would-be goatee.

"Well, I know it's not the usual," I agreed over our ritual Saturday brunch at the Fiddler Café. "But what have I got to lose?"

"Your dignity. Your self-respect. Your virginity."

"Lost, lost, and lost," I said, trying to get an egg yolk onto my buttered bagel without breaking it.

"Your illusions . . ."

"Left 'em in the maternity ward."

"Your life?"

"Oh, Marvin, you're so dramatic."

"Does he say if his name is Dahmer?"

———

71

The first two times I called I got his answering machine.

"Hi, I'm not here. Leave a message."

I hung up.

"His voice sounds nice," I told Marvin eight seconds later.

"What do you mean *nice*?"

"Well, he doesn't sound like a thug. He doesn't sound like a fruitcake. And he doesn't sound like he's from New York. He just sounds . . . I don't know. Nice."

"I'm from New York," Marv reminded me.

"Marv, you went to Bronx High School of Science. You went to Yale."

"Spoken like a true Choatie," he sneered, and hung up on me.

The fifth time I left a message.

"Hi," I said. And hung up.

I waited an hour.

"Hello?" he said.

"Oh," I answered.

"Hello?"

"Sorry. I didn't think I'd get a live person."

"I know what you mean," he said with a slight baritone laugh deep in his throat. "I'm Alex. What can I do for you?"

"I saw your ad in *Frontiers*," I managed to get out. "You sound great."

"What is it you're looking for?" he asked, a question that always floors me, for some reason.

I mean, what am I going to say?

Oh, I'm looking for a hot young stud of impossible beauty who will give me total pleasure and offer no resistance no matter what I ask. The stud in question will be sensitive and bright and have a great sense of humor and won't kill me after I cum. He will be respectful of his elders, but not want a daddy, and it won't bother him that I'm way past the gay expiration date and big enough around the equator to fit adolescent twins in my jeans.

What I said was:

"Well, I'd like to meet someone who looks like you say you look and who doesn't object to middle-aged men and who likes affection with his sex."

"Sounds like you found him," he said, and asked when he could come over.

"Tonight?" Marvin practically gagged into the phone.

"I like a man who goes after what he wants," I said, trying to sound blasé.

"No, you don't," Marv corrected. "You think Hamlet was impetuous!"

"Marv, all I said was I thought there were excellent reasons for not just killing his uncle—"

"What time?" Marv demanded. "I'm going to sit in my car in the street. If there is any trouble, you scream out the window. I'll bring the cell phone. I'll preset the speed dial for 911."

"Don't be ridiculous! I'll be fine. And besides, if he's as hot as he says he is, I won't want to know you're out there with your finger on the trigger. Or on anything else!"

At 10:02 P.M., there was a knock on the door.

He was late, but I forgave him, since I couldn't remember whether I'd set the clock two minutes ahead on purpose to trick myself.

I opened the little metal grate in the door to check him out. My eye was even with the canyon between his alpine pecs. I slammed the grate closed and opened the door.

"Hi," he said as simple as Simon.

"Hi," I said, thinking it was the wrong thing.

"I'm Alex," he said, extending his hand. I took it. It was the size of a small dog and as hard and muscular as a big one.

Alex was tall. Six feet five would be my guess. He was blond—naturally, unobnoxiously, and neatly groomed blond (his eyes were greenish blue). And he was built.

Colt Studios built. A brick shithouse in jeans, a red muscle shirt (and how well that shirt deserved its name stretched across his chest and shoulders), and flip-flops, like he just stepped off the beach. He had a face somewhere between a movie star and a choirboy in one of those states in the middle of the country that starts with *M*. He was carrying a little gym bag that looked like the kind of thing a cat burglar would carry his tools in.

I showed Alex in. I showed him the living room. The kitchen. The study. The bedroom.

"It's a really nice place," he said, looking over this and that. "Do you mind if I take a shower?"

"No, not at all," I said, thinking things were getting off to a weird start.

"I just got off a boat, and I'm kinda salty."

I gave him a clean white towel. He smiled as he closed the door behind him.

I paced up and down the hall, thinking how much I liked salt.

I nearly jumped out of my skin when the phone rang.

"Is it okay?"

Marvin.

"He is fucking gorgeous!" I whispered into the phone. "Where are you?"

"I'm out front."

"Go home!" I ordered.

75

Michael Lassell

"Where is he?" Marvin persisted.

"He's in the shower."

"You're already finished?"

"No, we're not already fi—I thought you said you were outside. How the fuck could we be finished? He just walked in the door."

"Shit, I just got here. I didn't even get a peek. What's he doing in the shower?"

"He's taking a shower, as far as I can tell," I said as the sound of the water went off. "And he's finished. Go home."

"I am staying right here."

I hung up on him.

I went into the study and looked at what I could see of my reflection in the one window you could see the Hollywood sign from. It was a flawless L.A. night. I heard the bathroom door open and went back into the living room. He wasn't in it. He wasn't in the kitchen, either.

Alex was in the bedroom. He was on the bed. He had wrapped the towel around his waist, but he'd folded it in half first, so it looked like one of those tiny sarongs the bar boys wear in Hawaii, only it was white, so it looked like all those boys in bathhouses back in the seventies. He had his hands up behind his head in perfect "do me" position.

Okay, I thought. Crude, but acceptable. I approached.

Alex had perfect tan skin without the trace of a hair or a blemish anywhere I could see. But he wasn't shaved. There just weren't any follicles. I felt like a yeti. I could not keep my eyes off his torso, his tiny little waist, those cobblestone abs, nipples like chocolate kisses. His thighs were enormous, and every muscle was defined. They seemed to be held on to his body by a network of veins that wriggled like indigo reptiles under his skin when he moved.

As I got near him, he sat up.

"Aren't you wearing too much clothing?" he asked.

"Possibly," I said, standing in front of him.

"Here," he offered, and pulled my sweatshirt up over my head.

He was Tarzan. I was Jane Curtin. Or Oliver Hardy.

"Very nice," he said when it was off, and shifted a bit so he could kiss the gray, hairy hollow between my tits. "I love hair."

He rubbed his hands over my chest. He plucked at my nipples with his fingers (callused—from weight lifting, no doubt). He put his hands on my hips and kept kissing my chest, my belly.

Then he made a single, quick gesture with both hands, slipping them between me and the elastic waistband of my shorts and, without hesitation, peeled them off me. They dropped to the floor. My rock-hard dick was aimed in the direction of his mouth.

He laughed.

"Too small?" I asked.

"Too soon." His laughter echoed in his chest cavity and resonated with the springs in the mattress. "Let's start with a little massage," he said, and stood up. "Facedown, head up by the pillows."

Now there's one thing I have learned in my life. When clear directions to a desired destination are offered . . . follow the directions.

The phone rang.

"Oh," he said. "You want to get it?"

"No, but if I don't, something paramilitary might happen."

"Huh?"

"Never mind." I picked up the phone.

"Hello?"

"It's me."

"Go home."

"Is he there?"

"Yes."

"Is he naked?"

"Yes."

"Is he big?"

"I'll call you tomorrow." I hung up.

"Do you mind if I use powder," he asked.

"Powder?"

"Talcum powder, instead of oil."

I didn't mind.

He reached into his gym bag, grabbed some classic Johnson & Johnson, and sprinkled cold talc on my back, butt, thighs.

Then he started rubbing my back as soft as he could. At first, there was barely any contact at all, just the hard, crusty ridges of those calluses. I was thinking of rose thorns, the skin of sharks, and every little nerve ending my skin ever thought of having was standing at attention like an army of microscopic erect dicks. Gradually he got more and more into it, massaging deeper and deeper. I do not remember telling him to stop at any point. The smell of the talc was heaven. As he was massaging my ass, I started dribbling out my dick, which was stuck underneath me. I wondered if I was having some kind of flashback to the nascent libido of my infancy, it felt so good. I made a mental note that my mother must have done at least one thing right, after all.

Then he reached underneath me and pulled my dick backward until it was breathing between my thighs as he worked on them.

When he straddled one leg, I realized with a not-unpleasant shock that he wasn't wearing his little white towel anymore. His seemingly heavy balls were rubbing on my leg, and his dick was obviously hard.

I rolled over onto my back. He straddled my hips and held my hands down on the bed with his. He was leaning over me . . . looming over me, I should say. It was like sailing past Gibraltar. His blond hair was hanging down over his face like the forelock of a billy goat. He could have killed me anytime he wanted, and I might have let him. He moved his face down to mine. I could feel his breath on my face as he moved his face toward mine. Then he veered off to the left and went to work on my neck.

I made a noise that was part purr, part gasp at the unbelievable sensation of it. I could not help but think that he had my jugular vein between his teeth for a time, but just when I was starting to get nervous, he started working the other side of my neck with his tongue. Like the good host I always tried to be, I was thrashing around on the bed, pushing up with my hips at his butt, the sweat-slick crack of which was making the perfect temporary home for my dick. That's when he looked me straight in the eye.

"Can I kiss you?" he asked.

"Of course."

And he did. And I kissed him.

Bells went off. Well, one bell. It was the front door.

"You expecting someone?" he asked.

"If I said no, I'd be lying. But I was kind of hoping he'd go away."

I opened the grate in the front door.

"You're still alive," Marv noticed.

"Yes, I am, although you won't be if you're still standing there in thirty seconds."

"I was just worried," he said with an indignant elevation of his left eyebrow.

"You just wanted to get a look at him naked," I hissed.

"I just wanted to get a look at him period."

"Well, then I guess we're learning the punctuality lesson all over again, aren't we?"

"Well, you get to look at him naked, and I didn't even get to look at him at all." He was a four-year-old caught red-handed with nothing like a plausible excuse at the ready.

"Yes," I explained, as if explaining the difference between little Jimmy's balloon breaking accidentally and popping it on purpose out of spite, "but that's because I'm naked, too."

"Gross!" he said, way too convincingly.

"Marvin, do you enjoy being a sighted person?"

"All right, all right, I'll go."

He kept not going.

"What?" I said, not the soul of patience.

"Well . . . I'm just a little . . . jealous."

I felt myself melting. "Oh, Marv. I'll always love you, no matter what."

And I meant it, too—at that moment.

"Breakfast?" he asked.

"Absolutely. Fiddler's at noon."

I blew him a kiss, which he blew back.

"Go home, okay?" I said.

And apparently he did.

"Who was that?" Alex asked.

"Jehovah's Witnesses. They weren't into group sex, so I sent 'em away to peddle their *Watchtower*s elsewhere. Actually, the cute one looked like he could be convinced."

Alex laughed. His stomach undulated.

"My turn," he said, and flopped down on his back.

There was no doubt about his beauty. There was something of a boy about him, most notably his seeming lack of shame, but he was, as they say, all man. He was stretched out there, his beautiful big dick as hard as they get and pretty much as big as any I'd ever seen up close. (It reminded me of the "pickle," the first musical instrument I ever played, in first grade, which was really just a kazoo in a kosher-dill-sized plastic casing.) His balls were tucked high around the base of it in downy, light brown hair.

It was too much. I went to work on him with my mouth and fiddled his nipples with my fingertips. I love sucking dick, and I was having the time of my life. His nipples were obviously of the highly sensitive variety, and he was rolling under my tongue and fingers.

I moved off his dick and onto his balls. He spread his legs, and I dove down between them. I put my tongue on his asshole, and I thought he was going to cum. I spit on my thumb and started playing with his asshole while massaging the whole area with my other hand. That's when he pulled his thighs back with his hands, and I realized what Alex had in mind.

A butch bottom, I thought with glee. God's perfect creation and as rare as justice.

I dove at his asshole with my lips and tongue. He was practically bouncing the bed off the floor and groaning like mad. I went at the pulsing sphincter with my thumb again, with more pressure this time.

"Oh, yes," he hissed, "please."

The magic word.

I reached across him to the bedside table and opened the drawer. I grabbed a new dick-shaped bottle of lube, pulled the top up with my teeth, and gobbed some into my hand.

There was no point beating around the bush. I went in with two fingers.

He pulled his vascular thighs so far apart I thought the tendons in his groin would snap.

I grabbed for a condom, but he took it out of my hand. He opened the pack with his teeth and rolled it down my dick. It had been a long time since I had actually been able to toss a fuck in a rubber, but I wasn't worried about losing this erection.

Then he did something I've only seen in circuses. He somehow wiggled his massive shoulders through his thighs so that his shoulders were holding his thighs down and apart, offering unobstructed access to his hairless asshole.

I went in with three fingers until I located the flat disk of his prostate. He was oozing all over his taut stomach. His little outie of a belly button looked like an acorn melting through ice in a spring wood.

Then I slipped into him, easy as a hand into a glove and just as warm. He was digging his hands into my chest and I was raking my nails across his glutes. He was practically having a seizure, and he was beating the pillows out of the way with his head, his hair falling into his eyes.

Now, there is nothing I like more than shooting a load into a man's asshole. There is no feeling like it on earth that comes close. Shooting into a condom, even if it is burrowed into the buggery burrow of a beautiful bodybuilder, doesn't touch it for a pure experience. I was, however, getting perilously close to shooting.

My knees were aching, and I was pumping, his dick in both my hands. I could see his ample balls shrink up into his body before he let loose, the first wad spurting out of him like a comet and splashing on the glass of the picture over the bed behind him. The second and third hit him in the face. The next few hit him in the neck, then the chest, then the stomach, puddling around his navel.

I pulled out of him, making him shudder with a sharp moan. I ripped off the rubber, flung it aside with a snap, grabbed my dick, leaned back, and gave myself a couple of fast, short jerks before I burst. I hit the wall, the pillows, his face, his chest.

Not giving a shit who heard what, I let out as massive a sex roar as I have ever bellowed, and Alex joined me, practically howling out his approval.

When my body finally gave up its last spasm, I collapsed onto him. He wrapped his arms around me and kissed my head all over.

After what seemed like hours, we managed to get ourselves into the shower. He was remarkably tender. I never did actually get soft until well after we were drying off. He wrapped me in the big bath towel, and I dried his sculpted back with the oversized bath sheet.

I watched him get dressed, smiling all the time. Because he wasn't wearing much in the way of clothes, it didn't take long for him to finish. His hair was plastered into a respectable arrangement. His skin was glowing with the day's sun and the night's . . . sin? Phooey!

"Thank you," I said as he was leaving.

"Thank you. Will you call me?"

"You have any doubt?"

"You wouldn't be the first who didn't."

I didn't believe him. I still don't believe that anyone could resist a second helping of him. Or a sixtieth.

I called the next day. Machine.

The next day. Machine.

"Well, he's not going to answer, that's all," Marvin said the following Saturday, finally giving in to believing the evening had taken place just as I described it.

"He was the one who was worried that I wasn't going to call him."

"He probably does see other people," Marvin suggested.

"Maybe he's out of town," I countered.

"Maybe he's dead," Marvin offered, always willing to trump my bid.

"Now who's being a drama queen? Maybe he's busy."

"Maybe he's some kind of weird, perverse straight man running around giving gay men exactly the kind of sex they want and then refusing ever to see them again, like some horrible heterosexual form of torture."

"I think that's it," I said.

"Yes, that's definitely it," he decided, letting a drool of grapefruit juice slip out the right side of his mouth.

The next time I called Alex, the phone had been disconnected.

His ad disappeared from *Frontiers*.

About two years later, I was wandering along the tourist shops and cafés that line the harbor of Paphos in Cyprus. It was a warm November, long after the tourists had, for the most part, departed. It should have been the rainy season, but the rain had taken a vacation elsewhere.

Suddenly, something caught my eye from the postcard rack of a refreshment stand. I pulled it out. There he was, Alex, sitting on a rock in the ocean surf I instantly identified as Zuma Beach. His blond hair carefully coifed, his massive upper body cantilevered over his impossibly thin waist, his prodigious thighs and beautiful butt were as naked as he was that night in my bedroom in L.A.

"Greetings from Cyprus," the card said.

There were no other clues.

I bought two—one to keep and one to send to Marvin.

A Little Past London

Kerry Bashford

On the fourth of February, I had £34 and 20p. The bank teller assured me that the money would arrive from Australia in two days. On the twenty-fourth of February, I had £4 and 10p. and the bank teller made no more assurances.

I had a choice. I either found shelter or food. As it was winter, it was clear I had to adjust my appetite. I hung around bars, hoping to exchange a feed for a fuck. It was a subtle form of prostitution as the men were rarely aware of their part of the arrangement. I would lie in strange beds, stating my terms with an orgasmic moan and a rumbling stomach. When my host fell asleep, I would creep into the kitchen, raid the refrigerator, and look innocently blank the next day when breakfast had vanished overnight.

On the twenty-fifth of February, I met a man who invited me to dinner. My table manners must have been appalling because, as we left, he gave me his name and number wrapped in a £50 note.

88

It was the best pickup line I'd ever heard.

(I've used it often since with little success.)

He said, "I'm going to the bar right now and when I come back, I'd like very much to talk to you. So if you don't want to talk to me, I'd start planning my escape now."

I didn't move.

(Reasons why I liked this approach: It is, above all else, extremely practical. It saves the predator the time and the embarrassment of working on an unwilling prey. It also allows both participants time to think of what to say next.)

The problem is, I can't think of what we said next.

He was late. I pretended not to care. I checked the back of the matchbox one more time. The hour and location had not changed. I stared at the shelves for a few moments before I came upon the book. I reached into my pocket and searched my hand. The name on the binding and the name on the box were the same right down to the hyphen that separated the surnames. The dust-jacket description cited him as better educated and better traveled than myself. The photograph demonstrated how I would have known him at a younger age. The comments on the back cover suggested that I wasn't the only one who thought of him fondly.

I looked up and saw him enter the bookshop. I felt

like I'd been caught reading a diary entry. I greeted him with one hand and hid the book behind my back with the other.

Reasons for feeling nervous on a first date:

1. He's better dressed than I am. His shirt is impeccably pressed and appears marginally less expensive than the tweed falling pleated from his waist. I am wearing an Oxfam jacket that barely conceals the cotton and the corduroy that have now seen more countries than Laundromats.

2. He lives in an apartment building with a rent equivalent to my income.

3. The plaque that rests above the front door bears his father's name, prefaced by the word "Sir." His father, he explains, is a member of Parliament. My father, I explain, is a member of the meat-packers' union.

4. On the other side of the door, his mother (whom I incorrectly address as "Lady") is fixing us lunch. Her son says, "Thank you, Mother, but we'll dine later," and takes me upstairs to fuck.

5. When we are finished, I return downstairs and his mother, without a sign of malice, hands me a towel and points to the bathroom.

The sex bit.

A standard romance has three components—encounter, deferral, and consummation. I have the opportunity to subvert this convention to a degree. You see, I've never been very good at deferring consummation. However, on this occasion the sex bit did not (does not) occur until the second date (page).

The other thing is, I've never been very good at writing about sex. Perhaps the reader would be kind enough to take over at this point. Here's a pen and a piece of paper and a list of words you might find helpful: cock, fuck, throb, thigh, tool, juice, thrust, manhole, jism, balls, pulsate, condom, lick, load, quiver, dachshund.

He studied at Cambridge
And spoke with a pain which
I never quite understood
He said I was brave
Because I behaved
In a way he never thought he could
And he'd often say
I spoke in a way
That betrayed my country and class
And I'd often pray
To know what he would betray
But there was never a way to ask.

A three-day rain and London is lapping at the windows. Asparagus on toast and tea-cake dessert. Trying to hold thin china in a heavily gloved hand. I tell him

I come from a desert island that dominates a southern ocean. An island whose inhabitants cling to the coast-line and their dreams of owning a piece of it. A country that works a whole week for amber fluid, works a whole season for amber skin, works a whole lifetime like am-ber streetlights waiting for the moment they can stop.

Only Australians, he says, really know how to mix their metaphors.

I have not been entirely honest with you. On the second page, I said that I discovered his book before his arrival at the shop. I didn't actually see it until much later.

However, he did suggest that we meet in a bookshop and I could have found it there. Perhaps that was his intention.

Gay men like to travel.

Gay men like to meet men.

Gay men like to meet men when they travel.

And they especially like to write about it.

But don't confuse me with those rich queens who buy their beauty in some foreign destination and then pass off their diaries as literature.

For a start, I've never been to Bangkok, and anyway, I've never found a country I couldn't starve in.

Love is, after all, the strangest coincidence. One meets another with the appropriate (a) appearance, (b) beliefs, (c) aspirations, and (d) tolerance.

Unfortunately coincidence has never played a major part in my life.

Appearance

You want to know what he looked like? Okay.

Age: 32

Height: 6 ft

Weight: 168 pounds

Complexion: Fair

Hair: Auburn

Eyes: Green

Oh, you want to know what he looked like to me. I don't know. A little like a cartoon I guess. A face that begged for caricature. (I sound cruel. I don't mean to be.) It's just that the curve of his cheek, the contour of his chin, came together in an almost comic conspiracy. (Note the unnecessary alliteration. I will add more.)

He was cute. Kinda cute. Quaint cute. Camp cute. Quite cute. ("When you say 'quite,' do you mean it in the English sense or the American? There is a difference.") And he was tall—a long expanse of stomach, chest, ribs, freckles, and nipples from his cock to his neck. And he had two arms, two legs, a full set of his own teeth, and I imagine most of his major organs.

Beliefs

One weekend, frustrated with his class origins, he became a revolutionary.

By Monday, he was over it. Later he said, "Always
remember that those who claim they would fight to the
death for your right to fuck will not be so willing if you
arrive at the barricades in an off-the-shoulder number
with clutch bag and pearls."

He was never again attracted to armed struggle. Except on one occasion. I praised Trotsky and he praised
the aerodynamic qualities of the ice pick.

Aspirations

I said, "Money won't buy you happiness, my dear."

He said, "No, but it would certainly make misery a
lot more interesting."

Tolerance

Unfortunately, tolerance has never played a major part
in my life.

He couldn't believe that he was my first lover.

"So what's kept you out of love for so long?" he asked.

"Good fortune, I guess. I've never felt at ease with
the idea. Even the vernacular of romance fills me with
suspicion. People 'fall' in love. People 'fall head over
heels.' People only fall by unfortunate accident or sui-

cidal design. Is it any wonder that after all this falling, they 'break up' and 'break down'?"

"So who'll be there to pick up the pieces for you?"

It was a Qantas steward actually. I couldn't help but feel grateful for the extra tissues on the tray.

It could happen in an airport lounge. Soft focus, slow pan, swirl of strings. Good (kiss) bye. I'll (hug) miss you.

But he will not let me steal a kiss before Customs.

"They'll see us."

"What does it matter? I'm leaving the country. Under those circumstances, they'd be pleased to let me go."

"But I'm staying."

"Don't remind me."

or

It will come with the mail. A letter postmarked London. He wants to hear from me. A Vegemite paw print. Anything. We correspond for a while. Then all the letters are local. I want to hear from him. A marmalade paw print. Anything

but

jam never touches paper

or

It will be two pennies left over from a £50 note

or

It will be a book. A book that he wrote that I read but never finished.

Chocomel

James Hannaham

Despite Amsterdam's reputation for liberalism, erotica, and tolerance—all euphemisms for loose morals—I have slept with only one person here, on the night I arrived, two weeks ago. I have been led on, however, by at least three other men. This is perhaps as much a result of the Dutch character as it is my ability to pick men who are unavailable to me. The last guy I "went out" with was having trouble deciding where he wanted to live—not within a particular city, but in the world. I came to Amsterdam because it seemed like a perfect place to get over someone—lots of easy sex, good humor, and "fries with mayo," if you know what I mean. But here's the difference: in New York, no one has a real boyfriend—in fact, most men are penalized for uttering the word—so guys will sleep with tourists and try to extend flings into long-distance relationships. It's an emotionally safe choice, the right one for a city where ambition conquers love. Here in Amsterdam these days, all the cute guys have boyfriends, so they won't sleep with tourists. But it doesn't stop them from sticking their hands down your pants. The guy I actually slept with wasn't Dutch.

———

I was in a bar, where I was being dogged by this guy on a business trip. "I leave tomorrow," he gloated, raising his eyebrows. His opening line had been to ask the length of my dick. "You're so romantic," I'd observed, trying to defer an answer. Curiosity may have killed the cat, but this tiger was not afraid to die. "Tell me," he'd insisted. "Sixty kilometers," I'd told him, thinking perhaps this was more black dick than he could handle. My idea of a suave pickup is not whipping out a measuring tape. Or whipping anything else, for that matter. Not in the Classic Bar Scenario, anyway.

I was trying to find an excuse to part ways with my unwanted suitor when Marco walked by. Seven feet of hulking Marco. He was wearing a shirt bearing a single word: *Tight.* I fumblingly suggested to the businessman that we should find out how tight, wanting more to evade his advances than anything else. So I struck up a conversation with Marco. His ears stuck out, his hair was kind of waxy and flat, and he had a little bit of an Arnold Schwarzenegger accent. When he smiled, he made you feel that he was simultaneously conspiring with you and making fun of you. I started to find him sort of charming.

I offered to buy him a drink and he told me he wanted chocolate milk. I was incredulous. I spent a few minutes trying to figure out if he was serious, and if the bar even served chocolate milk, a brand called Chocomel, which is popular here. He wasn't a teetotaler because he'd had a drinking problem, it seemed, but because he was a good boy, taking care of his health. It wasn't until later that I connected his desire for Chocomel milk to his desire for choco-men. I would have made a joke about it if I'd realized it earlier. Instead, I thought he was trying to get rid of me. "I don't believe that they serve that here," I told him. I thought the bartender would think I was crazy. "Are you always so afraid to embarrass yourself?" he asked. I went to the bar and made his request. I felt like I'd just been called on in math class. They were out of Chocomel.

When I returned, Marco and the businessman were talking, each in his own halting version of English. It was Marco's turn not to trust me. He didn't believe they were out of Chocomel, he thought I just hadn't had the nerve to ask, so he turned to go to the bar and find out for himself. I seized the opportunity to ditch the businessman and followed Marco so I could be there when he found I was telling the truth. "When you were gone," Marco reported as we went to the bar, "that guy kept asking me, 'Are you going to sleep with him?' "

"Well, what did you say?" I asked. It became clear that we were, in fact, conspiring. The businessman had disappeared.

More goofy stuff about Marco: He lives in the neighborhood by the Rijksmuseum but hasn't ever gone inside. He gets goosebumps—really big ones—when he hears a pop song he really likes. Not because it reminds him of anything, just because it makes him emotional. I asked him about that. He uses a lot of skin care products, including this white cream that made him look like a mime for a few minutes. He has two of the same picture of a handsome black guy cut out from a magazine taped to his refrigerator, with magnets shaped like bunches of bananas over their crotches. I didn't ask if it was a homage to Josephine Baker. He recently bought a couple of trays with pictures of fruit all over them. The trays make up for the fact that his apartment is too small for a kitchen table. He's proud of the fruit trays. His bed is a strange little love-nook: a couple of thin foam mattresses on the floor in the corner of his apartment, curtained off with white tulle. There's a jellyfish-like mosquito net hanging over the bed, wrapped in the same material. A train hangs from it that he tucks under the mattress at one side. On the wall behind the pillows, there's a huge wallpaper scene of a waterfall. He really loves to watch cartoons. I saw some comic books under the sofa, too. He put on Billie Holiday while we had sex. It hadn't occurred to him that wearing the word

Tight on a T-shirt might refer to anything other than the way the shirt fit him. I'd find most of this annoying in an American, I think, but in America all these peculiar facts would add up to something much less naive and endearing than Marco.

I have this theory that you can tell what a trick really thinks of you by the first song he puts on his CD player the next morning (if there's a next morning, you already have an inkling anyway, of course). Once a guy played the Indigo Girls' "In Love with Your Ghost" the morning after we slept together. I thought it meant he liked me, but in retrospect it probably just meant he wanted me dead. I got to Marco's CD player first and played Dionne Warwick singing "I Say a Little Prayer," for various ironic and nonironic reasons, and then Kate Bush's "Heads We're Dancing," because my favorite bass player throws a really strange riff throughout it. It turns out that the lyrics describe a one-night stand with the devil or something, though. Marco played "Maria" from *West Side Story*. I think it meant he liked Natalie Wood.

Marco had a part-time job as a doorman at a disco, but he usually worked at a hotel. He was the second person in a row I'd slept with who was in the hotel business. I don't think I have a thing for hotel workers. But isn't that the way people's tastes get shaped? You don't go out thinking, "I want to sleep with a horticulturist." Then you meet two horticulturists in a row, and

they happen to be good in bed. The next time you meet
a horticulturist, you're a little more curious than
usual. Then you become a horticulture queen. Perhaps just for the sake of continuity, or the comfort it
brings. Or the floral arrangements. But two's a coincidence, three's a pattern. Going by the rule of twos,
it would seem that I go for some pretty unconven-
tional "types": tax lawyers, actors from Chicago, Irish
Catholics born in July, guys named Jeff. Not exactly
the stuff of a fetish lifestyle. But whenever I run
across someone in one of those categories, a mallet
strikes my psyche's vibraphone. Maybe that's how
Marco developed a taste for "da flava," as I gradually
figured out he had. I could spend hours musing about
the implications of this subject, but I'm on vacation.
I've got Dutch boys to fuck.

We had breakfast. I followed him down to the grocery
store, we bought some muesli and yogurt drinks, he
mixed it all up. It had been a long time since I'd had
breakfast with a trick, though I prefer to, it seems so
civilized. He fed me this German zwieback toast thing
with coconut on it that I'm sad I'll probably never taste
again, certainly never with his thick fingers around it.
We watched cartoons and ate breakfast, balancing our
bowls on his prized fruit trays. I gave him the number
where I was staying. He massaged an assortment of
creams and astringents into his skin, took several vita-

mins, ate a scoopful of protein powder. Then he put on
the exact same clothes he'd worn the night before. I
followed him out of his apartment. He dwarfed the
staircase and had to duck twice to avoid decapitation.
He got his bicycle and started riding off to work. He
wouldn't give me a kiss good-bye, which I never demand, but which I feel should always punctuate even
the most casual encounter. "This is my neighborhood,"
he explained.

I ran into Marco in the street; he said he'd call. I ran
into him at the door of the club where he works; he
was acting weird in that way that guys do when they
don't want to express themselves. They insult you
obliquely, then they grab your butt. I didn't have time
for that. He called me a few days later, and then the
day after that, neither time leaving his phone number.
I visited him at work. He confessed that he didn't want
to get involved with a tourist.

"Involved?" I asked him. I just was hoping we could
get together again. I am, as I admitted to someone I
was trying to rebed recently, a repeat offender. If I enjoy an experience, I like to try it again. I suspect that
some men somehow interpret this desire for mere rep-
etition as "love." (This is the gay word for infatua-
tion.) "I'm going to Spain on Monday, the fourth. I'll
be back for a day on the twenty-third, then I'm going

home," I explained. Marco just screwed up his face. "Yeah," he said, "maybe we can get together then." "Sure," I replied, straddling my bicycle, "I'll buy you a Chocomel."

Room with a View

Barry Lowe

I was in the bathroom cleaning my teeth. I knew Geofferey liked to kiss and I was taking no chances. After
I'd gargled and rinsed, I took the time to floss. It was
not that I was reluctant, hell, I was so keen my dick
was screaming at me to hurry up.

I'd left young, good-looking Geofferey in the living
room watching porn. We'd been bantering sexually at
work for months, and when he turned up at the front
door, swathed in the unmistakable stench of testoster-
one and Calvin Klein's One, I knew I was on a winner.

Tito, my significant other, was as taken with Geofferey as I was, and so eager were we, I excused myself
to attend to my oral hygiene in preparation for an X-
rated bout of snogging.

Judging the time to be just about right, my cute little
erection protruding eagerly, I crept back to where I'd
left them fully aroused. Sure enough, my absence had
proven an aphrodisiac, and Geofferey was enthusiastically demonstrating his oral prowess on Tito.

My own dick, eager to share in the tongue-lashing,
led me into the room. Tito was expecting my approach
as we had refined our group-sex agreement right down

to the fine print—it kept our relationship from becoming as stale as last week's focaccia—and he knew it was to be a three-for-all.

As I approached, Geofferey looked up, thus interrupting his spit-polishing momentarily, and never one to let an open orifice remain unfilled for long, I guided my warmth-seeking cruise missile into his gaping gullet. Geofferey spat it out with ill-concealed contempt and hissed, "What do you think you're doing? I'm not interested in you."

He went back to his ministrations after throwing me the crumbs of "I suppose you can watch if you really have to." Tito was too far gone to complain and merely shrugged his resignation.

My cock shriveled in embarrassment and I would quickly have tucked it away had I not, inconveniently, left all my clothes on the bathroom floor. Quickly retreating to retrieve them, I dressed and headed for the front door but not before I heard Tito moan, "Get your tongue under that foreskin."

Rejection is rabidly esteem-deflating, particularly when your expectations have been cruelly shattered and your significant other is the preferred icon of lust. However, there were a number of mature options to consider:

ONE: I could burn down the house with both of them in it, claim the quite substantial insurance, and take myself on an extended holiday to the Caribbean, where I would live in sexual bliss with a swath of priapic Costa Ricans.

PROBLEM: Since we bought the self-igniting gas stove, and as neither of us smokes, matches are in short supply.

TWO: I could go one better and pick up the best-looking man in the universe and flaunt him in front of my treacherous friend and my traitorous other half.

PROBLEM: I had walked out without my wallet and I was not about to humiliate myself further by coitus-interrupting them again in the one night. Besides, in expectation of screwing Geofferey myself, I hadn't douched. Big mistake.

THREE: I could go to the bars and get pissed.

PROBLEM: (a) See above re wallet. (b) I'm an abstainer.

So, mature reflection over, I did what any seasoned gay man does under such circumstances—I consulted a clairvoyant.

Madame Acacia, occult friend to the gay and lesbian

communities, lives not far from the setting of the current perfidy, and she's accustomed to her friends popping around for a quick emotional cheer-up and tarot reading to see if the night's trolling is going to be blessed with union.

"Give me your watch," she said.

"But it cost $240," I whined.

"You have more money than sense," she retorted. "Anyway, Rolex or Lorus, it's all the same."

Madame Acacia was big on predictions and short on taste.

As she explained that she had not gone into bartering for payment, I handed it over, upon which she spasmed violently and dropped it. Hoping (a) that the watch had survived the drop intact or was at least repairable, but mainly (b) that it was a sign that Geofferey would die a screamingly wretched death before the week was out and that he would never ever have another satisfying sexual encounter after Tito, my reveries were interrupted by Madame Acacia's demanding, "Get rid of him. He's nothing but trouble."

"But I love him!" I protested.

"Rubbish! That's your dick talking."

It throbbed its agreement that Geofferey was one helluva sex kitten and probably phenomenal in the sack. And that bubble butt. The things I could have . . . but on all those points Tito was sure to provide an overly ample firsthand account.

Madame Acacia offered not the least consolation.

So with a dangly bit that simply would not dangle crying out for attention, I took the fifth most mature option of the night: I slunk back home and forlornly hoicked myself over our back brick fence as quietly as grazed knuckles and scuffed shins allowed and crept up the side to the double-glazed picture window where I had a perfect uninterrupted view of the goings-on in the living room from behind the shrubbery.

And from my darkened vantage point behind Tito's potted shrubbery, I admired my lover in full rampancy in each and every one of Geofferey's inviting but well-utilized passageways, fantasizing myself in his place. Eventually I found, if not release from rejection and humiliation, at least freedom from frustration.

The next day when Tito was watering the garden and complained of the awful coagulated, viscous mess that was blighting his greenery, I merely shrugged.

And blamed the pigeons.

Apple Tree

Wayne Hoffman

It was strange for an atheist to be quoting the Bible, but love tends to muddle the mind. Mark had me so starry-eyed, so goofy with love, that I was reciting poetry, talking baby talk, planning "a ceremony" at age nineteen.

It's enough to give a park-cruising, trick-turning gutter slut like me a reputation.

But I had a real live valentine for the first time, so I poured on the schmaltz. A love note. A selection from e. e. cummings. A verse from Song of Songs. In English *and* Hebrew.

Like an apple tree among the trees of the forest, so is my beloved among men.

Mark still has that valentine (possibly for future blackmail purposes) tucked away somewhere. It's been eight years since I answered his personal ad—something about a sense of humor "so dry it could blow away"—with an awkwardly self-revelatory (but apparently effective) note. And though we've certainly had our ups and downs, he still brings out the romantic in me.

It's hard to believe we broke up in 1991.

I thought nothing of it when he excused himself to use the bathroom on our first date. Little did I know he was secretly calling his best friend.

"But what will we talk about?" he asked. "He's so *young!*"

Mark had little to worry about; as I recall, I carried that conversation clear through lunch, several hours of walking around Washington, and all the way back to his Capitol Hill apartment. I hadn't yet learned that his genteel Southern ways made him reluctant to interrupt a Northeastern chatterbox like me. I figured it out at his place, as I sat on the couch waiting for him to stick something in my mouth and shut me up.

"You lure me back to your apartment, you're seven years older than I am, and you're going to wait for *me* to make the first move?" I asked impatiently, only half-joking.

(Well, it worked.)

We had a few good years as lovers. Really good years. Intimate dinners, cheap vacations, effortless conversations, family gatherings. And great sex, monumental sex that never wavered even in our worst moments. (We had our share of those, too.)

But our best years, many of our best times together, still lay over the mountains.

There was a gap after the breakup, nearly a year when we barely spoke. But, hard as it was to admit that I missed him, it was sillier to pretend that I didn't. We walked a precarious line for some time, unsure of our destination, until we realized that being a pair didn't mean we had to be a couple.

Our first trip together after we split up was to a writers' conference in Boston, when we were still negotiating exactly what our relationship would comprise. We could just be colleagues, two conference attendees who happened to know each other. Or we could be cruising pals, free to prowl the South End for a few days. Or we could be divorcés, some gay Odd Couple stewing and rehashing old arguments that we'd had years earlier on the same Boston streets.

Fortunately, we were both a bit bored by the conference, afraid we'd be forced to sit through some poetry slam or other, so we decided to skip the last day altogether. We borrowed a car and headed north; Mark had never seen Vermont, and foliage was at its autumn peak. As we spun around the mountain roads, stopping only for some clam chowder and to buy maple candies, we witnessed the first snow of the season.

It was pure New England kitsch, a moment at once hackneyed and new. But it was kitsch we shared, half-longing, half-laughing. And though it's only apparent in retrospect, that was the day we relaxed into our new relationship, comfortable and loving and just slightly postmodern.

If romance is nostalgia, we've got plenty of that: standing-room-only photo albums and hidden love notes. (I've got a few, too; I wasn't the only one writing earnest letters—although as I recall, Mark never got biblical on me.) I still pull them out occasionally, bringing back that old tingling buzz I remember so well. If romance is union, we've got that, too; we still finish each other's sentences, anticipate each other's calls, and speak paragraphs in total silence. (Baby talk, however, even unspoken, is a thing of the past.) And if romance is communication, we still confide more in each other than in anyone else (I've got the long-distance bills to prove it)—and our respective new boyfriends have simply come to understand.

He's still part of my family, although there's no ceremony where we can proclaim it; sometimes he's my parents' favorite child. When my mother recently drove up with him to visit me in New York, she found she preferred him as a traveling companion. "We sang show tunes the whole way up," she told me. "He didn't play any of that noise that you listen to." (I guess she quickly forgave him for breaking her little boy's heart; *Fiddler on the Roof* always did soften her up.)

Words, however, have finally failed me after eight years. I don't know what to call him. *Soul mate* is accurate but sounds too New Age—or too seventies, I can't decide. *Friend* seems inadequate, a term too generic to support our very specific baggage. *Ex-lover* is technically correct, but makes us sound like bitter, chain-smoking queens. And *buddy* is just too G. I. Joe for either of us.

In private—strictly in private—I call him Pooky (my reputation now utterly destroyed), although I never did when we were dating. It's a postdivorce pet name.

But he'll always be my apple tree: fruity, strong, and just a bit shady.

Extracurricular Activity

Larry Duplechan

Jimmy and I met in the showers at the Bally's Total Fitness health spa in Encino, maybe five minutes south on the Ventura Freeway from Woodland Hills, the somewhat sleepy suburb of Los Angeles where I lived with my partner of, then, seventeen years. While I hadn't noticed Jimmy in the weight room, I'd caught sight of him in the locker room—deep of chest and round of ass, with coarse, curly (and slightly receding) black hair and a pale olive complexion (if my skin was chocolate milk, his was Eagle-brand sweetened condensed) that suggested (to me, anyway) Italian or perhaps Greek extraction. (I'd later learn that he was actually half-Lebanese, half-English.) While lathering our respective anatomies beneath adjoining showers, Jimmy and I made quick eye contact and looked away, followed immediately by the sort of extended eye contact that never, but never, occurs between adult heterosexual males in America. We traded smiles. I was then treated to the winsome sight of Mr. Curly Hair's penis lifting its purplish head toward the ceiling. Followed by another exchange of grins.

"You look good," I said as we toweled off, standing

dangerously close to my still-smiling (if somewhat less tumescent) new buddy.

"Damn," he said through a wide smile.

"Damn?"

"Damn, you look so good."

We exchanged names and enjoyed a moist, rather prolonged handshake.

"Would you like to get together sometime?" I asked as we exited the spa side by side.

"Absolutely."

"Great," I said, rummaging around my fanny pack for a pen and a scrap of paper. Then I quickly added, "I'm in a relationship."

"So'm I. So I guess this'll be extracurricular activity for both of us."

"Yeah."

Okay, so I'm not so great at snappy repartee when standing in front of a San Fernando Valley health spa, swapping idiotic grins with a hot man while scribbling my phone number on the back of an old ATM receipt.

And Jimmy was definitely hot. And apparently hot for me. And married. What could be better?

It took a couple of weeks for us to schedule our first date—at my house: My Lover having left for a weeklong camping trip with a group of our friends (I do not camp in the sleep-on-the-ground sense of the term), and His Lover also conveniently out of town.

Closing my front door behind Jimmy, I asked, "Do

you kiss?" Because, let's face it, some guys don't.

"Absolutely," he said. And so we did. Jimmy's kisses were deep and sweet and tasted ever so slightly, it seemed to me, of coffee. As I'd learn over the next couple of hours, Jimmy managed a Starbucks. Consequently, the most intimate folds of his body smelled, and tasted, of coffee. Freshly ground, expensive coffee.

Jimmy was my idea of good sex: enthusiastic and affectionate, with a hard-muscled body—he worked out five days a week, and while he wasn't bulky, his entire body felt like a hard-on. Perhaps most important, Jimmy was vocally admiring of me.

"Come here, beautiful man," he said, pulling me down onto my bed and into another round of kisses.

"I could suck your dick all day," he said a bit later, between audible slurps. But he didn't. Instead, he traveled farther south. By the time he'd introduced his lips, tongue, and finally, a finger to my back door, it seemed pointless (and rather inhospitable) to mention that I'm basically a top. So I unrolled a Trojan over Jimmy's humid-headed boner and allowed him to boldly go where relatively few men had gone before.

After we'd both cum (Jimmy straddled me and sprayed my chest and belly with a truly impressive amount of hot liquid), we showered, cooked, and then ate dinner—Jimmy wrapped in my terry-cloth bathrobe, me in My Lover's. We sprawled on the living room sofa, toyed with each other's nipples, and in the great gay-male tradition of fuck first, converse later, talked.

Jimmy was thirty years old, eight years my junior (he made the appropriate noises about my not looking my age). He'd been with His Lover for three years. His Lover was considerably older, nearly fifty. His Lover was in some sort of sales and traveled a good deal; My Lover worked in a bank and traveled little. While my relationship with My Lover was officially open—that is, extracurricular activity was not considered a breach of fidelity or a breach of contract or a breach of much of anything—Jimmy's relationship with His Lover was not. What Jimmy did, he had to do on the sly.

"I'd like to see you again," I said as I walked Jimmy to the door.

"Absolutely," he said, treating me to another coffee-flavored smooch.

Months passed before we had occasion to meet again, this time at the Hollywood Hills condo Jimmy shared with His Lover. The lovemaking was even better the second time around (despite the nose-tickling fur in the bed from Jimmy's ancient Persian cat).

"This is the best," I said, lying across Jimmy's (and His Lover's) bed, Jimmy hot and sticky-wet in my arms. "I'm in a good relationship with a man I love, and every few months, I get to see you."

"You're right," he said. "It's pretty great."

"I've got an idea. I'll be your mistress, and you can be mine."

"Absolutely."

Later, we ate turkey sandwiches and discussed my writing (Jimmy had actually bought and read two of my books in the interim—who couldn't love such a man?), while Dionne Farris's *Wild Seed, Wild Flower* CD played in the background.

We met twice more over the ensuing eighteen or so months—again at Jimmy's, and then at my house. When Jimmy arrived at my house, a bottle of Korbel brut in hand, he seemed a bit agitated. When I mentioned it, he explained that he and His Lover had just quarreled, over Jimmy's desire to engage in extracurricular activity, and to do so openly. "I don't really want to talk about it," he said. "I certainly don't want to burden you with it." But a bottle of bubbly and some coffee-tinged lovemaking later, over grilled chicken and more wine, we talked about it.

"I love him," Jimmy said, gesturing with his fork. "I really do. But it's, like, I'm thirty-two years old, and I've never looked better in my life, and guys are, like, running up to me with their phone numbers, you know?"

I did know. My Lover had told me the same tale when he first asked to open up our relationship, a notion I fought fiercely for nearly two years. We'd nearly broken up over the issue, after fourteen years together, before I'd finally acquiesced.

"I'm thinking of leaving him," Jimmy said, as much to his corn on the cob as to me.

"I hope you don't. For the most selfish of reasons."

"What do you mean?"

"What I mean is, what makes you and me work is that we're both happily married. If all of a sudden you're single—well, it just won't work anymore, will it?"

How I do hate being right all the damn time.

The next time I spoke to Jimmy, on the phone, he told me he'd broken up with His Lover, during an RSVP cruise to the Greek islands. Jimmy had insisted on opening the relationship, and His Lover wouldn't budge.

"Don't worry," he said. "I'll keep in touch." But he didn't. That was half a year ago. His phone number has long since been changed. And I haven't heard from him.

Oh, well. Heaven knows, it was good while it lasted. And I'll always have Dionne Farris.

And to tell the truth, I still get a tiny bit horny every time I walk past a Starbucks.

PART THREE

ODD
ENCOUNTERS

If *Boys Meets Boy* were a self-help book, this last section might be titled "When Bad Sex Happens to Hot Men."

Sometimes an encounter takes an unexpected turn. When this happens, we might just go with the flow, because we are so startled it is the easiest thing to do. Or it may be too late to back out, or we can't think of a delicate or graceful way to avoid a situation so we submit to it.

And afterward, as we recall the moment or relate it to our friends, we laugh and ask ourselves, incredulous, "What was I thinking?"

The writers fearlessly recount some of these painfully embarrassing moments, which will leave you wincing in recognition of "having been there" in similar situations, while at the same time laughing at the absurdity of the imbroglios they have wound up in.

In that way, it may serve as a sort of self-help book after all, as cautionary tales of possible pitfalls when boys meet boys, or provide comfort when your own encounters take a turn for the unexpected, and you recall these episodes and realize it could always be worse.

Sex Tips for Boys

Or, What to Do When the Guy You Met in the Steam Room Wants to Get to Know You Better Before He Lets You Put His Penis in Your Mouth; or, Dates from Hell

David Feinberg

Recently, I've had an unrelenting stream of bad dates. Indeed, were it not for my shining knight in Montreal whom I met at a bathhouse so sleazy that the dryer was broken and consequently patrons were given wet towels, I believe I would have completely lost hope in all humanity, or at least that portion of humanity with which I might possibly get laid. For some reason, nobody wants to have sex with me these days, save that occasional bulimic Adult-Child-of-Alcoholics novelty dancer who keeps calling me at odd hours. There *was* a rather enjoyable hour of foreplay *interruptus* in the hotel room of an extremely attentive young man last week, but then again, he was from L.A., which more or less negates any possibility of consummating the deed in the future, near or distant. Before that was the cute but unfortunately overly introspective neuropsychiatric resident whose ex-lover was dying of leukemia who told me that he was initially drawn to me because of his subliminal death

125

wish and perhaps given my serostatus I could be an agent of his death, whereas I in fact preferred to be known as an instrument. And before that was the gentleman (although perhaps it would be a stretch to refer to him using this descriptive, since *douche bag* would be more appropriate) whom I picked up at the gym, had sloppy and not particularly memorable sex with, and then, two weeks later to the day when I saw him at the gym as I was doing forty-pound curls, had the following conversation with:

"Hi, Mike."

Genially: "Hi." Pause.

(Figuring he'd forgotten my name) "It's Dave."

"Oh." Bigger pause. "I know I know you from somewhere. I'm sorry, but I just can't place it."

Huge pause. "The gym."

Quick beat. "Oh, yeah. You came over that evening."

Brief pause. "It must be my new haircut." The one that looks identical to my previous 'do.

Of course, what I should have said was, "It's quite understandable that you wouldn't remember me because, being a clone, I look exactly like the last fifteen men you've had sex with, whereas your quite distinct acne scars make you what Natalie King Cole sang last year in the necro-incest duet with her dead father, *unforgettable*."

But now everyone I meet wants to have *relationships*. I refer specifically to the failed actor I met last month under extremely tawdry circumstances at my gymnasium whose testicles I have, in fact, felt in the palm of my hand, as if I were comparison-shopping for produce at the local A & P. Quite exquisite, I might add. Well, Walter (not his real name) decided that he wanted to get to know me better before we did the nasty. Gleefully, I referred him to the local bookstore, thinking that perhaps he could purchase and read both of my admittedly autobiographical novels. Since he felt a need to get to know me better and I didn't necessarily feel the same need, I didn't understand why I had to be physically present as he "got to know" me. Nonetheless, I proceeded to undergo a series of quite enjoyable (and to my mind, quite beside the point) dinners and movies and the occasional shopping expedition with him: I believe they're known as "dates" in common parlance. Still no nooky. Walter still felt that I was primarily interested in having sex and that the only reason he was the object of my interest was physical proximity. Frankly, I didn't understand how we could have sex otherwise.

I decided to do what I usually do, which is make a list, comparing reasons to sleep with someone immediately and reasons not to.

David Feinberg

Reason Not to Sleep with Someone Immediately
1.

I decided that I would write the second list first, and by the time I finished the second list, perhaps one or two reasons to wait would spontaneously occur to me.

Reasons to Sleep with Someone Immediately
1. Your combined T cells taken as SAT scores wouldn't get either of you into the tiniest, most decrepit community college in the state of Iowa, and they have open admissions there.

2. To know, know, know you is *not* necessarily to love, love, love you. As a matter of fact, the more appropriate proverb here is "familiarity breeds contempt."

3. "I'd love to blow you but I just did pentamidine" doesn't really cut it as a good excuse. Why else did God invent breath mints and peppermint-swirled candies?

4. Just because he suffered the humiliation of having his braces entangled when he kissed his second cousin Matilda when he was fourteen, there is no reason to repeat the trauma at thirty-five by getting his IV entangled with yours at some future date. *Carpe frenulum!* Seize the dick!

5. Sexual intercourse can be an extremely intimate form of nonverbal communication. If he really wants to know you better, what better way than by fornication? Indeed, sex can function as an excellent "icebreaker" in

terms of breaking down barriers and thus facilitating future intimacy. On the other hand, if he wishes to keep his distance, sex can be had in a multitude of ways that would not necessarily impinge on anyone's personal space.

With Jeffrey Dahmer in prison and Roy Cohn most decidedly dead, I still haven't come up with any adequate reasons not to sleep with someone on the first date. I suppose there's always that character issue. You could fall asleep next to some gorgeous hunk and wake up next to a design professional or, worse yet, an actor. But, hey, why be picky? Discrimination is against the law. Moreover, it's tacky. If anyone knows of any good reasons to wait, please let me know. You know where to find me.

129

Bridge-and-Tunnel Tony

Tim Driscoll

Everyone in the cast has been teasing me today because I have a date after the show, and he's picking me up right down the road from the afternoon dinner theater where I work, which is right on Route 17 in Wood-Ridge, New Jersey. His name's Tony, and he's Italian, and he's picking me up in his black Trans Am at White Castle. When I told Tony I did musical theater in New Jersey, it was hard enough to explain the concept of afternoon dinner theater (the producers bus church and retirement groups in from all over New Jersey—the cast members call this type of audience "blue hair"), hard enough to explain *La Cage aux Folles* (a show he'd never heard of since the American movie hadn't yet come out), and hard enough to explain my role in the show (Phaedra the Enigma), but trying to give him directions to the theater was even harder, since I never drive there myself—I take a bus out of Port Authority to get there every day, and I don't pay attention to where the bus is going.

So as I'm talking, I'm trying to think of clues to tell him how to get there. "Well, I know it's right on Route 17 . . . and it only takes us like twenty minutes out of the city . . . and it's this big brown building that faces the freeway . . ."

"Wait—is it right down the road from White Castle?"

I guess that's all I would've needed to say.

So we decide that I'll page him after I finish the show and that I'll meet him at White Castle instead of at the theater, so he can pick up a pack of the famous little frozen hamburgers for his little brother. As I'm walking the stretch of Route 17 in between the little-known theater and the famous fast-food restaurant, there's a sudden cloudburst that comes out of nowhere. It's summer, so I have shorts and sandals on, and I start running as rain starts pelting down on my freshly scrubbed face and freshly slicked-back hair. As I'm running along against oncoming traffic, I can hear my sandals slapping along the gutter of the access road to Route 17 in my desperate attempt to get to an eating place built to look like what it's called—a big white castle. When I get inside, the air-conditioning's on full blast, because it's July and it's hot, so there I am—wet, out of breath, and freezing, but afraid to go to the bathroom to dry myself off, because that would be the moment that Tony'd drive up. I order and pay for a package of the twelve little burgers to save time, then stand right in front of the entrance doors, shivering in the air that's chilly and filled with the smell of grease and ketchup.

All of a sudden I see a black Trans Am make a right off of Route 17. He speeds past the glass doors, making water spray up onto the sidewalk, as he sees me waving the burger bag to let him know he doesn't have to come in. He gasses it all the way to the end of the parking lot, then spins the car around and stops right in front of where I'm standing at the top of the stairs to the castle. I guess he wants the passenger door to be convenient for me. From where I am at the top of the stairs, I can see through the smoked glass of his T-top. I see his black hair trying to stay combed straight back, and he looks up at me with this smile that says, "Get in!"

As I go down the stairs, I think about how weird it is to be meeting his mother on our first actual date. The only other time Tony and I have been together is when we sucked each other off in a buddy-booth bookstore on Christopher Street, conveniently located (for Tony) near the PATH train to New Jersey, and (for me) right down the street from where I live in the Village. When he first saw me, Tony tried for a long time to get me to go in a booth with him, but I was afraid of getting reprimanded by the Middle Eastern mop men who run the place.

"What, are you afraid they're gonna go tell your mom or something?" Tony jeered at me a couple of times. I thought he said it as a joke, just to get me to realize how ridiculous it is to be afraid of these men who make money to send home to their wives in other countries off of gay guys who put quarters in slots to be able to suck dick. I definitely wasn't concerned about my own mom finding out, since she lives all the way across the country. I didn't know until later that it'd be *his* mom I'd have to be afraid of. Tony's only twenty-three, and he still lives at home. I'm twenty-nine and live alone in Manhattan. I hadn't really planned on dating him, because both his age and his bridge-and-tunnel status were working against him, but also because I'd had my heart broken recently and had sworn off relationships (which are rare and take too much work for what they're worth) and I was striving for anonymous sex (which, especially when you live in the Village, is plentiful and easy to attain at any time). But Tony had been so adorable, making out with me and saying stuff like, "Okay, my turn," as he bent over to suck my cock in the 2½-by-2½ foot buddy booth, that I'd agreed to go out with him even though one of the three numbers he'd written down for me when we'd parted had "MY MOM" scribbled next to it.

Today Tony's taking me to meet his mom at their house in Chatham, New Jersey. His Italian mom. Italian from Italy.

So I get in the car, and of course he has the air-conditioning on full blast. "It's freezing in here!"

He grabs my hand and holds it while he steers with the other. I think it's so sexy when a guy can so confidently do that. I bring the hand that he's holding mine with to my mouth and kiss his part of the fist we're forming.

"Oh my God, I was just gonna do that to you. Y'know,

you are so hot. You're so hot you make my blood boil."

Out of anyone else's mouth, a comment like that would make my eyes roll, but for some reason, coming from him it sounds so adorable.

So after an hour of driving and holding hands the whole way (he never lets go and neither do I), we finally get to his house. As we walk along the curving concrete walkway leading to his front door, Tony tells me, "Y'know, when I told my mom I was bringing you over today, I told her I really like you. I told her I thought you were really hot."

"You told your mom you thought I was really hot?"

"Mm-hmm. My mom's like my best friend—I tell her everything . . . and you are—you're hot. I told you . . . you're so hot you make my blood boil."

It's all in the way he says it. So adorable. Except now I'm walking into the house of an Italian mother who's probably wondering in what way I'm so hot.

So Tony opens up this huge carved oak door and steps into a marble-floored entryway and bellows out like a teenager, "Mommmm! We're home! . . . Um, we're here!"

We walk past the stairway toward the kitchen, and there she is . . . his mom . . . with a full head of silver hair, but a young face, showing no signs of aging, and showing no signs of welcome.

"Hi . . ." I awkwardly half-smile at her, standing there

in my sandals, which are still soaked from running along
Route 17.

She just leans back aggressively against a huge
wooden table in the middle of an enormous kitchen
with her arms crossed. She nods slightly as if to say,
"So you're the one who's so hot, huh?"

So Tony tells her, "Mom, we're gonna order Chinese."

And she almost shouts that she already made something with beef, but Tony turns to her and says sternly,
"Mom, we want Chinese."

So she throws me a dirty look. Then she really gives
me a scary glare when Tony motions me over to the
door to the basement. What better place to suck off and
butt-fuck her son but the rec room basement? As we're
hopping down the stairs, she starts rattling off demands
to "Antonio" in Italian, and Tony just yeses her back in
English. She leaves the door to the top of the stairs wide
open and every once in a while hurls some message in
that fiery language down at us.

So me and Tony receive our order of spicy beef and
vegetables with white rice, and Tony wants me to watch
his favorite movie of all time, *Terminator*. He has the
whole three-movie collection set in a special carrying
case that he shows off to me. As we eat, he explains
parts of the movie to me in ways I'd never have expected
Terminator to be interpreted. Again, it's adorable. Trust

me. We finish our food, and Tony trots up the stairs to take the plates to the kitchen, and I hear his mother scream something at him right before I hear him close the rec room door at the top of the stairs on his way back down. He sits down next to me on the couch and holds my hand. The door swings open, and although the couch is out of her view, she stands at the top of the stairs and screams one more thing, this time partly in English—about mowing the lawn tomorrow.

"Okay, Mom, okay!"

She slams the door shut again as Arnold blows someone away. I change my vertical position to lie across his lap, and he starts to get hard, and that makes me get hard, too, and all the motorcycle and machine-gun sounds seem to actually exacerbate our horniness. Tony whispers that he wants to suck my dick, and we roll into an easy sixty-nine, as Arnold scrapes a car along a concrete barrier. Tony then slowly pushes us off the couch to do it on the floor, I guess in respect for his mother. The carpet isn't thick, so Tony pulls a crocheted afghan off the back of the couch and says quietly, "We gotta be careful with this—my grandma made it."

So we suck each other, with Tony stopping his noiseless slurping every once in a while with a one-third-worried, one-third-horny, one-third-disinterested look on his face, like he loves what he's doing, but kind of wants to get it over with before she opens the door again, but also wants to see what's happening on the screen.

Now if times were different, we would at least not have had to worry about keeping the place clean—we could simply swallow each other's load. But in the nineties, neither of us is gonna take any cum in his mouth, so when I get close, I suddenly pull off of his lips. Unfortunately, I time it too closely, and I shoot before I can roll onto my back and have the load project onto my belly as I'd planned. Instead, my jism spurts out—not strongly enough to spray all over Tony, porno-style, but inefficiently and awkwardly—onto the afghan.

"Shit!" Tony whispers, afraid to touch the stuff for fear of rubbing it in. He slides up carefully, trying not to make the folds in the fabric touch together for fear of causing the thick, milky fluid to spread further.

As Tony goes to the bathroom to get some tissue, his hard-on boinging out of his boxers, any slight fears I have are washed away as I notice that Grandma must make her afghans out of acrylic. My load stays intact on top of the nonabsorbent synthetic fibers, glistening in the glare of the television screen, as Arnold swings his ridiculously large loaded weapon around.

Luckily, I'm fully tucked back in and zipped (but also still fully hard) when the door at the top of the stairs swings open—just as Arnold mutters, "I'll be back."

As Tony's mom rattles off some new unintelligible command, I watch the screen, wishing I could hear how Arnold would say, "You're so hot you make my blood boil."

Rock 'n' Roll Groupies

Peter Burton

They don't get as much publicity, but male groupies are every bit as in evidence around stage doors as their more notorious female counterparts. I should know, I took advantage of enough of them when, between 1972 and 1977, I left England to crisscross America in the entourage of the rock band Rod Stewart and the Faces.

And it was all so easy.

Picture the backstage area of a large American concert hall or stadium—be it in New York, Los Angeles, or somewhere in the Midwest. The band have finished their set and the obligatory encores. Now they are ensconced in their dressing room—drinking, smoking, as likely as not fighting about the merits and faults of the evening's show.

The stage area is abuzz with activity as the road crew dismantle the stage set and the lighting and sound equipment, loading it onto the trucks that will haul it to the next venue. Elsewhere Bill Gaff—one of the few rock managers to have publicly come out—might be collecting the great bundles of cash and stuffing them into his briefcase. The night's take.

Others of us drift more or less aimlessly—awaiting

that moment when we can climb into our limousine and speed back to the hotel in which we're staying. Mingling with the tour personnel will be youths and young women who have somehow managed to acquire back-stage passes. They're dedicated fans—and probably dress in the style the band were wearing on the previous tour. It's also likely that they're drunk or stoned, possibly both.

The fact that I have access to the dressing room will have drawn attention to me. As I make my way through the door—in search of another drink—a boy of around eighteen stops me. He has floppy blond hair, the kind of tan that simply doesn't exist back home in England, and is dressed in aging Levi's jeans and a form-hugging white T-shirt.

"Hey, man. Are you with the band?"

I nod. "Sure."

"Can you get me in there?" He gestures toward the dressing room.

" 'Fraid not. Boys are busy."

I stare at the boy. He's really rather cute. I relent a little. "Would you like a drink?"

"Gee! Wow! Swell! Great!"

"I'll fetch you one when I come out next time," I promise as I push my way through the door and into the room. By this time I've made up my mind. I fill a plastic beaker with red wine and replenish my own drink. Then I'm outside again.

"Hi," I say as I hand him his drink. "I'm Peter." I find myself adopting a mid-Atlantic accent.

Brick stretches out a hand. I do likewise. We shake hands. His grip is firm.

"Hi, Brick," I acknowledge, and give a smile that I hope isn't too predatory.

"What d'you do?"

"I'm the group's publicist."

"Gee! Wow! Swell! Great!"

"It's a living," I reply nonchalantly.

"Wow! Hey—what's Rod like?"

"He's a nice enough guy," I say, and then add, almost as an afterthought, "He'll probably drop by my room for a drink later."

"Wow! Hey—are Rod and Woody gay?"

He's certainly got the picture.

"No way," I say.

"They sure act it sometimes."

"Well, they're not."

"I'd sure like to meet Rod. I think he's real neat."

"Why don't you come back with me then? I might be able to arrange something."

No chance. Rod will have his own fish to fry.

"Gee! Wow! I can't believe this is happening to me."

This is probably the moment when Billy reappears, clutching the cash-laden briefcase. He gives me a knowing wink. "Let's go," he says, and hurries away to the area where the limousines are parked.

Brick and I follow, climbing into the car after him. "Billy, Brick. Brick, Billy," I say by way of introduction. "Billy's Rod's manager."

This information elicits another "Wow! Gee!" from Brick.

The car speeds away back to the hotel. There's always food and drink in my room—sometimes music, too, if I've bothered to pack a cassette player and tapes. And there's so much luggage spread around—totally covering the second bed in the room—that the only place to sit is on the bed I'm using. Brick settles himself.

"Drink?" I offer, holding up a bottle of Scotch. He nods. I pour hefty shots into two glasses and add no more that a dash of soda water. "Food?" I hand him his drink and gesture toward the cold cuts, salad, and fruit on the room-service trolley in the center of the room. Brick swallows about a third of his whiskey. He shakes his head. He swallows more of his drink.

"Hey, would you mind if I take a shower?"

"Go ahead," I reply with a sense of anticipation. But he drains his glass and, fully clothed, disappears into the bathroom. After about ten minutes, Brick emerges from the bathroom. Damp and pink, a towel round his shoulders, a towel round his waist, and his discarded clothes in his arms.

He deposits the clothes on the floor and—still towel-clad—sprawls on the bed. "Another?" I ask, holding his empty glass. He nods. Over what is probably another

141

hour, we empty the bottle of Scotch and consume most of the food. We are "merry" rather than drunk and I'm both tired and enjoying an anticipatory erection.

"I'm bushed," I admit. "I think I'll turn in."

Brick doesn't say anything.

"You can stay the night if you like."

"Great."

"You might as well get in with me. It's too much hassle to shift all *that*." I point at the luggage-laden spare bed.

"It's okay. I'll sleep on the couch."

This I hadn't planned for.

Brick takes the cover from the end of my bed and puts it over the seat of the couch. "Shall I do the lights?" He turns out the lights and in the moonlit room he is but a shadow as he removes the towels and slides under the cover on the sofa.

Naked in bed and still gently erect, I ponder my next move. Brick is breathing easily, but I'm pretty sure he isn't asleep. I ease myself from the bed and across to the sofa. As I kneel by the side of him, I gaze down on Brick. He really is very appealing.

The cover from my bed is only over the lower half of Brick's body. Cautiously I stroke the smooth, still-boyish skin of his shoulder. He neither flinches nor responds. I venture further, letting my fingers tease his nipples. There is still no reaction. I incline my head and kiss—then suck—one nipple after the other. He certainly doesn't seem to object to my advances.

Manipulating the cover, I slide my hand under and let my fingers stroke his stomach, working slowly down until they graze his pubic hair.

Brick is quite inert, yet clearly wide-awake. My fingers move into the bush of his pubic hair and I rub at the base of his cock. He is entirely flaccid. Abandoning all caution (he's clearly not going to thump me), I begin to manipulate his cock in the hopes of arousal. No response. What can I do to get him hard?

"I can arrange tickets and a backstage pass for tomorrow night's gig," I whisper. There is a low sigh. "It should be a great show."

My hand continues to tug at Brick's cock. Is it finally beginning to respond? It is . . .

"I could let you have some money to get there," I continue. He's definitely stiffening. "Twenty-five dollars. Maybe fifty."

Brick's cock is now fully erect. I push the cover completely away from his body and plunge my mouth down onto his cock. I suck at it for a few minutes before coming up for air. "Come to bed," I say.

Brick nods. In what now seems an idiotic gesture, I scoop him up into my arms and carry him over to the bed. "Don't fuck me," he says as I lower him onto the bed and climb in beside him.

Nor did I—though we did everything else.

And from the point of view of a rock 'n' roll fan, Brick's night wasn't entirely wasted. The following morning, while I was shaving, the telephone rang.

"Can you get that, Brick?" I called.

The ringing stopped as the receiver was lifted. I could hear the murmur of Brick's voice. Then he was at the bathroom door, shaking with excitement. "It's Mick Jagger. He wants to know which room Woody's in . . ."

Sibling Rivalry

Dean Durber

My sister was just leaving the house when she teasingly mentioned that her latest boyfriend was waiting upstairs. She changed them all too regularly, an indecisiveness on her part that really pissed me off. She was bronzed, with long, flowing hair and a well-toned body. She could—and did—have any boy she wanted. I, on the other hand, was pale and puny. And male. The closest I ever got to such pleasures was a sneaky brush against the leg of her latest as we sat on the sofa watching television, and it took weeks for me to build up enough courage to get that far. And given Sam's indecisiveness, time was not always on my side.

I waited until she had disappeared and then raced upstairs to meet him. In my haste, I accidentally bumped into him as he was stepping out of the bathroom, causing his loosely tied green towel to fall seductively to the floor. I knew then that this one had to last. He bent down, ever so slowly, to retrieve the fallen towel. My face was burning red. Embarrassment or not, I still had time to check out the fresh cleanliness of his cock, slightly too stiff at that particular moment to be dangling naturally between his legs. I guessed that the

145

rubdown he had just given himself in the shower had excited it to the point where just a little bit more work might have provided a full erection. I could easily have offered him this service by reaching out my hand. But I stopped myself. John was my sister's new boyfriend. I could at least afford to wait a little longer.

"Sam's out," he told me without the slightest hint of shame at what had happened to him. He didn't even attempt to divert his stare from my eyes as he said this. Instead, he slowly brushed his cock with the palm of his hand, slipping it neatly inside the towel again. Was he the one for me? I needed to consult a copy of my sister's *Girlfriend* magazine for the right answer.

> *Q: I am in love with a guy who is five years older than me. We spend heaps of time together and I really miss him when I'm not with him. I like him so much, I told a gorgeous babe at school the other day to go jump. Should I stay with him and try to make it last or should I go back to the schoolboys? Confused, NSW.*

> A: You'll probably change a lot between now and the time you want to get married. You might decide he's not right for you—so don't pin all your hopes on him. However, there's no reason to break up with him just because you might not marry him. Enjoy the time you spend with him and evaluate your relationship as it goes along.

That settled it. I waited patiently until he had finished dressing in my sister's room and then raced to find his wet towel in amongst the dirty laundry. I smuggled it into the bathroom and took a hot shower of my own. I imagined how he must have looked there, surrounded by steam, covered in soapy suds. I sniffed hard and smelled every part of his body where it lingered on the towel. My sister and I had similar tastes. She went for the likes of John because she knew my mother expected better, as if John and his muscles were not good enough for our family. I went for him because he belonged to my sister and I wanted to one up her.

I followed them everywhere. My sister never once complained about having her younger brother in tow. She was too fond of flaunting her affections in my face. And was permitted to do so, whilst I was forced to reserve my feelings for the solitude of my own bedroom. Talk about a love that dare not speak its name!

I encouraged Sam to never miss out on her nightly aerobic class.

"Just think of those thighs and that arse," I urged. "John will go wild for all that."

The more often she was out of the house working on her body, the greater the chances of getting John to work on mine. That was the plan.

I watched them as they caressed and tickled each other unashamedly on the sofa. My eyes were fixed directly on the television ahead, but I sat close enough so as to be able to make out their reflections in the screen.

They kissed and cuddled with sound. I took those pictures and noises with me everywhere, waiting for the day when I would take her place. I sat at the dining table eating pizza and drinking Coke, sharing every meal they had. I fetched him food and drink, acting as his servant, fighting with my sister for every last drop of his attention. I would have done anything he asked of me. The only time I ever left them alone was when they stepped inside my sister's bedroom and closed the door. I would have gone inside, too, if they had let me. And maybe just watched. But, for now, I was forced to retreat to my own room next door and merely listen. It was at times like this that my need for comfort and advice was at its greatest.

Q: I'm really nervous about getting a boyfriend. Everybody else around me seems to have one. People bully me and tease me, so that makes it worse. My friend has a really nice boyfriend and I'm jealous of her. I don't want to hurt my friend by telling her how I feel. Please help. Jealous Girl, Queensland.

A: There's heaps to look forward to. Just because life seems glum at the moment doesn't mean it always will. You can't survive in life if you compare yourself to others—you'll always find someone who seems to have it better. If we're jealous of others, it poisons our hearts. Make the most of what you've got. Life goes in circles—good and bad things happen to us all. Don't mention your feelings to your friend. It's your prob, not hers. Just because you've never had a boyfriend doesn't mean there's anything wrong with you. It's all part of learning who's right for us. In the meantime, be happy for your friend.

I could always tell when they had finished. Usually long after me. My sister stepped out with a smile on her face as if to let me know she had won again.

"Don't you ever work out?" he asked me one day just after they had reappeared from the bedroom. He was in total innocence of my fixation. How could I? I would never be able to show my full body at the gym to the likes of him. I mapped out the shape of his upper torso through the tight white T-shirt that clung to his body. I could just make out the darker shades of his nipples.

"Get yourself some muscles," he said. He flexed, pausing to see if I would dare to stroke them. If my sister had not been standing behind him, ready to steal that chance away from me, I might have taken him up on his offer.

We spent most of our time down at the beach. For once in my life I was glad to have been living so close to the sea. It gave me ample opportunities to ogle more of his body than I might otherwise have had the chance to see again. My greatest dream in life was to see him naked, to relive the memory of the fallen towel—and this time find the courage to act on my desires!

If my mother had ever found out that I was spending time in the midday sun without a drop of factor-15 cream for protection on my face, she would have freaked. Even more so if I had tried to explain to her how my limited chances of actually seeing his naked body would be placed in serious jeopardy if I were to spend my entire life hiding in the shade. I was burning for this boy. I needed every possible moment to follow the slim contours of his body, admiring the thin patches of hair that jutted out from the crevices of his armpits and hoping that soon, very soon, I would have the chance to taste the clean flavor of his Speedo-locked cock. Each day became more of a frustration.

And so when John headed off alone toward a small patch of nearby rocks, looking back with a smile that stayed on his mouth for longer than was necessary, I took it as a sign to follow.

"Why don't you get undressed then," he said.

The thought of him doing to me here, in the open air, what had been the focus of weeks of masturbation sessions forced an erection so fast I was unable to re-move my clothes without a struggle. My cock to atten-tion, I stood waiting for him to slip out of his skimpy swimmers, knowing that I would let him do to me now whatever he wished. At last, I had managed to defeat my sister for his attentions! I would be the one he loved. I could see that I was already drooling with anticipation. A wonderful feeling that disappeared the moment I saw the rest of his gang appear behind him, heads poking out from the jagged rocks, laughter filling the air. A hideous stream of cackling bronzed and muscular bodies now surrounding my pale and naked skeleton.

My sister was amongst them. As if to help me in my shame, in a totally uncharacteristic gesture she asked, with seeming innocence, why I hadn't thought to change at the house. John followed her as she walked away, and I was left alone to cope with this full exposure of my desires.

She got rid of John a few days later and soon found herself a new one. She claimed that she'd grown tired of him, but I think she knew this time how close I had come.

Looking for a Hot Time

Alistair McCartney

Someone on the other side of the dance floor caught my eye. I could barely distinguish him through the haze of pineapple-scented fog pumped out by the smoke machine: tall, dressed in black, he was just an attractive outline. But that was enough. For me to want him. For me to use my imagination, coloring in what I didn't know about him. Which was everything.

We were at a favorite alternative club of mine in Kings Cross, Up To the Elbow. This was the place where boys who liked boys, no longer under the yoke of house music, could dance to songs by angry girls with distorting guitars. I'd paid my two pounds to the bouncer hidden beneath his padded parka and gone inside—where it was warm. There had been a brief snowfall that afternoon. Not enough to fill me with childlike wonder, openmouthed as the world disappears beneath a layer of white; just enough to make everything seem brutally cold. I'm slim now, but at twenty-two I was much lighter, my body a magnet for temperatures below freezing. I had run out of change to feed the coin-operated heater built into the wall next to my bed. My lips were turning the deep blue of the comforter. A chill had settled into my bones for the evening. Rather than following suit, winding down for a long, cold night at home alone, I went out in search of warmth.

I looked across the dance floor at him and he looked back at me. I averted my gaze, then returned his gaze. My neck creaked like the hinge on a door in need of a good oiling. He avoided my eyes, then directly met them, and so on. A coy game of catch in a hall of mirrors. A situation I'd been in countless times before: cruising a stranger in a bar on a Saturday night, a man who might or might not have something precious to give me.

It all took place in silence, without a sound track. The deejay's equipment had blown a fuse, and he busied himself, trying to fix it. I shifted awkwardly from side to side in my dirty black-and-white Converse boots, on the threadbare brown carpet patterned with swirls of orange roses. I switched my pint of beer from one hand to the other. The outline of my dreams smiled, and that broke the quiet. I walked over and asked his name and we began to talk.

Up close I could see that Richard possessed an odd, alien beauty. A shaved head set off his finely chiseled face, with its impossibly angled cheekbones. He had deep-set eyes black and hard as anthracite. His right eye twitched every few seconds, the mark of someone with a taste for amphetamines. A shiny gold piercing stuck out from the center of his chin, lending him the appearance of a less ostentatious version of Pinhead from the movie *Hellraiser*. His torso was almost gaunt, but at the same time he had broad shoulders. Large, powerful hands, his left nursing a pint of Guinness, his right cradling a cigarette. His skin was not so much white as silver, faintly cratered like the surface of the moon. The drugs at work again.

There was something familiar about him, and I realized I had seen his photograph in one of the gay rags, *The Pink Paper*. He was in this thrash-cum-performance-art band Minty, which was causing a lot of stir at the time. The antics of the front man, Leigh Bowery, who had a habit of splashing his HIV-positive bodily fluids over the audience, were getting the band barred from most venues throughout the city.

The sound system working again, My Bloody Valentine's "Feed Me with Your Kiss" came on full blast: a dense wall of feedback (not quite) crushing a lazy melody, the singers' tinny, lovelorn whispers. My favorite song, I was transported into the queer-core equivalent of a Harlequin romance. I couldn't hear anything of what Richard was saying to me, even after slinking my body conveniently closer to his. Sick of yelling "What?" and "Sorry, I still didn't hear you," I gave up and just nodded and smiled, batted my eyelashes in time to the trapdoor movement of his mouth. My eyes trailed down to his piercing, which created an obstacle course to his crinkle-cut lips. The thought occurred to me that I could nick myself on him. I brushed the tip of my index finger against its razor-sharp edge. As if I had pressed a magic button, the volume was lowered and things were set in motion.

"Have you ever been someone's slave?" Richard asked, his polished lance grazing my earlobe.

His question didn't startle me. I wasn't a fool. With him pierced and shaved, decked out in black shirt and trousers courtesy of army surplus, and the biggest give-away—the crudely drawn tattoo on his upper left arm of a hairy muscle guy walking a pouting blond boy on a studded leash—it wasn't difficult to work out that he was into S/M.

"No."

"Have you ever thought about it? Fantasized about it?" he continued politely.

His dry tongue dusting my cheek, I could tell he had eaten corner-shop curry earlier that night.

"Hmm, not really." My fantasy life, although rich and varied, had never flowed in the master/slave direction.

"Well," he said, growing a little impatient with my reticence, "what do you fantasize about?"

Doing nothing to dispel his annoyance, I answered, "I don't know, different things I guess." I hadn't come here to be given a survey.

The possibility of anything coming from this meeting

wasn't looking so good. Even so, I had a bulging hard-on in the camouflage pants I'd bought earlier that day at Camden Market.

Richard glanced at my crotch and raised his eyebrows. "What's that all about then?"

I shrugged, a question mark burrowing behind the skin of my face. "Well, what exactly are you into?"

He quickly recited a grocery-like list of things that left me nonplussed. Moldy terms I associated with bearded men from two decades ago.

"Handcuffs or other forms of restraint, shaving, domination and subjugation, verbal abuse, water sports, hitting, fisting? It all depends on who I'm playing with, how far we both want to go."

Songs blurred into songs. Richard bought me another pint. I danced. Searching for something to furnish the empty spaces of the evening, I smoked one of his Gauloises, even though I don't smoke.

"I'm going to head back now. Feel like coming home with me?" In light of our clumsy sex talk, his offer felt like nothing more than a display of good manners.

"Yes," I said, surprising both of us. "Yeah, uh, sure, I mean, I guess that would be okay," I said, coming on all Molly Bloom, but without the passion or the clarity.

"Whatever this ends up being like," I told myself as we took the night bus, crowded with bleary-eyed drunks of all nationalities, from Saint Pancras Station to his apartment in Soho, "I won't forget this."

He lived on the second story of a remarkably plain white stucco building. A fish-and-chips shop resided on the ground floor. Its blackboard indicated that the special of the day was battered baby eel: a dozen for five pounds. He led the way up two flights of narrow stairs that reeked of fish, newspaper, and vinegar. I noticed a dent in the back of his head, in the shape of a horseshoe.

"If you want out at any time, just say so."

I didn't answer him. We arrived at his door, which was blackened, as if it had recently been set on fire. He turned around, the bones of his body and the floorboards moaning.

"Are you sure?" he asked.

"Don't ask me that."

His hands grabbed my shoulders roughly, and he turned me around.

"Face the wall. I'm going inside to prepare. Don't move an inch until I come to get you."

"Can I pee first?" I entreated, scratching my nose.

"No, not yet. Just stay here." I did as he told me. I knew that I wouldn't have a problem with following his orders. Since I was a child, I've had a talent for eagerly complying with what others want me to do.

He opened the door a crack; it creaked just like my stiff neck.

"Oh, and from now on I want you to address me as 'father' or 'sir.' Understood?"

"Yes, father-sir," I replied, unable to settle on a title.

The door closed again and he was inside. His Doc Martens clunked off into the distance. I waited, I'm not sure how long. I don't wear a watch. Obediently, I kept my eyes fixed on the off-white wall the entire time. A plaster scar the length of my appendectomy stitch-mark ran at eye level. It's amazing what can hold your interest.

Eventually he came back out. An Altoids mint failed to conceal the curry that had colonized the root scent of him. He dictated another no-no into the nape of my neck, as if a recording device had been planted in there: "Don't look at me." In his firm grip, he led me into the apartment, down a hallway as nondescript as the landing, then directed me into a room empty except for the baroque metal frame of a bed.

"Undress quickly and put this on."

He left me alone again. I looked down. There in my lap was an extremely ugly chocolate-brown apron with a white border. This was not so much slutty French maid as overworked checkout chick. I undressed and put the apron on; one size too big, it hung loose on me. The way it left my ass exposed reminded me of a hospital gown. I felt distinctly unsexy, but remembered the scene in *My Own Private Idaho* where River Phoenix dresses up as a maid for an eccentric German client, and this kept me going.

With the Van Sant movie still running in my head, Richard reentered.

"Kneel down on the floor. Rest your head on the bed frame."

"Yes, sir."

Cold metal kissed the side of my face; raw wood scraped my knees. I worried about getting splinters. He spread my legs and manacled them: cool metal locked shut against my shinbones.

"Put your hands in front of you, like you're praying."

I heard the loud crackling noise of cellotape being unwound. He wrapped the sticky plastic around my wrists, then blindfolded me with a strip of black cloth that let in a sliver of light. He fastened a studded collar around my neck. My ensemble was now complete. The collar buckle bit into my Adam's apple. Sniffing like a bloodhound, I could tell the leather was brand-new. I was the first to use it.

"You're my dog now. My little puppy. Bark for your master!"

This struck me as a bit too obvious. All I could think of was that tyrannically batty old English dog trainer, Barbara Woodhouse, the one with her own TV show. The Maggie Thatcher of the four-legged world, she'd boss her beagles and corgis around, then end each show by putting the kettle on and bringing out the biscuit tin.

"Ruff!"

"Ruff, sir!" he corrected.

How was I to know he wanted a talking canine? I let out another bark, this time with his name tagged on the end.

"Good dog," he affirmed, patting me on my rump. "Good boy, stay."

Panting happily, I wagged my ass in need of a tail, allowed my tongue to loll out of my mouth and touch air. Dehydrated from the beer, I hoped he might bring me a bowl of water.

Suddenly he changed tactics. Raising himself up, he placed his boot on my lower back.

"You piece of shit, you're not even a dog. They're better than you are. At least they're alive."

This last statement didn't strike me as being quite so obvious. I squirmed beneath his heel.

"You're a chair. A table. A vase. A window."

Was this guy a master or an interior decorator? I resisted the temptation to suggest that more accurately at that moment I was his footstool. I wondered if we were having sex yet.

Richard shifted his foot down to the crack of my ass. My groin tingled slightly, finally registering a sensation close to pleasure.

"Crawl!"

The toe of his boot prodded me to another part of

the room. The wooden floor gave way to a sheet of plastic.

"Lie down on your back! Piss all over yourself like a baby!"

My master evidently suffered from a short attention span. Back in the realm of the animate (if infantile), I lay on my side and tried to pee. I've been pee shy for as long as I can remember. At least ten minutes must have passed before a trickle slid down my thigh and onto the sheeting that seemed way too fussy for a sadist. My mother used the same technique, covering the arms of her imitation-suede, emerald-green couch with rubber doilies—to avoid tea stains.

My father (or mother?) could see my regression wasn't going so well.

"Get back on all fours."

As I scrambled up, I heard what I assumed was the fly to his trousers being unzipped. At last, thought I— a sucker for tradition—a cock! I knew what to do with one of those.

But I would have to wait. An aerosol hissed, and a lathery, wet substance was applied to my asshole and balls. Richard proceeded to methodically shave this whole area. No Bluebeard, he took the utmost care. I've always loved submitting to the barber's scissors and clippers, and it was like that, but a little different. As the razor glided gracefully over my skin, my cock rose.

A curious memory came to mind. Twelve years old, I

was sitting on the gray concrete stairs behind my parents' house. Armed with one of my father's blunt, rusty razors (but without the aid of any soap or cream), I hacked off the newly sprouting hairs on my legs in a backward drive to delay puberty.

My hard-on fled along with the memory. Having accomplished his task, my master examined the finished product: my hairless ass, smooth as a porn star's. He stuck a finger in. Had it been attached to someone else's hand, this might have turned me on. But under his somewhat clinical touch, it was about as exciting as a doctor taking my temperature. It's the one and only time I've yawned while being finger-fucked. Pulling his bony thermometer out, I sensed frosty air enter me. He stood up rather hurriedly, clicked off the lights, and split.

Alone once again, I began to experience a mounting frustration. This subordinate business was starting to tax my patience. So far—at best—I had been moderately aroused. My body was now more than ready to be astonished. Brusque sounds of drawers and cupboards opening and closing traveled up the hallway. Forgetting how thoroughly he had sealed me in, I tried to do my favorite yoga stretch, but of course I couldn't.

This constrained ability to move triggered a minor panic. I could hear the tension in my breath; it was surfacing sharp and shallow. Noise from the kitchen meant only one thing—knives. Paranoid, I produced an unambiguous motive. My master, observing my lack of interest, had gone off in a huff to find something nice and pointy. "Let's see how tedious it is being gutted," he broods. "Yes, that'll teach the uppity little slut."

A scene from the movie *Cruising* sped through my mind: the murderer in the tinted shades—with the Robert Plant haircut and the pockmarked face—has the beauty with the dark curls and the awesome basketball-like ass in bed, on his stomach, his wrists securely bound in rope with the sheen of licorice. He's begging for his life: "Please, please." With a deceptively small steak knife, the psycho enthusiastically sets to work on the muscular shoulders of his soon-to-be-not-so-handsome victim. Fine red bloodlines spurt across pale flesh, off the screen. The movie over, I struggled to free up my arms and legs, but to no avail. I wobbled hopelessly back and forth, like a broken-down rocking chair.

After what seemed like forever, Richard returned with, as luck would have it, a joint. Its rich, sweet odor was unmistakable. He dragged a real chair over and, propping his boots up on my chest, converted me back into his pouf. Nestling the joint between my lips, I took in deep puffs. It did the trick. My breathing decelerated. Everything did. Wrapped up neat as a brown-paper parcel, I knew I was helpless. And that was dandy. That was just fine. In the odd mixture of hallucination masked as lucidity that dope can bring, my fingertips swept along the mazelike tread of my master's boots.

Having suddenly developed the ability to read braille, I stroked secret erotic codes out of industrial-strength rubber. The Helen Keller of the sensual world, I was open to anything.

Maybe not quite anything.

In between his draws, Richard flickered ash onto my skin, stinging black snow.

"Ouch!"

As he reached down to balance the last of the joint in the final resting place of my mouth, something fell out of his wallet, landing with a dull thud on the by now clammy plastic.

A moment later, some round, flat objects were inserted into my asshole.

"What's . . . ?"

"Here, piggy piggy! Here, piggy piggy! You're my little piggy bank now. Let's keep that money in you for a rainy day, shall we?"

My vision of wanting to undergo a sexual odyssey had well and truly passed. The pot had hit my stomach, and my reveries had begun to take on a very different nature: pepperoni pizza, Swiss milk chocolate.

"Um, Richard, you know, I think I want to stop now."

"Are you sure?"

"Yeah, I don't think this is quite up my alley."

"That's a shame. I was just about to piss on you."

"Oh, sorry."

Ever the gentleman, even when denied his grand finale, he emancipated my limbs, granted me back my sight.

"I hope the cuffs didn't leave any bruise marks?" he inquired gently, briskly rubbing my ankles as if I had been subject to exposure.

I checked. "I don't think so."

Nurse had one more piece of useful advice.

"Oh, and as the hair around your ass grows back, it will be pretty uncomfortable for the first few days. But don't worry, the itching will go away. Try petroleum jelly."

"Thanks."

Once dressed, I followed Richard to the kitchen for a glass of water. I was giddy from having been recently unfettered, and the blue-green paisley linoleum lurched beneath me. Since I was still a little sensitive to light, the fluorescent-purple polka-dot wallpaper, an op-art throw-off, made me long for my sunglasses.

There was not much to talk about, shy as high-school sweethearts. I put it down to first-date jitters.

"Look," he said brightly, holding up an empty jar of peanut butter, pointing to a tiny fragment of brownish gray rock. "I have a piece of the Colosseum."

"Wow, that's really nice." If I wore a watch, I would have checked it. "You know, I really should get going."

"Oh, sure. Well, thanks. Give me a call. We should do this again sometime."

"That would be fun. Bye now."

165

Alistair McCartney

I folded up his number, written in perfect handwriting on the back of a flyer for an S/M march, and shoved it in my pocket.

Back in my icebox of a room, the sky outside the window did a slow fade from umbrella black to milk-bottle blue. It was Sunday morning, almost 7 A.M. Weary with adventures, I was preparing to go to sleep. Turning on flannel sheets in an endeavor to heat up, something jingled in my ass. I rolled over. There it was again. As if I had gas, I pushed down on my asshole, still wet with lube. Out popped three silver coins, the equivalent of seventy-five cents. There was no question in my mind as to how to spend this unique memento. Without opening my eyes, I climbed out of bed and dropped all three coins into the heater's slot. They clinked into place; then the machinery growled, and a musty waft of fuel told me that I would soon be warm. Satisfied, I slipped back under the covers.

When in Rome . . .

Stephan Niederwieser

Before I went on a business trip to Rome, my friend
Tenor warned me to keep my hopes down. The Romans
are arrogant, he said, and the gay scene is shit. Ah, I
thought, what does he know?

Rome is particularly hot in September. A shine of sweat
was on all faces, as if they were painted with a layer of
clear lacquer. Even the ever-so-cold churches were
stuffy and hot. And forget the subways. They were
crowded and hotter than hell.

I was down at Termini, the main train station, where
the train I had just missed threw up a cloud of dust. It
was 6 P.M. rush hour; people stood so close I felt like
the clichéd sardine in a can. I pushed myself against
the marble wall, which seemed to be the only cool thing
in this capital of heat, chaos, and heterosexuals (for
three nights I had walked the streets at night, without
meeting a single hot Roman lover).

The sweat was running down the back of my neck. I
was reading the sign that warned, in five languages, of
pickpockets when I became aware of this guy stumbling

toward me. As he drew near, his eyes went wide, as if in shock; the circles of sweat on his light blue shirt grew bigger. Everything that followed occurred in a split second. First, I thought, he is going to kill me, he will put a knife right between my ribs. Then I wondered why anybody would do that, especially in a crowded train station. So I decided he was having a heart attack and just needed somebody to hold on to. Automatically I opened my arms to catch him—there was actually something exciting about the prospect, since I hadn't held a man in my arms for weeks—then I heard him whisper gently into my ear, "Come to my house tonight!" He put a business card in my hands. Then he quickly turned around and left; I watched him pushing through the crowd. He must have been in his forties, a businessman in a suit, the jacket neatly folded over his muscular arm. His skin was tan and his hair black, a bit balding in the back. He'd spoken in such a nice accent that it had gone down like honey; the whole guy was screaming for love.

He was an older guy, and usually I like younger guys, but in the desert you grab the first sip of water you find. I ran back to my hotel, took a shower to cool off, put on fresh clothes, and tried to figure him out. There was fear in his eyes—no, it was the guilt and pain that only an Italian mother could inflict on a man. He wouldn't be one of those wild lovers, I feared, one of those sex-

crazed hunks. It would probably just be lots of kissing.
But that didn't matter to me. I wanted a good polishing
of my helmet, and if he didn't know how, I was going
to teach him. (In retrospect I still have to wonder why
it never occurred to me that he might have been after
something else but sex.)

Federico Castelli, Via Aurelia 4, 2⁰ piano. By the time
I got to his house I was dripping with sweat again. I
rang the bell. Upstairs a woman opened the door. She
was in her early forties, quite attractive, her hair all
done up, wearing a simple walnut-colored linen dress
and a thick chain of pearls around her neck. She was
quite the Sophia Loren type with a big toothy smile.

I wondered if I had rung the wrong bell, but she
wrapped her arms around me and said, "You must be
the young guy Federico invited. And perfectly on time
for dinner. How typical of you Germans." Her face was
bright with happiness, and I was so stunned I let her
lead me into the apartment. There Federico shook my
hand and smiled a shy, quiet smile. He was freshly
shaved, his hair still wet from a shower; the smell of
Paco Rabanne assaulted me as soon as he grabbed my
shoulder.

"Nice you could make it," he said with his sweet,
sweet accent; he had the slightest bit of a lisp. The guy
looked like those models in Armani ads—broken,
pained, suffering—that make you want to put your arms

around them and comfort them. I wanted to take him right there on the spot, and would have, if there hadn't been this woman standing next to us.

He guided me into the dining room. The table was set with crystal and silver; the entire apartment was decorated with a lot of style and money. I thought he must be a banker, a lawyer, or a doctor at least. He sat me down at the table, poured me some red wine, while his wife (I can only assume that that's what she was) served us huge tortellini stuffed with truffles and meat, followed by little birds that were tied up with string and roasted and now floated on top of an herb sauce.

"So what do you do?" Her voice was loud and dominating, but at the same time comforting.

What had he told her? I wondered, and what was I supposed to answer? "Oh, I'm in business," I said, trying to be as vague as possible. "That's how I know Federico," I added quickly.

Wrinkles appeared on her forehead. "Oh! I thought he just met you on the subway. Federico?"

I blushed and turned to him for help. And he did. He smiled shyly and put his big, warm hand on my shaking, cold one, as if to say, "It's all right. Don't worry." I wanted to melt away from embarrassment, but couldn't, of course, and anyway I'd already survived the intense heat.

"I see you two are getting comfortable," she said, and her face brightened again. "Let me look after dessert."

As soon as she was out of the room, Federico leaned back and let out a deep sigh. "Hot night, no?"

I nodded, growing more and more uncomfortable.

"Why don't you take off your shirt?" he said. His wife—or whatever she was—appeared in the door, smiled a sweet smile, and disappeared again.

"I'm fine, thanks," I lied, sweat running down my spine in big pearls.

He got up and grabbed my hand. "Come on," he said, as if I knew what he was up to. At this point, I was so uncomfortable that I didn't care what was going to happen next as long as *something* was happening.

We walked past the kitchen, with him holding my hand like a lover or a child. His wife was picking dust off raspberries, carefully placing them on a plate of white sauce. She must have heard us, because she turned around and smiled again. "Have fun!"

"Pardon me?" I said, confused.

"Isn't that what you say?" she asked.

I had no idea, but I nodded as if I were in a trance and followed Federico. Behind the main entrance door he went up a winding staircase that I hadn't noticed when I'd first entered. I was tempted to grab the opportunity to leave. But there he was with that crushed look in his eyes, his hand holding mine even tighter. I followed him.

Upstairs was a bedroom under the attic. An extralarge bed, fur, mirrors, the whole bit. Federico undressed. I watched him fumbling with his belt, the zipper, beads of sweat forming on his pate. I looked around me, toward the open door, where I heard the woman clamber around the kitchen.

He turned to me. "It's okay," he said, and I almost laughed. Nothing was okay, absolutely nothing!

His pants went down with a jingling of coins, and his old man's undies followed. Naked, he looked even more vulnerable and innocent. He came over and put his thick, hot tongue in my mouth. What lips! But what a terrible kisser!

When he didn't even make an attempt to undress me, I jumped out of my clothes and into bed with him. I just wanted to close my eyes and make believe he was somebody else. I felt like I needed a Roman to salve my ego and justify my visit, and this was my last chance.

Federico seemed even more helpless in bed, lame, as if he didn't want this at all. I sucked on his nipples and he closed his eyes. "Ah, Stephano," he sighed. "Sì, sì, yes, yes." I ran my tongue across his hairy chest, which smelled of white flowers; I dug my tongue in his deep belly button, which made him giggle, and I bit his groin. Again he sighed and finally his fleshy penis erected. I took it in my mouth, and it grew bigger. It was quite a pleasure to feel flesh in my mouth again—and he must have enjoyed it, too, because finally there was some response. While I continued to eat his dick, a hand ran through my hair and down my back. Soon after that, I felt a tingling in my ass. It felt silky, but turned out to be a hungry tongue. Quickly it went deep, it felt damn good. It felt so good that it took a while for me to wonder how Federico could manage to eat my butt while I was doing him.

I jumped up in shock and found myself staring into the face of this woman. She wore some silken, see-through bathrobe the color of clouds.

"Delicious," she said, licking her lips and giving me that toothy smile again. She was just getting ready to dive again when I jumped out of bed.

"I'm s-sorry," I managed to stutter, cold shivers running down my spine. I looked at Federico. He shrugged his shoulders and gave that pained look again. I grabbed my clothes and ran for the stairs, followed by her screechy voice: "How ungrateful you are! So typical of you Germans!"

As I hurried down the stairs, zipping up my pants, I thought: Tenor was right, Rome is shit for cruising.

The Sound and the Fury

Matthew Linfoot

I met Simon through our mutual friend, Patrick, who was visiting London from the Isle of Man. This small island off the north coast of England was very fashionable as an upmarket holiday resort between the wars. The pleasant countryside and long beaches also attracted genteel retired couples, who repaid the island's generous tax advantages by providing highly reactionary political views. For this reason, homosexuality was still illegal. Understandably, Patrick came over to London often for some light relief, staying in a flat in Earl's Court that belonged to one of the rich, closeted gay men from the island.

I'd gone by Patrick's for a visit, but he seemed distracted and anxious. I put this down to acclimation and his anticipation of going out later to have some fun.

Then Simon arrived. He was shorter than I, with a plump, round bum. He wore a baseball cap that he kept on even when indoors. When he took it off much later, I realized he kept it on to make him look younger. We spent the evening talking about politics and how awful life must be for Patrick on the island. It was quite late, past eleven, when we got up to leave. I imagined Patrick would be going out to a bar, but he said first he was expecting a call from his partner on the island. I contrived to leave at exactly the same time as Simon so when we were both downstairs on the pavement, I could casually offer him a lift home—even claiming that Fulham was perfectly on my way home, whereas in fact it was completely in the opposite direction. By this point, my mind was made up. Simon was good-looking. He didn't have many other qualities, but that was enough to make me want him. I assumed he felt the same way.

Simon lived in a desirable part of London—a leafy avenue of largish terraced houses.

"My side of the street is all owned by the Council," he explained. "They used to be whole houses, but they've been converted into flats. I really want to buy mine from the Council—I'd get a huge discount. But . . ."

I swung along Fulham Broadway.

". . . there's a problem with noise. It was such a cheap conversion, there's no proper sound insulation. And I've got a family from hell living upstairs."

Simon's street was lined with parked cars, some even double-parked, which I thought was illegal. I found a space some way from Simon's front door.

Simon got out immediately, then turned. "Are you coming in?"

This struck me as fairly direct and to the point. Less ambiguous than, say, "Would you like a coffee?" I can

175

remember, incidentally, a young man I met in a super-market. I shoved my hands down his tight denim shorts as soon as we got back to his place, and he said ingenuously, "When I said, 'Would you like a cup of coffee?' I meant, 'would you like a cup of coffee?' "

I followed Simon down the street, mentally warming my hands for that first contact on his buttocks. Through the outer door, I could hear someone's appliances and began to understand what he meant when he'd earlier mentioned a problem with noisy neighbors. Simon unlocked his front door and we walked through into the apartment.

To my surprise, this was where the noise was coming from.

Simon had said he lived alone, yet sound and music seemed to spill from every direction. In the front room, a stereo was blaring techno at full volume. In his bedroom, voices from the television boomed out. And in the kitchen, a radio further contributed to the cacophony.

I realized that relations with his upstairs neighbors must have sunk to this level, that he did this simply to annoy them.

I assumed that Simon would turn everything off now that we were there, but in fact he seemed to go through the apartment raising the volume on each of the appliances. I guess he'd grown immune to the sound after all this time.

Simon made me a cup of coffee— he wasn't having

one. And then he lay on his front on the bed and stared at the television screen. The noise continued, and there was no attempt at further conversation.

I sat next to Simon, trying to follow the dialogue on the television. My hand grazed Simon's jeans. I shouted to ask if this was okay. No response.

So I touched him again, and again, each time getting bolder. Finally, I was massaging his legs, his back, and his buttocks through his clothes. At last Simon turned his head and smiled, a kind of assent, I suppose, and I started to undress him.

I kissed and caressed and licked his body, making hungry, growling sounds deep in my throat as I devoured him, but all the time he seemed strangely inert and unresponsive. Things seemed very one-sided.

I hadn't really attempted to shout over the noise. But eventually I had to ask, "Are you all right? Is this okay?"

No reply.

I tapped him on the shoulder. Simon looked round, rather startled.

"Sorry. What is it?"

And then I saw. He had earplugs carefully inserted in each ear. I was as distant to him as the moon. Nothing was going to penetrate him, not even the din of my ecstasy. I continued my beleaguered attempts at lovemaking, only now it really was just sex. The tactile hand movements became mechanical, the kissing was quick and dispassionate. I didn't even bother to get fully undressed. And all the while Simon just lay there. I think he mouthed some words at one point, but I couldn't be bothered to make them out. When I had finished (Simon had never even started), I began to wipe up.

I wondered what I could do to make my exit graceful. Even though Simon was oblivious to me, I didn't feel I could just get up and walk out.

Then I noticed the telephone by his bed. The whole instrument was flashing. I'd seen one before, in the office of a deaf colleague. Simon got up, pulled out an earplug, and shouted into the receiver. He obviously couldn't hear anything—I got up and turned the television and radio off. My ears ached with the sudden change in volume. A loud thumping bass continued to reverberate through the ceiling from the floor above. Simon glowered at me, but then his expression changed as he listened to the other end of the conversation, finally able to hear.

"What?" I asked when he hung up.

"That was Patrick's boyfriend, Grant, calling from the island. Patrick's locked himself in the bathroom. He says he's going to do something stupid."

"I'll go back and see to him," I said, grabbing my coat and the excuse to get out of there.

Simon didn't answer—except to turn the volume up again on the telly and the radio.

Tom, Dick, or Harry

Lawrence Schimel

One of the advantages of getting a book published is running your photo on the back of it. This makes it easier for your fans, groupies, and stalkers to identify you. I have had a handful of stalkers, more than a handful of groupies, and not nearly enough fans. Still, the fans I do have seem to be loyal—almost as loyal as the stalkers—and I'm inordinately fond of all of them. But I never remember any of their names.

I get so nervous before I do a reading or a signing that I would forget my own name if it weren't printed in every copy of the book. And I know which book is mine only because it's got a photo of me on the back.

Of course, there are those illiterate sorts who haven't yet discovered my writings, on their own, and for them (who, alas, seem to outnumber the fans, groupies, and stalkers combined) I'd like to evoke all the glamour that accompanies the writer's life. . . .

One sweltering night I was at the Big Cup—an oh-so-trendy fag coffeeshop in the Chelsea neighborhood of Manhattan—because it has air-conditioning and I don't. I was on deadline, and when I'm trying to work in my small studio (New York rents, writer's income), it's so easy to procrastinate by calling friends or washing dirty dishes or what-have-you.

Despite my relocation, I wasn't getting any work done—I was too busy staring lustfully at the Latino guy at the table next to mine. His unattractive blond friend was leering at me with the same intensity with which I was leering at his tablemate (a configuration of frustratingly misdirected lust that practically defines modern gay life). At least they weren't a couple; this gave me some hope of bagging Señor Sexy. If I could ever work up the nerve to talk to him.

"Are you a writer or something?" Blondie asks out of the blue, indicating the sheaf of papers spread out before me.

"Yeah," I said, and smiled at Señor Sexy, ready for him to swoon over my celebrity status. Before he had a chance to even return my smile, however, Blondie broke our connection.

"So, have you published anything?"

I hate this question, although it's better than "Have I read anything you've written?" (as if I'm supposed to know what anyone else has read). I was stumped for a moment—wondering how to convey that I've published more than a dozen books, and hundreds of stories, articles, and poems, how to make my body of work sound important enough while not appearing to be, myself, too immodest. If I make myself out to be *too* famous, they'll wonder why they haven't heard of me before.

"I've written for a number of magazines and I've published a few books," I admitted.

I clearly didn't strike the right balance with that response. It stymied Blondie into silence (not that I minded), but the dead air didn't lend itself to drawing Señor Sexy into the conversation.

I was mentally scrolling through my possible next lines when, as if on cue, a stranger came up and asked me, "Didn't you write *The Drag Queen of Elfland*?"

I looked him over, trying to figure out if he was a fan, a groupie, or a stalker. He wasn't cute enough for me to want him to be a groupie, thus reducing the options considerably. With a glance at Latino Sex Stud, who was indeed now paying close attention to our conversation, I intimated that I was indeed the responsible party.

"I can't believe this!" the Fortuitous Stranger exclaimed. "I've read that book three times, and as I was standing over there on line, I couldn't help thinking you looked just like your author's photo. Well, actually, I was thinking you look much younger and cuter than the photo, with this new haircut."

I am not making this up. I wouldn't have the nerve to try to pull something like this in my fiction—no one would believe it.

I smiled, made some appreciative murmurs for his praise of my work, and the Stranger, again as if on cue, giddily got back on line and then left with his latte or whatever.

Hooked by this exchange, Señor Sexy gracefully ditched his friend and set about the admittedly not very difficult task of picking me up. I didn't get much work done that night, despite my deadline, though I did sleep, contentedly exhausted, in Latino Loverboy's blissfully air-conditioned apartment.

Unfortunately, all too often (i.e., every single other time in my entire life), the Fortuitous Stranger misses his cue, the Sexpot I am cruising goes away without noticing me, and I am left with yet another story of The One Who Got Away. And sometimes the Stranger himself, unaware that he has been cast as a walk-on, causes a rather sticky situation. . . .

One night, my gym partner and I headed over to A Different Light bookstore to pick up some titles we'd been arguing about all during our workout. Said workout partner stubbornly insisted that some not-to-be-named writer was actually talented and promising.

"You're wrong," I calmly reasoned as we wandered along the shelves, "he's the most execrable writer I've ever had the misfortune to read."

I could tell by the look on his face that my gym partner was about to cite literary theory, the history of gay writing, Foucault, random quotes from *All About Eve*, and whatever else he could find in his rhetorical bag to justify his untenable position. Just then, however, I was paged over the store intercom. This surprised me since usually only the staff are paged for a phone call, and anyway, no one but my querulous gym buddy knew I was there. But I cheerfully walked to the front of the store, thinking, "Saved by the bell," as this interruption gave me the last word.

The clerk had seen me come into the store, he explained when I got to the front counter, and as someone had just bought my latest collection, he wanted me to sign it for him. I smiled my "professional author pleased to meet one of his many fans" smile and turned to greet the customer. Luckily, I was smiling when the shock set in, and I was saved from betraying my true emotions. The customer was a man I'd tricked with a few weekends previously. Unfortunately, though our sex had been unforgettable—and I mean that in all the most negative connotations of the word—I could not recall his name.

We had cruised each other on Eighth Avenue in Chelsea—the world's largest flea market of available men—and started talking. I was on my way to get something to eat, so I invited him along. During dinner I learned that he was a thirty-eight-year-old electrician who lived in New Jersey with his mother, and while wonderfully gifted in the brawn department, he was all but a flat line when it came to brains. We really weren't clicking, as far as I was concerned, and though I did my best to wriggle off the hook, I was the Catch of the Day for him and he wasn't about to let me off the line easily. He walked me home and was just so earnest that I felt obligated to go through with the encounter. How bad could it be? I reasoned.

Pretty bad, I soon discovered. Afterward, I was more than happy to send him home to his waiting mother without giving him my phone number.

I hadn't told him I was a writer, but my apartment was in a bit of disarray, with copies of the aforementioned *Elfland* collection piled up on the floor. Because there's a photo of me on the back cover, it was not hard (even for him) to put two and two together.

Now, here I was facing him again. He'd gone out of his way to come into New York City to buy my book— perhaps the first one he'd owned since *Curious George*— and even though he'd been one of my worst lays since puberty, I felt like a heel that I couldn't remember his name. And to inscribe the book for him, I'd have to humiliate us both by asking him.

To forestall this ugly confession, I told him I didn't know what to write for him, that I liked to write something special for people I knew and not just the usual trite clichés that we writers use for strangers' books. It had the ring of truth to it because, as luck would have it, it is true—although he counted as a stranger to me, which may have just been wishful thinking. I asked him if he was hungry, hoping I could pull his name out of my faulty memory or get him to inadvertently reveal it during conversation. And our departure insured that I'd won my argument with my gym partner—at least for the moment.

During the meal, I used all my wiles to wheedle his name out of him. ("My mother, unfortunately, calls me 'Larold.' Does your mom have a special nickname for you?" "Junior.") Without success.

The next thing I knew, he was walking me home again and I had a sinking feeling in the pit of my stomach. I could see where he thought this was heading, and as I hadn't yet figured out his name, I couldn't figure out a graceful way out of this. Even remembering how inept he had been in bed, I invited him up. (I was feeling generous since he'd gone out and bought the book after sleeping with me.) After we'd gotten our clothes off, I was as bored to tears with him in bed as I recalled.

Luckily, he had a bladder as small as his intellect, and during his trip to the bathroom, I jumped out of bed, fished his wallet out of his pants, and started digging for some ID. I was terrified that he'd come out of the bathroom as I was riffling through his wallet and get the wrong impression—and more terrified that he'd get the right one! But it was too late to back out now. I continued my search and dug out his driver's license with his name right on it: Tom.

I rearranged things exactly as they'd been and leapt back into bed just in time for him to come back and attempt to resume our uninspired sex. This was too much to bear—even in the name of graciousness—and I feigned sleep.

Alas, I did actually fall asleep—and so did he, missing the last train back to New Jersey. Once I'd discovered his name, I'd planned to sign his book, send him home, and immediately forget all about him. But I didn't have the heart to kick him out, since he'd be stranded, and thus spent the rest of the night fuming, unable to fall back asleep. His snoring was actually louder than the construction crew that was working in the lot on the corner.

In the morning, it took everything I had to get him up and out of the apartment—he wanted us to spend the day together and all I wanted was some uninterrupted sleep. Hardening my heart to his crestfallen looks, I locked the door behind him. I eagerly threw myself onto my bed, planning to spend many hours there alone, but as my head fell toward the pillow I caught sight of something that startled me wide awake: my own face, staring up at me from the back cover of his book. It was sitting on the bedside table where Tom had left it last night atop the Different Light bag—still unsigned.

About the Contributors

PATRICK BARNES is an actor and songwriter who lives in New York City. He has written various librettos, and his works of prose appear in the anthologies *Two Hearts Desire*, *Flesh and the Word 5*, and *Hard at Work*, among others.

KERRY BASHFORD was editor of the magazines *Pink Ink*, *Kink*, and *Campaign* and now edits *The Sydney Hub*. He lives in Sydney, Australia.

PETER BURTON worked in the music industry for many years before switching to journalism. He is one of the leading figures in British gay letters, through his own published books—which include *Among the Aliens* and *Talking To . . .* —and as literary editor for *Gay Times* and commissioning editor of Millivres Books. He lives in Brighton, England.

JAMESON CURRIER is the author of the novel *Where the Rainbow Ends* and the short story collection *Dancing on the Moon*. A prolific literary critic and contributor to various regional and national magazines and newspapers, he lives in New York City.

TIM DRISCOLL is a performance artist whose works include *Creative Fluid, My Whole Life,* and *Genders Collide Inside My Dance Belt.* His short stories and essays have appeared in various anthologies, including *Men Seeking Men* and *New York Sex.* He lives in New York City.

LARRY DUPLECHAN is the author of four critically acclaimed novels, including *Blackbird* and *Captain Swing.* He lives in Los Angeles, with his life partner of twenty-three years.

DEAN DURBER is the author of the forthcoming novel *Johnny, Come Home* and a one-man stage show about River Phoenix, *Rising from the Ashes,* among other works. As a journalist, he has contributed to diverse press all over the world, including *The Sun Herald* (Australia), *Faces* (USA), and *The Daily Yomiuri* (Japan), and is a regular columnist for *Capital Q.* He lives in Sydney, Australia.

DAVID FEINBERG was the author of two novels, *Eightysixed* and *Spontaneous Combustion,* and a collection of essays, *Queer and Loathing.*

JAMES HANNAHAM is a journalist whose work has appeared in *The Village Voice, Details,* and *Out,* among other periodicals, as well as in the anthology *The Mammoth Book of Gay Erotica.* He lives in New York City.

MARC J. HEFT left his job as executive vice president of a public relations consulting firm to travel the world, and fell in love in Saigon, where he now lives. His work has also appeared in the anthology *Men Seeking Men*.

WAYNE HOFFMAN is a widely published journalist whose work has appeared in *The Advocate, XY, Torso*, and other national and regional magazines. He is co-editor of the anthology *Policing Public Sex: Queer Politics and the Future of AIDS Activism* and is currently arts editor for *The New York Blade News*. He lives in New York City.

MICHAEL LASSELL is the author of a collection of short stories, *Certain Ecstasies*; three volumes of poetry: *A Flame for the Touch That Matters, Decade Dance* (winner of a Lambda Literary Award), and *Poems for Lost and Un-lost Boys*; and a collection of essays, stories, and poems titled *The Hard Way*. He is the editor of numerous anthologies, including *Men Seeking Men, The Name of Love, Eros in Boystown*, and *Two Hearts Desire: Gay Couples on Their Love* (with Lawrence Schimel), among others. A former editor of *L.A. Style* and *Interview* magazines, he is the articles editor for *Metropolitan Homes* magazine. He lives in New York City.

MATTHEW LINFOOT is an award-winning radio producer and presenter for Greater London Radio. He lives in London, England.

BARRY LOWE is a playwright whose work includes *Rehearsing the Shower Scene from* Psycho, *The Death of Peter Pan,* and *The Extraordinary Annual General Meeting of the Size Queen Club.* He contributes regularly to Australian periodicals, and his writing appears in various anthologies, including *The Mammoth Book of Gay Erotica* and *Men Seeking Men.* He lives in Sydney, Australia.

ALISTAIR McCARTNEY is a twenty-seven-year-old writer from Australia, now living in Los Angeles. An M.F.A creative writing student at Antioch L.A., he is currently working on his first novel, tentatively titled "T/here."

JOHN McFARLAND's poems and essays have appeared in many periodicals, and are also included in various anthologies such as *The Badboy Book of Erotic Poetry* and *Letters to Our Children.* He lives in Seattle.

STEPHAN NIEDERWIESER is the author of the novel *An einem Mittwoch im September* as well as eight books about alternative medicine. A frequent contributor to various periodicals such as German *Vogue,* he has also published a story in the anthology *Sexperimente.* He lives in Munich.

MATTHEW RETTENMUND is the author of the novels *Blind Items* and *Boy Culture,* and the nonfiction books *Encyclopedia Madonnica, Queer Baby Names,* and *To-*

tally Awesome 80s. He lives in New York City, where he works as a magazine editor.

D. TRAVERS SCOTT is the author of the novel *Execution, Texas:1987* and editor of the anthology *Strategic Sex,* as well as guest editor for *Best Gay Erotica 2000.* He lives in Seattle.

SAM SOMMER is an actor and writer who lives in New York City. His work also appears in the anthology *Queer View Mirror II.*

AUBREY HART SPARKS has written for *Drummer, The James White Review, First Hand, In Touch,* and other periodicals, as well as the anthology *Doing It for Daddy.* He lives in Seattle.

Copyright Acknowledgments

About the Editor

As he writes this biographical note, LAWRENCE SCHIMEL is the author or editor of twenty-seven books, and happens to also be twenty-seven years old. As he commented in a recent interview, he neither smokes nor drinks, although he does have his vices—namely, boys and a sweet tooth; presumably, if he had different vices, he would have published fewer books.

He is the author of the short story collections *The Drag Queen of Elfland* and *His Tongue* and the editor of numerous anthologies, including *The Mammoth Book of Gay Erotica*, *PoMoSexuals: Challenging Assumptions About Gender and Sexuality* (with Carol Queen; Lambda Literary Award winner), *Switch Hitters: Lesbians Write Gay Male Erotica and Gay Men Write Lesbian Erotica* (with Carol Queen), *Two Hearts Desire: Gay Couples on Their Love* (with Michael Lassell), *Food for Life and Other Dish*, and *Kosher Meat*. His stories, essays, and poetry have been included in more than 150 anthologies, among others: *Best Gay Erotica 1997* and *1998, The Mammoth Book of Gay Short Stories, Gay Love Poetry, The Mammoth Book of Fairy Tales, The Random House Book of Science Fiction Stories,* and *The Random House Treasury of Light Verse.* He has also contributed to numerous periodicals, from *The Saturday Evening Post* to *Physics Today* to *Gay Scotland.* His writings have been published abroad in Catalan, Dutch, Finnish, French, German, Italian, Japanese, Polish, Portuguese, Russian, Spanish, and Swedish translations.

He currently divides his time between his native New York City and Madrid.

EZEKIEL'S EYES

EZEKIEL'S EYES

ONE MAN'S ABILITY TO SEE
THE REALM OF EVIL AND G

JOHN PEAS

FRANKLIN GREEN
PUBLISHING

ACKNOWLEDGMENTS

To God the Father for his blessings and for keeping me within his grace and mercy. For giving me the mindset to write a fictional story that highlights God as the ultimate power and protector, and shows that through God, all things are possible with faith and prayer.

To my mother, Joy Roberts Pierre. For the many hours of her time she spent listening and exchanging ideas. For pointing me in the right direction when looking for inspiration within my bible. And for never tiring of reading my story after so many changes and rewrites over the course of me finishing my book. I don't know what I would have done without her love and constant support.

To my brother Jeffrey Pease, who planted the seeds in my mind that inspired me to write this book. I might never have taken this journey if not for you.

To my wife, Nina, and my son, Jaiden, whom I love more than words can express, for putting up with me when I shushed everyone in the house until I could complete my thoughts and write them down. Thank you for putting up with me.

To Pastor John Ramirez, my mentor, who was like a never-ending battery that constantly recharged my mind and my spirit. There were times unbeknownst to him, when I was feeling lost and unsure of what to do. He would stop by with a pleasant word or quote that would lift me up and out of that dark place, and onto a brighter path. Thank you so much for your positivity and support, for your love and belief in me. And for the cheesecake you would send from New York. LOL God bless you.

The grass withers, the flower fades, but the word of our God will stand forever.

—ISAIAH 40:8 (ESV)

*Do your best to present yourself to God as one
approved, a worker who has no need to be ashamed,
rightly handling the word of truth.*

—2 TIMOTHY 2:15 (ESV)

CHAPTER ONE

The Rebirth

*In the beginning, when Ezekiel saw the face of evil
in the shadows, it had always been blurred. But
this time it was crystal clear and horrifying!*

EZEKIEL STOOD IN THE FOLSOM CALIFORNIA STATE PRISON
courtyard, with a bloody knife in his hand, looking over the
bodies of two men. One of the men was in pretty awful shape;
the other would pull through with care. He could hear the sirens
sound as the prison guards quickly made their way toward him.
Strangely enough, his mind wandered to his past . . . and everything that had happened to him leading up to this moment.

As long as Ezekiel could remember, he had always been a little
bit faster, stronger, and smarter than the next guy. Whatever the
occasion called for, depending on his situation, he was up for the

task. He never really gave it too much thought—at least not until recently. As far as Ezekiel could remember, he was four years old when he began noticing things—scary things. He could see evil, or demons, or whatever you chose to call it. It hid inside of people and used them like puppets, doing everything within its power to corrupt people. Some spiritual types would say that what he saw was a person's aura. Some were bright, others were dim, and some were dark—but whatever you called it, he could see it as clear as day. Now you might imagine that this was a good thing. It was like having a one-up on things, so to speak. The only problem was that evil doesn't like to be seen; and when it is, it will make sure that it's not. So when someone like Ezekiel comes along pointing it out to others, he becomes its target.

The spirits who lived inside people were the easiest for Ezekiel to deal with, because he could spot them right away and usually avoid them. These people had very dark auras. However, it was the spirits that didn't need permanent hosts that were the hardest for him to spot, and consequently the most dangerous.

Now I know what you are probably thinking: *So what? How can a spirit, evil or good, be of any real consequence in our world?* Well, have you ever heard of Ted Bundy, the Son of Sam, or Adolf Hitler? These were very unassuming people at first glance, but what lived inside of them was pure evil, and we all know what they did. And oh yeah, there's something else I forgot to mention, something I left out about Ezekiel. Not only could he see the evil that lives within a person, he also had the ability to pull it out and destroy it. The downside of this seemingly wonderful power was if it wasn't done correctly, the host would be destroyed as well. To do it correctly took preparation, prayer, and fasting. Demons played for keeps. When they possessed a soul, they meant to take it to hell.

A soul, once released from a possession, must stay close to God, because that demon will always lurk around waiting to redeem that soul unto itself. In fact, it will not only return, but it will also bring along seven more demons to assure the victim remains bound. If the host is killed, the soul is also lost.

Ezekiel's journey began when he was born, or more accurately, when he died. Ezekiel was a breach birth, and when the doctor turned him around, the umbilical cord wrapped around his neck, cutting off his air supply. He died within moments of his birth. Seven minutes later, the doctors successfully revived him, but he had changed—he had the sight. And though his memories of that time remain cloudy, as they are for most people, Ezekiel truly could tell when evil was present from birth. Of course, all he could do to let anyone know was cry.

It is said that people who die and come back sometimes become conduits for the spirit world. Ezekiel believed that was what he was, a conduit; but he was much more than that. When he was young, he saw shadows that seemed to move on their own. Most everyone has had that happen to them: you see a movement in the shadows and take a second glance, and nothing is there. But it was different with Ezekiel; when he looked, he would see something looking right back at him. Sadly, to his dismay, as time went on, these occurrences only became more frequent.

Sometime around Ezekiel's fifteenth birthday, an old black woman who smelled of lavender and lilacs stopped him on the street and said, "They will be coming soon."

"Who?" Ezekiel asked.

"The faces in the shadows—they will be coming soon!"

Her words caused chills to run down his spine, because he suddenly realized the things he had been seeing were not his imagination but were, in fact, real. And something beyond his reasoning told him they wanted him. For what, exactly, he didn't know.

He asked the old woman, "What are they?"

She shrugged and said, "The devil's hands. They're the devil's hands."

He frowned and shut his eyes for a second, and when he opened them, she was no longer there. This type of thing began to happen to him more and more often. People would walk up to him and say, "They are coming," or "Get ready." It was surreal.

It was around that time that he also began to dream about a man named Joshua who would show him things, people, and places to avoid. Once, he dreamed that he came upon an alley, and Joshua told him to avoid it, but he didn't listen. A homeless person was sitting on the ground in the alley asking for help. He approached the person, ready to offer help, when he heard Joshua's voice whisper in his ear, "Don't do it! Stay away from him. You're not prepared." Ezekiel turned to ask Joshua what he meant, but he was gone.

Ezekiel couldn't explain why he didn't just listen to Joshua in the dream, because every fiber of his being was telling him that everything was not as it appeared to be. Instead, Ezekiel walked toward the man and extended his hand, offering him a few dollars. The man grabbed Ezekiel by the wrist and began to pull him closer. His grip was cold and strong. Ezekiel could feel his essence draining from his body. He tried to break away but he couldn't, and there was a strong smell of vinegar and rotten eggs. Ezekiel could feel his life force escaping him as the thing lifted its head, revealing its face. In the beginning, when Ezekiel saw the faces of evil in the shadows, it had always been blurred. But this time it was crystal clear and horrifying! It pulled him closer with ease, almost shattering his wrist as it did.

"We got you! Ha ha—oh yes, we got you now!" it screeched. Ezekiel shuddered as the putrid odor of its breath assaulted his nostrils and the creature's slimy tongue licked the side of his cheek. The heat of its foul breath burned as it whispered in Ezekiel's ear, "Now we will have you—yes, we will have you and he will be pleased."

Ezekiel peered into the eyes of his impending doom and cried out in horror. He woke up abruptly, with a shrill scream resonating from his throat. He could still taste the creature's foul breath in his mouth, and there were angry red bruises on his wrist where it had grabbed him in the dream. Ezekiel was rubbing his wrist when he heard Joshua's voice whisper in his ear, "Stay out of that alley and stay away from that man. The time will come when you must confront him, but that time is not today. You're not ready. If you don't listen, you will surely die!"

Later that same day, Ezekiel was walking down that very same street from his dream, only this time he was wide awake when he heard a voice call from the alley, "Spare change, mister?"

It was just like in the dream, only this time Ezekiel didn't need Joshua to warn him. He went past the alley as quickly as his legs could carry him, ran as fast as he could to his bike, and rode back to his apartment. He sat on the couch and wondered if it had happened at all or if he had imagined it. Then he looked up and saw Joshua in his living room mirror. He met his gaze, and Joshua said, "Well done." And then he vanished.

Ezekiel had many dreams like that in the years that followed; unlike the first, he always listened to Joshua in them. These dreams became a training ground. Ezekiel learned how to spot evil; Joshua taught him how to fight it. He showed him what he had to do before he went to sleep. Joshua taught him to always be on his guard and to control his thoughts.

Ezekiel discovered that the lines between the spirit world and our world merged when he dreamed, and he found that he served as a bridge enabling them to cross over. That was one of the reasons why they wanted him so badly. Joshua assured him that he would be coming to help him soon, but for now, he could only speak to him through dreams and occasional whispers.

As time went on, Ezekiel learned that these spirits existed just outside of our perception but that they were always around; they had the power to cross over and inhabit a person, prematurely trapping that soul and condemning them to hell.

But they could only do this with cooperation. The person would have to be a dark soul, or they would have to break a rule that would open them to a foul spirit. Some souls go willingly; these are the dark souls that attract these spirits. Very rarely, however, these entities will occasionally take a pure soul. Those are trophies, and nothing tastes as sweet as the innocent. Nothing, perhaps, but the capturing of a soul like Ezekiel's, which would in fact be monumental—if it were possible—because it would cut into the very fabric of all creation.

Many other things lurk in the dark; creatures such as vampires—oh yes, they're real too, but they are nothing like what we've been led to believe. Rather than draining your blood, they drain your life's essence. But it's easy to see how the story got twisted over time. The victims of these things usually sought psychiatric help. Some would commit suicide; others would be turned, becoming one of the night's creatures. The real name for these beings is "vimpies."

Then there are also beings referred to as "shades." Some angels fear them, and all demons do. They are demigods—supreme devils if you will—and they don't follow the rules. Rumor has it that they can kill angels, but no one knows for certain if this is true.

There was so much for Ezekiel to learn, but he was sure that at the appointed time Joshua would prepare him and show him who he was. And once he was properly trained, Ezekiel would possess the power to destroy a demon before the seven seals are broken; that's something not many angels can do without permission. Ezekiel would have the power to kill a shade, to destroy demons, and to vanquish many others—possibly even an angel, once he came into his own. This would make him a desirable commodity to both sides. Ezekiel would indeed be a phenomenon—before him, only an angel could kill a demon.

Now demons are old, powerful, and exceedingly shrewd. They are lesser beings than angels, but that does not negate the fact that they can severely harm one. If it were possible for one to somehow corrupt Ezekiel, it would be a catastrophic assault against the kingdom. There are numerous other creatures in the spirit realm—too many to mention them all. The important thing Ezekiel needed to know was that he was wanted by all, which meant he should always be mindful and stay focused and ever prayerful.

One Friday evening, Ezekiel was at the library, researching facts for a school paper. He stayed a little later than usual, and when he left, he was tired and headed straight for home. Just before he arrived, he heard a woman cry out for help. He moved in the direction of her cries and saw her fighting what he thought was a man. He ran over to break up the fight, ignoring his inner voice, which told him to stay away. Instinctively, he pulled the man off the woman, but to his surprise, the man vanished and the woman grabbed his throat.

With her free hand, she began pressing her fingers into his chest. He tried to move, but he couldn't break free of her grip. It felt like she was trying to reach inside of him spiritually.

He could feel himself fading, and then he heard Joshua's voice screaming in his head: "DO NOT LET IT TAKE YOU! FIGHT IT, YOU CAN PULL IT OUT OF HER!"

He heard other voices saying, "NO!" And then he heard someone say, "HE'S NOT READY. HE CAN'T! HE DOESN'T KNOW THE RULES."

And Joshua replied, "WOULD YOU HAVE ME DO NOTHING? I CAN'T WATCH THEM TAKE HIM, HE'S TOO VALUABLE; I WILL SPEAK THE WORDS AND PRESERVE HIS LIFE! I WON'T LET THEM HAVE HIM."

Then Joshua spoke in a tongue that Ezekiel did not understand. Hearing this, Ezekiel found renewed strength. Believing Joshua, he fought with everything he had. He grabbed the woman by the neck with his left hand and began pulling backward with his right, like he was drawing back on a bow. He pulled with all his might, and though he believed he was pulling with his hands alone, it was not just his hands that were doing the pulling; it was also his mind. It was instinctual.

The woman screamed, and so did the thing inside her, but still Ezekiel kept pulling. He could feel himself growing stronger as he did. The thing was scratching and pulling on his arm. Ezekiel's aura grew brighter and brighter, and the evil inside the woman fought hard, but Ezekiel held it with an unbendable grip and ripped it out of her. It let out a scream and burst into flames, disintegrating and dispersing into the air. Before Ezekiel could collect his thoughts, he heard Joshua's voice say, "Well done, Ezekiel, now get up and leave quickly, there is no time to waste, they know of you now and they will be coming."

What Ezekiel didn't know at the time was that the moment he ripped the evil from the woman, he earned the attention of both angels and demons alike. This action changed him. This was the moment of his spiritual birth; he was something else now! Ezekiel could hear Joshua's voice whispering in his ears, telling him to leave. The woman did not survive the ordeal. He had broken her neck during the struggle with the entity. He tried to get up to leave, but he was just too exhausted, and he passed out. When he regained consciousness, the police were there, and he was in handcuffs. He was just fifteen, but he was charged as an adult with involuntary manslaughter, and that was how he ended up in prison. Initially he was given three years with the possibility of parole at six months, but because of his age and prison being what it is, his time was extended for multiple incidents with other inmates.

That was two years ago, a few days after the New Year began. Ezekiel was seventeen years old now. Aside from having to constantly ward off unwanted sexual advances from inmates, he also had to be vigilant of all the nasty things that lurked in the spirit world. Every once in a while, when he allowed himself to fall asleep without performing the prayer ritual or when relaxing unmindful of his trend of thought, he would drop his guard—and they would see him and come. So now he stood in the prison yard holding the bloody knife, waiting to feel the unwelcomed kiss of the guard's wooden batons, which would pummel his body until they brought him to his knees, and be dragged off to the hole. At least there, he thought, he'd be safe for a while—safe until they released him back into the general population. Then the fighting would start all over again. But that was OK with him. It was short work compared to the war being waged in the spirit realm. He was no longer afraid, because he had hardened. Let them come, he thought, because he'd be ready, and he would not be taken, nor would he fall, so long as it was the will of God and Joshua was with him.

*He sitteth in the lurking places of the villages; in
secret places doth he murder the innocent; his eyes
are privily set against the poor.*

—PSALM 10:8 (KJ21)

CHAPTER TWO

Robbie Harrison

*Two blood-red eyes glowed briefly and a slight
smile, barely visible, crept over its face, and
then it just faded back into the shadows.*

IT WAS THE NOT KNOWING THAT WAS KILLING ROBBIE—NEVER
knowing on what corner Joey would be waiting with all his bully
friends. *It isn't fair that he gets to do whatever he likes just because
he's bigger than me,* Robbie thought. If his father were still here, he
wouldn't let Joey pick on him. He would have worked it out, even if
it meant putting them in a ring and letting them duke it out.

Robbie's father had been a boxer in the Marines, and he
believed in fair play; he was just that kind of person. All the neighborhood kids knew him; he was "that guy"—the one you would
see playing stickball or touch football in the street with the kids.

He was the one everyone looked to when something shady went down on the block. He stopped kids from picking on one another. It was just what he did; it was a part of who he was. It was this sense of fair play that had gotten him killed. He stopped a robbery at his neighborhood bar, and during the altercation, he was shot twice in the chest. He still managed to hold onto the thief until the police arrived, but he died on the way to the hospital. Robbie never got a chance to see his father that day—he'd left his house earlier than normal to avoid bumping into Joey and his gang at the school gate.

Joey lived closer to the school than Robbie, and he would always get there before him. Joey and his boys harassed everyone who came through the gate, but for some reason Robbie didn't know, Joey's favorite victim was him. In fact, the reason was that one day Joey had overheard his girlfriend talking with her friends and saying that she thought Robbie was cute; this infuriated Joey. *How could she even look at this little punk,* he thought, and this was the source of Robbie's current predicament. If Robbie had just stayed home a little later that morning, he would have seen his father one last time. That was six months ago, but it felt like yesterday to him.

When Robbie entered the school, he stopped at the end of the hallway and peeked around the corner, poking his head out just enough to see if the coast was clear. He was a good-looking kid, with large doe-like eyes that were as blue as the sky. He didn't see Joey, but James and Brian were there. They hung out with Joey, and they were just as mean. He decided it would be easier to turn around and go down the back stairway to his homeroom. It might take a bit longer, but at least he wouldn't have to deal with any of those guys. Before he could turn around, however, everything went black. There was a sharp stinging sensation on the right side of his face. His head had just been smashed into the cold tiles on the wall. He could feel one of the tiles cut into his cheek as his head collided with the wall. His books dropped to the ground and everything seemed warped and distorted. He tried to regain focus and get some clarity, but he just couldn't make anything out. Everything was blurred and shadowy, and he thought to himself, *What just happened?*

He could hear people talking all around him, but he couldn't understand what they were saying. "GAAT UUP, PUNNK," someone roared.

At least that's what it sounded like to Robbie. His focus returned just in time for him to see a fist heading toward his face, but he was too dazed to block it. Later, Robbie thought it was funny how his mind was able to remember the smallest details in a fraction of an instant. Like people covering their faces and saying, "OOOWWW!" in reaction to seeing blows delivered to his face, or some writing on the wall above the lockers that said, "*SCHOOL SUCKS!*" or the name *Joey* on a ring just before it crashed into his eye and everything went black.

"GET UP, PUNK. GET UP!" Joey shouted. "I thought I told you not to walk on my side of the hallway, TARDO. Now look at you."

After a moment, Robbie could see again. He looked up from the floor and saw Joey looking down on him with his boys, Brian and James, cheering him on.

Joey was a good deal taller than Robbie, with a full head of black unruly hair that had a stubborn cowlick that went pretty much its own way. He was lean, but not skinny. He was hard and muscular, and at this moment he was clutching his fist and waving his arms about.

"I caught him watching you guys like a little punk, acting all gay and whatnot, so I just surprised his punk behind with a little wake-up call to the head."

Joey roared. Robbie's head was killing him, and he could feel his right eye closing and warm blood rolling down his face from the cut on his cheek. He raised his arms to protect his head as he slid down the side of the wall onto the floor. He heard a voice in his head say,

"GRABS HIS BALLS, AND DON'T LETS GO."

He heard the voice over and over again.

"GRABS HIS BALLS, AND DON'T LETS GO."

So when Joey approached him to inflict more damage, he grabbed hold of Joey's balls with everything he had. Joey was wearing baggy jeans, the kind that keep sliding off even with a belt on. This new fashion fad turned out to be a bad choice for Joey on this day. The saggy jeans made it easy for Robbie to get a good grip—that and the fact that it was probably the last thing in the world Joey was expecting Robbie to do.

"TWIST THEM! TWIST THEM!"

Robbie followed the instructions of the voice.... Each time he did, Joey cried out a little more. The voice continued,

"PULLS THEM, THEN TWIST THEM. MAKES HIM HURTS THE WAY HE HURTS YOU."

By this time Joey was screaming out in agony. He screamed for help from his friends, who were momentarily stunned into inaction by what they were witnessing. They emerged from their stupor and rushed toward Robbie, trying to pull his hand away, but he would not let go. Instead, he held on even tighter. Brian put Robbie in a headlock while James repeatedly punched him, trying to get him to let go.

"DON'T LETS GO! PULLS THEM OFF, BUT NEVER LETS GO!"

It was a chilling sight! Even though James and Brian were pounding Robbie, and a teacher joined in to try to get Robbie to release his grip, Robbie simply *would not let go.* Robbie felt no pain; all his thoughts were of ripping Joey's balls off. A smile seized his face as he proceeded with his anfractuous torture. By this time, Joey was on the floor, lying on top of Robbie. He could no longer speak, and drool and snot were running down his face. His eyes had rolled up into his head. Robbie wondered if Joey could see him smiling, and he tugged on his balls a little harder. It was a rapturous moment for Robbie—until a kick to the head rendered him unconscious. When he woke up, he was in a hospital. He had a concussion, and his perfectly straight nose was broken. He had a bruised larynx and a black eye. There were cuts and scratches on his arms and hands from nails trying to pry his hand open, and his body ached all over from being kicked. He could hear the doctor speaking with Nina, his mother, outside his door. "He's resting now," said the doctor. "He has a concussion and a few bumps and bruises. His nose is broken, but he will be fine. However, the other boy, Joey, he's going to be here for a while. His parents want to speak with you. There was some damage done to his right testicle. The scrotum was torn, and his left testicle is badly swollen. He may not be able to have children." The doctor shook his head sympathetically.

"Yeah," whispered Robbie to himself, "who's the punk now, Joey?" Then he smiled.

Nina couldn't believe what had happened. This was not like her Robbie. He was not a violent person. He was quiet and thoughtful. She knew he was suffering due to the loss of his father, but she wasn't aware it had become this serious.

Robbie closed his eyes; he was oddly at peace. He felt strangely euphoric and pleased with what he had done. He had no remorse—none. From the very beginning of the school year, Joey had been a thorn in his side—beating on him, taking his money, and humiliating him, just for the fun of it. Because of Joey, he hadn't seen his father the day he died. Now Robbie pictured Joey, lying in bed wondering if his little balls would ever work again. He relished the thought of Joey's pain and contemplated how he could get in his room when everyone was gone and finish what he had started and *rip his balls off!*

Robbie was different now. He had changed; he no longer felt the emptiness in his heart, and the fear was gone. Even his eyes were different; the light was gone from them. They were dark pools of murky blue. His innocence was gone too. In its place was hate: hate for anyone who had ever teased him. Hate for everyone who just stood by and watched it happen. Hate for anyone who ever laughed, or talked smack, or instigated the foolishness that had caused so much pain in his life. In a split second, the Robbie Harrison that everyone knew had died. It was like he had been reborn and turned into something else—something dark and malignant. Robbie had completely given himself over to the voice in his head and would do whatever it told him to do. This was the first time in Robbie's life that he felt confident. He felt bold and strong. He lay back and closed his eyes, and a moment later he fell off into a deep sleep.

Behind Robbie, in the corner of his room, a malignant shadow emerged from behind the curtains and hovered over his bed. The presence moved forward and looked down over the boy. Two blood-red eyes glowed briefly and a slight smile, barely visible, crept over its face, and then it just faded back into the shadows. Robbie Harrison belonged to him now.

Nina entered Robbie's room, walked over to his bed, and looked down at him. He was asleep and looked so vulnerable. His face was swollen, and his eye was black and completely shut. It was not in her son's nature to do what he had done. He was just defending himself the only way he knew how. *That boy was way bigger than he was,* she thought as she sat in the chair next to his bed. Nina fell asleep and didn't wake until a nurse entered the room, later that night, to give Robbie a pill.

In the weeks that followed, a different Robbie emerged. He was exercising regularly and lifting weights, practicing the jabs his father had taught him. He no longer slouched when he walked. Instead, he held his head up with a newfound assurance, appearing taller, confident, and unafraid. His full lips stretched across his face more often, displaying even white teeth as he smiled; the difference was like night and day.

After the fight with Joey, he had earned himself a rep as a badass. Everyone knew what he had done to Joey, who was still not back in school. But the true test of his new rep came when James and Brian jumped him in the stairwell. It didn't come as a surprise to Robbie. He had been expecting it.

It was Friday afternoon around 1:15; James and Brian lay in wait for him in the stairwell. He was on his way to math class when he noticed a crowd forming in anticipation of a fight; strangely, Robbie felt no fear. He was excited and confident as he walked through the corridors. And he looked sharp too, with his new leather jacket and his Calvin Klein jeans. He'd had taps put on the heels of his shiny new black boots, and he was feeling himself. This type of situation would have terrified him in the past, but now the adrenaline surged through his veins. He was pumped up with energy.

He entered the stairwell and faced his nemeses. James and Brian were talking smack to impress the crowd. When James saw Robbie, he reached out to push him. But just as James's hand touched Robbie's shoulder, he made a quick maneuver and put

James in a headlock, astonishing the crowd. Then Brian approached him from behind and Robbie caught him with an elbow to the nose, instantly breaking it. He then began pummeling James. He could hear Brian behind him saying, "You broke my nose! You broke my nose, you stinking little punk! I'm gonna kill you, you little turd!"

The instigators in the crowd made *ooh* and *ah* sounds, and Robbie smiled as they did, still holding onto James. He answered, "Not if I kill you first," in a surprisingly calm tone.

James was a husky and muscular kid. He was a little shorter than Robbie, but bigger in girth. He was very fair, with platinum blond hair. His face was red, and purple bruises were materializing on his cheeks and chin. His right eye was completely closed now from the punches Robbie had delivered. Robbie's hand, now covered in blood, reached out and grabbed James by the hair. He slammed his face into the metal handrail that divided the staircase in two. It made a bong sound and then a humming noise as Robbie let go of James and he slid down the steps. He turned to face Brian as James just lay on the floor.

Brian, still holding his broken nose, blood running between his fingers, became filled with rage. There was just no way that this little punk was going to get away with this. *First he messes over Joey and now he thinks he can mess with James?* He clenched his hands into fists and screamed, "Come on!"

Robbie heard the voice in his head again, saying:

"FINISH HIMS, SHUTS HIS MOUTH NOW."

Brian rushed him and pushed him back into the corner of the wall, causing his backpack to fall off his shoulders. He pulled his hand back, intending to bring his fist down across Robbie's face, when Robbie smiled and winked at him. Brian paused, just for a moment, but that was all it took. Robbie brought his knee up and struck Brian in the testicles. Tears immediately fell from Brian's eyes as he tried to hold onto Robbie's shirt, but Robbie kneed him again, almost in the same spot as before. Brian, a thick, brawny black fellow with wooly hair, fell to the floor, holding his balls, unable to do anything but cry and whimper. Robbie looked down at James and then at Brian. He smiled, turned around, stepped over James, and picked up his backpack, slinging it over his shoulders. He walked to the top of the stairs and proceeded to math class. The crowd looked on in awe.

He looked at his watch. Four, maybe five minutes had passed. He still arrived at his class on time and went to his desk and sat down. He was reflecting on what had just taken place. When he noticed that he still had some of James's blood on his hand, he stared at it and tasted it; he decided that he liked it and wanted more, but he rubbed at it until it came off. About five minutes into math class, the school's security officer arrived and took him out of class. He was suspended for a week. The parents of the two other boys wanted to sue the school and Robbie's mom, but Nina beat them to the punch. She sued the school *and* the parents, because in each incident there were witnesses that confirmed that Robbie had acted in self-defense. Everyone knew that Robbie was quiet and that Joey and his gang were the school bullies. So the school and the parents agreed to settle out of court.

That was almost a year and a half ago. Robbie was a senior now, no longer that skinny young teenager. During high school, he put on a little weight and grew a few inches. Although he'd captured the attention of many young ladies, he still basically kept to himself. Joey, James, and Brian didn't say anything to him anymore, and if they happened to see him in the hallways, they just moved to the side and let him pass. In fact, from the outside looking in, it would seem that Robbie's life took a positive turn for the best. But what most people couldn't see was the emptiness in his eyes and the malignant force behind his smile. Everyone admired him—everyone except Vera, who had seen the look on his face last year on that stairwell. She saw him smile just before breaking that other boy's nose, but most importantly, she heard the voice in his head!

For every one that doeth evil hateth the light, neither
cometh to the light, lest his deeds should be reproved.

—JOHN 3:20

CHAPTER THREE

Vera McNulty

…and just for a second, she could have sworn
she saw a shadow or something standing
next to him, watching her as well.

AT THREE O'CLOCK, VERA MCNULTY WAS ON HER WAY HOME
from school with her friends. They stopped at the candy store like
always. Vera was seventeen years old, and she wouldn't be getting
any older if he got his way—and he always does. She approached
the counter to pay for her Cherry Coke and Cool Ranch Doritos,
when suddenly a chill ran down her spine, causing the hairs on the
back of her neck to rise. An eerie feeling engulfed her, as if she was
being watched. She turned sharply, causing her long curly hair to
whip around and cover her cheeks. Scanning the interior of the
store, she only saw the clerk. He asked, "Hey, you gonna pay for
those, or are you waiting for the sun to set?"

She turned around, pulled five dollars from her pocket, and gave it to the clerk. He gave her some change, and she stood at the counter staring at the change in her hand.

"Is something wrong? Did I shortchange you or something?" the clerk asked.

As if struggling to look away from her hand, she looked up at the clerk and asked, "Is anybody else in here with you?"

"What?" the store clerk replied.

"Is anyone else here in the store with you?"

"Nope, just you and me. Your friends are outside waiting for you. Why?"

Vera looked back down at her hand, noticing that there was a strong odor of vinegar and rotten eggs in the air as well.

"It's just that I feel like somebody else..." Her voice drifted off in midsentence.

"You feel like somebody else what?" asked the clerk.

"Never mind," she said, shaking her head as if to clear it.

She put the change in her pocket and walked to the door. As she pushed it open, she heard the bells jingle overhead and looked up. Then she turned back around and saw the clerk watching her, and just for a second she could have sworn she saw a shadow or something standing next to him watching her as well. She raised her hand and rubbed her eyes, and when they refocused, the shadow was gone.

"You be careful, little lady," said the clerk. "See you tomorrow."

He smiled, and then the phone rang. He went to pick it up as Vera turned around. She had been feeling a little off all day. She kept seeing things out of the corners of her eyes, but when she would turn to look, there would be nothing there. She wondered what was making her feel this way. She attributed it to nerves—her final exams were coming up.

She left the store and rejoined her friends outside, and the friends made their way up the block to the bus stop, where they waited for the bus to arrive. Vera never turned to look back again, but if she had, she might have glimpsed something emanating from the clerk, something that lives in the shadows, something ancient, and something completely evil. If she had waited just a moment longer or looked into the clerk's eyes a little deeper, she might even have drawn it out into the open. For that reason alone, the hidden figure wanted her. It craved her flesh. It wanted to taste her soul. And if it got its way, she would be its next meal that night . . . and Vera McNulty would cease to exist.

*But when He, the Spirit of truth, comes, He will
guide you into all the truth; for He will not speak on
His own initiative, but whatever He hears, He will
speak; and He will disclose to you what is to come.*

—JOHN 16:13 (NASB1995)

CHAPTER FOUR

The Warning

*"Stay away from the shadows, that's where he
lives; that's where he gets his power."*

VERA HAD BEEN FEELING JUST A LITTLE OFF FOR QUITE SOME
time. But lately she was feeling even more uneasy. She was also
finding it hard to focus. She'd been having blackouts and losing time.
She would go places and have no idea how she got there, and she
even sometimes did things she didn't remember doing. Now and
then, she would have a dim memory of an event, but she couldn't
be sure if the memory was real or if she had dreamed it. However,
she was beginning to doubt that they were dreams. She was beginning to believe, instead, that they were memories of things that had
actually happened, and this scared her.

She was seeing things—shadows moving in her peripheral vision. When she turned to look at them, they would fade or disappear into the shadows. She always felt as if she were being watched; like something bad was about to happen to her, but she didn't know what to do about this ... or who to tell. After all, who would believe her? She tried to tell her mother, but her mother just thought she had been working too hard on her school projects and needed some rest. She couldn't tell her friends; they just wouldn't understand and would probably think she was crazy. And honestly ... maybe she was, or at least on her way.

Yesterday, outside the grocery store, she had been talking with her friends when she suddenly began yelling and pointing at some fat guy. Her friends told her she had said some crazy things and the guy almost fell. She just couldn't shake the feeling that she was not alone. She felt weird, like someone else was in her head. *Maybe my mother's right,* she thought. *I need to rest more.* But she could swear that something else was guiding her and telling her what to do. Vera had believed these were her thoughts at first, but lately, it didn't feel that way. She knew it was something else, like a presence, guiding her, and even protecting her, but from what?

One day, on her way home from school, she noticed an elderly woman trying to pull her shopping cart up onto the curb. Without thinking, she went over to help her. The old woman thanked her, and as she took hold of the cart, their hands touched and she stumbled a bit. Vera grabbed the woman's arm to steady her and asked if she was OK. Suddenly, it seemed as if they were transported somewhere else. She felt like they were in the clouds. The woman looked her in the eyes. She never moved her lips, but Vera could hear her say, "Stay away from them shadows; that's where he lives. That's where he gets his power."

"What? I'm sorry," Vera said, confused.

"Start praying, girl. He lives in people, people you won't suspect. That's how he deceives you. Use your sight, girl. He can't take you unless you let him. Never trust him, never believe him, and never give in to him. He is a liar. Stay out of them shadows, and whatever you do, never let him take you into the shadows after dark."

Vera recoiled as she asked, "Who are you? What are you talking about?" But the old woman held on to her firmly and continued to speak.

"There is another who seeks you as well. He is your guardian, although it may not seem that way to you at first. Trust with your heart, not your eyes; do not lose faith despite your circumstance, for it's your faith in God that gives you strength."

The old woman let go of Vera, and they were back on the street. The woman started pushing her cart down the block, and Vera just stood there watching her, unsure of what to say or do. She wanted to call out to the woman, but she couldn't find her voice. She looked around to see if anyone else had seen what just took place, but no one had, and when she looked back at the old woman, she had vanished. Only a sweet scent of lavender and lilac remained.

Vera had been brought up in a semireligious environment. She believed in God and all the stories in the Bible. One of her favorite movies was *The Ten Commandments*, with Charlton Heston and Yul Brynner. She often wondered what Moses thought when he first came back with God's commandments to his people. Did he think himself to be crazy as he spoke with a burning bush, or did he know right from the beginning that he was speaking with God? And how hard must it have been to follow God's instructions when it seemed like everyone and everything around him was falling apart. The reason she was thinking all of this was she believed she had just spoken with an angel. She couldn't explain her feelings, she just somehow knew it was true. She also knew that no one would believe her if she told them.

"Stay out of them shadows and keep the faith." That's what the woman had said, but there are shadows everywhere. How could she avoid them all? *She also said he lives in people I wouldn't suspect and to use my sight.* None of this made any sense to her.

She closed her eyes for a minute and rubbed them, and then someone tapped her on the shoulder, and said, "Are you all right?"

"Yes," she said as she turned around to see who was asking. To her surprise, it was Robbie Harrison.

"Are you sure you're all right? You look a little lost." He took her backpack off her shoulder and put it over his. "I've seen you around before. You're Vera, right?"

She was shocked and surprised that he knew who she was. She was also a little frightened of him—she had been ever since that day in the stairwell when he got into a fight with those two boys. She could have sworn she heard a voice talking to Robbie, an evil voice. She mostly avoided him after that, but looking at him now, he didn't seem so bad.

His dark blue eyes almost seemed to hypnotize her. She answered, "Yeah, and you're Robbie, right?"

He smiled and said yes.

"You can give me my books back," Vera said. "I'm OK, really. I was just thinking…about something, that's all."

"It's OK; I don't mind. Let me walk you to the bus stop."

She smiled and thought to herself that he didn't seem like what she thought he was and in fact he was kind of cute. So she said, "OK."

They walked to the bus stop and talked while waiting for the bus.

Across the street, in the shadows of a nearby building, a figure watched and smiled. It thought to itself that if it could not reach her directly, it would take her through an indirect route. Either way, she would be his.

"Behold, I am sending you out as sheep in the midst of wolves, so be wise as serpents and innocent as doves."

—MATTHEW 10:16 (ESV)

CHAPTER FIVE

The Shade

"Reveal yourself, demon, and shed your mortal guise, for I see you plainly. I am a cup bringer for the one true God."

"Did she see me?" he wondered. "How frightfully intriguings. There are so few who cans sense me, much less sees me. She smelled so goods. I could almost taste her. Sooo sweet, sooo innocent, I must haves her," he thought.

Nestor exited the store and, avoiding the light and creeping through the shadows, he followed her. When there were no shadows to hide in, he moved into a person. Riding a person was easy as long as their aura was dark. But to possess someone, now that required some work and a bit of cooperation on their part. Nestor had been around for thousands of years, tormenting humans in one way or another. He was a soul reaper. In a sense, what Lucifer was to God, he was to the Devil—not as powerful, but just as evil. Some even suspected that it was he in the guise of the snake that tempted Eve in the garden, but that was only an assumption. Nestor's only purpose on earth was to harvest souls and deliver them to his master, Lucifer. His only weakness was that he now needed to feed on souls himself; he had become addicted. And over the years, he developed a taste for human flesh as well. It was not so in the beginning, but now, when he took a person, he truly would devour their mind, body, and soul. There was a time when he would have to possess a person to get them to do things. But now, he found that a simple touch was more than enough. He wasn't sure if that was because it was closer to the time of ascension or if was just that he had gotten so much better at what he did. Although he couldn't do it to everyone. Not if they were close to God. He hated those souls and took great delight when they fell short of God's expectations. He listened in on the thoughts of the people he inhabited as he stalked Vera from afar. He slipped inside a man in his mid-fifties as he exited his car.

The man wondered how old they were. He guessed about fifteen or sixteen, something like that. *Just right,* he thought, as he imagined getting with them. Then he gave a short, choppy laugh and thought, *Nah, I'm just kidding, I would never do that; they're way too young.* He then began to critique their parents, thinking they should never have let them come out dressed like that. Got him all hot and bothered.

Nestor was always surprised by how a person's thoughts could differ so greatly from their appearance and actions, and this man was a prime example of that paradox. Then suddenly, Vera turned around quickly, without warning, and stared directly at the man. Her hazel eyes locked with his, her lips slightly parted as she tilted her head ever so slightly. It was as if she was looking right through the man and directly at Nestor. This caught him completely off guard and caused him to recoil, almost as if someone had shoved him. She walked toward him, and Nestor took a few steps back as she did. He found he was unable to turn away from her penetrating gaze; the girl had momentarily immobilized him. "WHO IS SHE?" he thought. Her aura was so bright! "How does her gaze hold me?" Then she spoke.

"Reveal yourself, demon, and shed your mortal guise, for I see you plainly. I am a cup bringer for the one true God, and all who stand opposing shall surely fall, so saith the Lord God, Amen."

Her voice was akin to thunder—sharp and resonating in his mind. The words she spoke were unnaturally compelling to him and he thought, "Somehow this whelp has called me out."

Maybe it was being caught by surprise or being seen. Or it could have been the words she spoke or a combination of all three, but whatever it was, for the first time in over two thousand years, a mortal—a child at that—had given him cause to fear and doubt himself, just for a moment. But that was enough.

He leaped from the man's body and back into the shadow of a nearby alleyway and watched her from across the street. She was still pointing her finger and shouting at the man, even though Nestor had left his body. Then she paused for a moment, continuing to stare at the man but saying nothing, almost as if she were examining him.

"Look, little girl," said the man, "I don't know what you're talking about, but you need to get out of my face." He stepped away, a little embarrassed. Vera looked around and then slowly back at the man.

"I'm sorry; I thought you were someone else," she stammered. She turned around and went back to her friends, who looked even more confused than the guy.

"What was that all about?" they asked.

"I made a mistake. Come on, let's go."

They shrugged and continued on their way.

"Who is this little girl, and where did she come from?" he thought. "She's special, rare, not for many millennia have I felt anything like that. She may be one of the chosen, extremely rare indeed, a genuine find. I will have her, and she will taste so sweets. I'lls be peeling her young flesh from her bones and hearing her screams as I eat her slowly piece by piece," he thought. "I have to plan this just right. She's not one that I can just sneak up on. No, she can sense me somehow. I'lls makes her tell how it is she can see me, while I'm peeling away her flesh. She'll tells me, oh yeah. She'll be beggin me to stops. That will makes its so much sweeter, hen, hen, hen."

He followed her from a distance, staying in the shadows, always dropping under a nearby car or into an alleyway whenever she would turn around. It frustrated him that she instinctively knew where he was. She walked down the street, stopping periodically and looking in his direction. Her gaze felt as if it were burning his skin.

"Who is she, this little thing, this human that her looks could cause one such as I to be uncomfortable? I who has walked among gods, and crumbled empires, should suffer a look from a whelp?" thought Nestor.

Make a chain: for the land is full of bloody crimes,
and the city is full of violence. Wherefore I will bring
the worst of the heathen, and they shall possess their
houses: I will also make the pomp of the strong to
cease; and their holy places shall be defiled.
—EZEKIEL 7:24

CHAPTER SIX

And the Innocent Perish

Hector watched in horror as the blood that fell to the
floor drew itself upward into the demon's mouth.

LIDIA DIAZ CLIMBED THE STAIRS TO HER THIRD-FLOOR APART-
ment in a five-story walkup. The stairs always wore her out after a
long day of work. She just wanted to catch a nap before the boys
got home from school. A drunk driver had killed their father, and
now she was the sole breadwinner. They'd left Columbia when
Hector was two and she was pregnant with Rico. Joey, their father,
was a mechanic. She'd dropped out of school when she became

pregnant with Hector and had been forced to take a job as a maid after Joey passed away. She still cried at night whenever she thought about Joey. *He shouldn't be dead,* she thought; they were so hopeful and excited about their new life here in America. They were doing so well. If Joey had lived, she would have been studying nursing. She shook her head, refusing to think on it further. "I'm not going down that road," she said aloud. *At least I have Hector and Rico,* she thought. *They're my life now. It's up to me to give them the life that Joey and I planned.* When she reached her door, she took her keys from her handbag and opened it. When she passed the kitchen and saw the dishes in the sink from that morning's breakfast, she stopped and said, "Maybe I'll straighten up before I lie down." Lidia couldn't help herself. She liked things tidy and wouldn't be able to rest knowing the dishes were in the sink. Having cleaned up the kitchen, Lidia walked into the living room, laid down on the sofa, and dropped off to sleep.

At 5:30 p.m., the after-school program where Lidia sent the boys was letting out. Rico burst out of the door and down the steps, heading straight for the candy store. Hector got out a few minutes later and stood outside the door waiting for Rico, as his mother had instructed him to do. He waited for about five minutes and then walked back inside the school toward Rico's classroom. Rico's teacher saw him and wondered what he was doing back inside.

"Is everything all right, Hector?" she asked.

"I was looking for Rico," he said, now feeling worried.

"Rico left about five minutes ago, Hector. Didn't you see him?"

Hector realized that his brother had probably gone off to the candy store because they had just gotten their allowance that morning. He didn't want to cause a commotion, so he quickly said, "Oh, I forgot: Rico told me to meet him at the candy store. I'm sorry, Ms. Brown."

"That's OK, Hector. You boys had better hurry home and not dilly-dally around and worry your mother."

"We won't," Hector said cheerfully, hiding his anger as he turned and ran off to find Rico.

How many times had their mother told Rico to wait for him? Hector was furious. They were supposed to come home together.

Rico wasn't willful; he was just very impulsive. When he got a thought in his head, he just went with it. Hector was more mindful of what he did. Of course, Hector was two years older and a very responsible ten-year-old. Hector skipped down the stairs and raced up the block toward the candy store. He was almost at the end of the block when he spotted Rico walking back toward the school, looking into a little brown bag. He looked up and saw his brother running toward him, and a broad smile swept across Rico's freckled face. He ran toward his brother, shouting, "Hey, Hector, I bought you a jawbreaker too!"

Hector had a frown on his face as he readied himself to chastise his younger brother. When they met up, though, Rico stretched forth his hand, offering the jawbreaker to his older brother. Hector's face softened as he reached forth to collect the offering and he said gently, "Hey, Rico. You know Mom told you to wait for me."

"I did," Rico said with a smile. "I didn't leave you—I'm here." Rico plopped the jawbreaker into his mouth and said as he took off running, "Be I can beat you to the house!" And they both took off running down the street.

At 5:49, almost two hours had passed since Nestor's encounter with the young girl. The sting of her gaze was still fresh in Nestor's mind. He was angry, and he hungered, and he craved flesh. He would be denied no longer. The sun was setting and, as it did, he felt his power growing within him. He owned the night and all who dwelled within it. A few blocks away, two boys were racing each other. They were on their way home from the recreation center on Figueroa and Sixth, close to the science fair parkway.

"No fair, Rico, you cheated! You have to count to three before you can go," Hector said. "You didn't even count."

"You're just mad cause I'm beating you," Rico shouted. "Loser has to smell the winners' farts!" He laughed.

They both raced up the street, and Rico took the shortcut through the alley and came up the back way to their house. He hated losing to Hector. He was such a jerk. "Oh, no you don't," Hector shouted as he doubled back and tried to overtake his brother. They were the best of friends. They were so busy trying to outdo each other that they never noticed the dark figure emerging from the shadows until it was too late. Rico was running too fast and unable to slow down in time before he ran into him.

"Slows down little sir. Slows down."

It caught Rico off guard, as this man, this incredibly tall man, seemed to just appear out of nowhere. He had to be at least ten feet tall, and he was so thin it was unnatural. Then the stench of vinegar and rotten eggs hit him. It was overwhelming.

He stopped dead in his tracks, looking up at the man.

"Sorry, mister, I didn't see you," he said nervously.

"It's OK, I saws you, and you looks so good."

Then, without warning, Nestor reached out and grabbed Rico's arm, violently jerking the boy toward him. It felt to Rico like he'd pulled his arm out of his socket, and he shrieked out in pain. Rico looked at Nestor's face and saw roaches, millipedes, and every kind of nasty insect crawling around. The part of his eyes that should have been white was red, and the irises didn't have pupils— they were pools of blackness. His skin, if you could call it that, was pale gray and clammy-looking. He could hear his brother Hector shout, "Get off my brother, you freak!" Hector then charged him, intending to tackle him to the ground and free his brother; then the two of them could run home. It was a good plan. He could see it playing out in his mind.

Suddenly, he felt a sharp pain deep in his chest. It felt like his soul had been pierced as well. *How did he get me—how could he? He was at least ten feet away a moment ago.* Hector opened his mouth and tried to speak, but no words came. Nestor had reached deep into the boy's chest with a hand that looked more like a claw. It only had three fingers and looked deformed. His fingers wrapped themselves around the bones in his chest plate, and Hector winced in pain. His touch was like poison. Both boys felt nauseous, and neither had the strength to fight back.

Then Nestor's mouth began to grow. The bottom jaw seemed to dislodge and unhinge itself, expanding like a snake. His back arched and his head lurched forward, guiding Rico into his mouth. He began swallowing the boy's head and shoulders, slowly inching him down bit by bit. Hector managed a scream as he heard his brother's bones popping and saw the blood pouring down on the lower half of his body. Hector watched in horror as the blood that fell to the ground drew itself upward into the demon's mouth. He could still hear the muffled voice of his brother crying out in pain. Rico's legs were still thrashing about violently as Nestor continued devouring him. His neck enlarged as he swallowed Rico whole. Pushing his feet into his mouth, the demon spit out his sneakers and licked his fingers afterward. Then he looked at Hector, his red eyes glowing, as he said,

"Soo goods, soo goods."

Hector tried to cry out, but the only word that made it out of his mouth was "Mommy..."

Nestor smiled at that, thinking how much sweeter this would have been had he been able to fill his belly with that little girl he desired. He needed her, and his hunger would forever be unquenched until he had her. Maybe she would call out for her mommy as well when she realized she was his. He would have to figure out a way to get to her without being seen by her, at least until it was too late. A brief laugh escaped his lips at the thought of that. Then he refocused his attention back on Hector and said, "You'll just have to do for now, though, won't you."

A block away, Lidia was waiting by the window for her boys to get home. For some strange reason she could not explain, she couldn't help worrying about them. It was as if she could hear them calling for her. It caused the hairs on the back of her neck to rise. As she rubbed the goosebumps on her arm, she waited, wiping away an occasional tear from the corners of her eyes. She couldn't figure out why she felt this way.

Suddenly, she had the urge to leave the house and look for the boys. She grabbed her jacket and ran out the door and down the stairs. She stood in front of the house for a second and then started walking to the corner, hoping to meet them on the way. This feeling she had of foreboding and dread overwhelmed her; she just needed to see her babies. She couldn't explain it—she just knew something was wrong.

She turned to walk toward the bodega but switched directions and took off running into the alley, accidentally bumping into a man and knocking him off his feet and onto the ground. She was sorry for that, but she didn't have time to stop. She knew the boys would sometimes come that way even though she wished they wouldn't. Suddenly, she saw him, Nestor, holding Hector in the air, dangling him over his head with his mouth open. It was impossible, but it looked like he was about to eat him. She screamed out, "LET HIM GO! SOMEBODY HELP ME!" Nestor looked up, surprised that he had an audience, but not alarmed. After all, this type of thing was bound to happen from time to time. What he was not prepared for was the large, glowing figure standing behind her.

"Let him go and leave from this place. You have done enough harm this day."

The voice was like thunder to Nestor, but Lidia, who was now rushing toward him, heard nothing. He pulled the boy's foot out of his mouth and frowned at the glowing figure.

"**What brings you down to my neck of the woods, Gabriel? It's not like you to interfere in these matters.**"

Then he tossed Hector to the ground. Lidia grabbed him up into her arms right away, saying, "Are you all right? Where is Rico?" But Hector couldn't find his words. He did, however, notice the shining man who had told the demon to let him go. He wished he had gotten there a few minutes earlier—maybe Rico would still be alive.

"**No matters,**" uttered Nestor. "**Tomorrows is another day.**"

He looked down at Hector and said: "**Be seeing you, boy.**" His eyes glowed wildly as he faded back into the shadows and vanished.

The glowing man that Hector simply knew was an angel had also vanished. He told his mother and the police everything that had happened, and while the police dismissed most of what he said, believing he was trying to get attention by telling a shocking tall tale, his mother believed in her heart that he was telling the truth. And nothing would ever be the same for them, ever again.

Thou wilt keep him in perfect peace, whose mind is
stayed on thee: because he trusteth in thee. Trust
ye in the Lord for ever: for in the Lord Jehovah is
everlasting strength:

—ISAIAH 26:3–4

CHAPTER SEVEN

Evil Can't Prevail Over Faith

"He is old and powerful, and he can't know of you
yet, because he will know what you are, and what you
can do, but more importantly, how to use you."

Five Years Later, Present Day

IT HAD BEEN SOME TIME SINCE EZEKIEL'S LAST ENCOUNTER
with any demons. Joshua had been with him more than ever these
past few years, trying to keep him focused on what was coming. It
had been hard trying to keep himself off the Devil's radar. Ezekiel
had become more spiritually perceptive, which Joshua had told
him would happen a long time ago. The more he fasted and prayed,

the stronger he became. What Joshua failed to mention were the visions he was having. They were so vivid and intense that he couldn't tell whether he was awake or dreaming. They were always of the same girl, somewhere in the city. She was special too, like him, but different; and the dark one wanted her. The dark one wanted her because she could see him, and that scared him. But there was something else. She could push him out of his host body just by looking at him. Ezekiel wondered how she was able to do that. He wondered if Joshua knew about her; he would have to get to her soon. He could feel the dark one's rage getting stronger and knew that he would be coming for her. It was almost like he was in its head, hearing its thoughts—so dark and so full of hate. It was like poison in his soul. The funny thing was, though, that Ezekiel thought if he meditated and pushed very hard, he really could get into the thing's head and hear its thoughts. He could even make it say or do what he wanted it to. Ezekiel would play with its mind to see how far he could push it, but the thing's mind was just *so* dark he couldn't stand to be in there for very long. He found himself wondering why he and the creature were so closely linked. And there was something more, something that Joshua hadn't told him, or maybe Joshua didn't even know. Things were going to be happening soon, and whatever they were supposed to do had to happen immediately. That meant he had to get out of prison if he was going to be of any use in this fight.

Then Joshua spoke to him: "Be patient, Ezekiel. Everything is as it should be for now, and the girl is safe; but she will need you to help her, just as I helped you. And be warned, Ezekiel, the dark one is not to be trifled with. Stay you out of his mind for fear of losing your own to his. He is old and powerful, and he can't know of you yet, because he will know what you are and what you can do, but more importantly, he will know how to use you."

"Well, then, how can I fight him if he's so powerful? How can I stop something like him?" Ezekiel asked.

"Know you this: for all his formidable powers, he is nothing compared to the Father, and the Father resides within you. But you need to be stronger in Christ. There can be no doubt; you must believe with all your heart, all your mind, and all your soul. And Ezekiel, whatever you do, wherever you go, go with God, and no power on earth will be able to stay you from your course."

Ezekiel had suffered the hole for about three months after his last encounter with two of the newer inmates who had tried to build a rep by taking him down. He had been back in the general population now for over a week. And to his surprise, no one had approached him. The guards as well as the inmates had concluded that there was something strange about Ezekiel; the beating that he'd put on the last two inmates had made quite an impact on the others. In the past, they had given it their all trying to take him out. They tried to shank him when he passed in the yard, and there were several attempts made to overtake him in the shower. But no matter what they did over the years, he always seemed to know when they were coming, and the outcome was always the same. Whoever attempted to harm him was permanently maimed—never killed, but usually wishing they had been. A man they called Bones could testify to that; Bones was a big man, almost seven feet tall, with a huge, odd-shaped head. His eyes were small and set deep into his face, causing his forehead to protrude. To call him ugly would be an insult to ugly people. However, he was built like an ox and had the strength to go along with it. He had gotten the nickname Bones because anyone he got into it with always ended up with something being broken, like an arm or a leg, and anyone who had a bout with Bones would tell you it was a no-win situation. Well, one day Bones got it in his mind to focus his attention on Ezekiel—the young buck who had yet to be broken, the one everyone called choirboy. Tonight, he thought, the choir is going to sing. The outcome surprised everyone. Bones had to be airlifted out to Los Angeles County General Hospital. The guards on the scene reported that Bones's genitalia had been removed, and both of his arms and his collarbone had been broken. He also had a ruptured spleen and several shattered ribs. Bones spent the better part of the year in the infirmary recovering. The doctors did what they could, but after something like that the body just doesn't work the same.

There were plenty of similar stories like that surrounding Ezekiel. And there were more than a few men walking around the prison who were either blind, limping, or missing a body part because of their dealings with Ezekiel. They thought at first that Ezekiel was just lucky, so they just kept coming. But after five years of the same thing, they realized that this guy was just untouchable—and scary too. You couldn't get close to him, because he didn't trust anyone, and he always seemed to be talking to himself. And now, after the latest episode, no one wanted any part of Ezekiel. Word got out that Jake, one of the guys who had jumped him in this latest fight, was in a catatonic state. He just sat in his cell staring at the wall with drool running out of the corners of his mouth. So Ezekiel found that when he walked through the yard, the men parted like the Red Sea did for Moses. They scattered like flies, putting out their cigarettes and shifting their gaze downward, afraid to make eye contact with him. And Ezekiel just chuckled to himself, because it was quite funny to him. After all, they were the ones who had brought the trouble to him, but you would think it was the other way around.

Ezekiel wasn't the same man who had been ushered into the prison five years ago. His eyes were knowing, his jaw had hardened, and his once-lean body was full and muscular. He was a ritual-istic being, with a daily routine that brought meditation at dawn, after which he would study the scriptures, and then Joshua would come. He showered with the others, always maintaining a watchful distance. He ate breakfast alone and always seemed to be writing something while he ate. He knelt to pray every day in the gym, just before a vigorous workout. He always kept to himself, very rarely speaking to anyone, except the guards…and Joshua, of course.

Take a scroll and write on it all the words which I
have spoken to you concerning Israel and concerning
Judah, and concerning all the nations, from the day
I first spoke to you, from the days of Josiah, even to
this day.

—JEREMIAH 36:2 (NASB1995)

CHAPTER EIGHT

The Book

Her aura was bright, and he felt nothing but
warmth and love emanating from her.

WHILE COMPLETING HIS USUAL WORKOUT, EZEKIEL WAS approached by a guard who told him that he had a visitor. The guard said that it was his aunt, but Ezekiel didn't have any idea who that could be. His mother had died while he was in prison, which pained him, and she had no sisters that he knew of; his father was unknown to him. Ezekiel knew that he had to be careful. Just because his fellow inmates had decided to let up on him, that didn't mean that he was out of danger. There were still other things he needed to worry about. He followed the guard down the corridor toward the visiting area, ever mindful of his surroundings. He was led into a room that resembled a cage; a place he'd never seen before now. There was an oblong table and eight chairs lined up in a row in front of it; the table itself was partitioned off into sections that measured about a yard between each partition, to allow for privacy. The table was fastened to the wall, which had a long window that started just above the table and went all the way up to the ceiling. This cage-like room separated the inmates from their visitors but allowed them to see each other. Ezekiel entered the room and cautiously approached the window, but he stopped short before sitting down. He recognized the woman and was shaken—he started to back away.

"Come on, come on, child," she said, waving him to be seated. "Come and talk to your old aunt Sarah, it's been a long time. How have you been doing?" she asked.

Ezekiel sat down slowly, still uncertain but no longer shaken. Her aura was bright, and he felt nothing but warmth and love emanating from her.

"Joshua sent me," she told him. "And I have something to give you."

"I've seen you before," Ezekiel said. "Many years ago, you warned me that they were coming. You were right."

She just smiled and said, "I know that this is a hard task you shoulder, but the real journey is about to begin." She produced a small book from the inner pocket of her coat. "Now, quickly before the guard notices…" She placed the book against the window, and the glass shimmered, rippling like water. The book passed through to his side. Ezekiel took the book and placed it on the counter. A guard glimpsed the glass rippling and walked over to make sure everything was OK. He saw the book and picked it up, examining it suspiciously. He opened it but only saw blank pages.

"What's this?" he asked.

"It's mine—it's my notebook. Can I have it back now, please?" Ezekiel stood up, looking down at the guard. The guard looked at the old woman, who was smiling at him, and then back at Ezekiel. He put the book down on the table in front of him and then walked away.

"Sit, child, time is short, and I have things to be saying to you. Guard this book with your life, Ezekiel. It's ancient; study it along with your Bible. Read it when you are in the book of Revelations. Things will be revealed to you. things that very few know, things that only a handful can know. Now, put your hands on the glass, Ezekiel," she urged him, and when Ezekiel placed his hands on the glass, she put her hands on the glass so that their fingers were lined up.

"Close your eyes," she instructed him. And Ezekiel closed his eyes.

"No enemy shall defeat him, nor shall the wicked oppress him. For I shall crush his foes before him and those who hate him, and I will smite his enemies before him, so saith the Lord God of Host." She took her hands away from the glass. "Open your eyes Ezekiel." And he did. "How do you feel?" she asked.

"Rested," he said, surprised at how refreshed he felt. "What did you do?"

She smiled and replied, "I've given you rest, so you can use your eyes."

"What?"

"Read, Ezekiel, read."

She pointed toward the little black book she had given him. Ezekiel looked down at the strange little book. It looked ancient, and the words engraved into its cover read *Ezekiel's Eyes*. He looked up to ask her what it meant, but she wasn't there anymore.

You will not be afraid of the terror by night,
Or of the arrow that flies by day;
                    —PSALM 91:5 (NASB1995)

CHAPTER NINE

Danielle Walker

She could feel him reaching places
inside her that were unnatural.

2001, 20 years ago

IT WAS A WARM JUNE NIGHT IN NEW YORK, LOWER MANHATTAN, on the west side. A young lady was leaving a nightclub called the Tunnel on Twenty-seventh Street and Twelfth Avenue. It was almost three o'clock in the morning, and she'd had a few drinks and was feeling tipsy. She didn't live far, so she figured she would leave her car in the valet parking and walk home. She hoped the walk might sober her up, and she knew the night air would do her some good. As she turned the corner of Twenty-third, she noticed a tall man standing under the light pole. She might not have paid any attention to him, except for the fact that he was wearing a trench coat and a hat on such a warm night. It just seemed odd.

She hurried past him and as she did, she thought she heard him say something quite strange: "It's not safe for you here; hurry home and do not tarry, for the unclean one is near." But how could he have said all of that in the one second it took for her to walk by him? She turned around to look at him, but he was gone. Goose-bumps ran down her back and arms. *This is crazy,* she thought as she continued on her way. She couldn't shake the feeling of being watched as she hurried home. She got to her apartment building a few minutes later and breathed a small sigh of relief as she reached into her purse and fumbled around for her keys. She thought she heard something behind her and whipped her head around to see what it was. Somewhere in the back of her mind, she knew it was nothing. She told herself she was just a little unnerved by the strange man earlier. However, when she turned around, Nestor was standing in front of her. She tried to scream but he had already placed his hand over her mouth, keeping all sound from escaping. His touch was cold and clammy, and yet it seemed to burn at the same time. She struggled to break free from his grasp, but it was no use. He had her.

"You're specials, I can smells it on you. You were chosen, weren't you?"

He walked her through the doorway and into the hallway of her apartment building, dragging her under the staircase into the shadows. Tears were running down her cheeks, and the smell of vinegar and rotten eggs in her nostrils combined with the alcohol she had consumed earlier caused her to begin vomiting. Nestor smiled at that, and instead of trying to avoid it, he wiped some of it off the bottom of her lip and licked his fingers and then her face. His tongue was black, slimy, and surprisingly rough, like a cat's, and it caused her to shrink into herself as silent tears fell from her eyes. He drew in deep breaths of the bile that spewed out from her as if he were smelling flowers. He placed his hand on her stomach, and incredibly his already inhuman smile grew broader.

"You're with child, darlings, did you know this? This is going to be soo much the sweeter. Two for one."

He cackled, revealing what seemed to be hundreds of teeth. He licked his dry, cracked lips and then bit her on the neck long and hard. Her flesh was sweet in his mouth. He planned on eating her, but not just yet; he still had plans for her at the moment.

She could feel what could only be venom or poison entering her system from his bite. Her body began convulsing, and she began to feel a numbing sensation spreading throughout her body. She wanted to call out for help, but she couldn't get the words to leave her mouth. She was now paralyzed, and she figured it was his bite—what else could it be? Then she felt him push up on her. She looked into his eyes and realized his intent. She could feel his member stiffening, and she screamed a silent scream. Tears poured down her cheeks as she felt him entering her.

Nestor was an empathic being and could feel the terror and horror within her, and if that were not enough, her eyes made it clear what was in her heart. He pushed deep into her, thrust after thrust, ripping into her delicate womb and shattering her pelvic bone.

She could feel him reaching places inside her that were unnatural. Still unable to call out, she began praying. "Dear God, please make him stop. How could you allow this monster to do this to me? Please, God, help me. Please!" Tears running down her face and running short of breath, with tremendous effort, she screamed "NO!" and the last of her energy was spent.

Not even a second later, she heard a voice say: "Let her go, demon; she is not for you."

Nestor looked up, smiling:

"Ah, but I have already hads her. She is no longer clean in his eyes. Leaves now, angel, you have no business with this one, or me."

The angel pulled his coat back, revealing a golden sword. He lunged forward and cut Nestor across the face with it, slicing through his ear and taking off the tip as he did. Nestor fell to the floor holding his face and looked up at the angel who had struck him in disbelief.

"You cannot," he said, muffling his voice as he held his cheek. "It is not your time. The truce—it's forbidden."

Nestor's speech had changed; He was no longer speaking with a lisp and purposely dragging his Ss as he spoke. The angel swung his sword again. Nestor put his hand up to protect his face as the blade whizzed by, taking his index finger and pinky and leaving two long, claw-like fingers on his hand. Black blood spewed from his hand as he dropped the young lady to the ground, shrieking.

"You're dead, angel, dead—do you hear me?" He stood up, clutching his bleeding hand.

"You have broken the truce, and no one can deny my vengeance . . . "

"Be silent, you vile thing, or by God and all that I hold dear, I will split you from your groin to your gullet. Call me false, demon, and I shall lay thee low for all to behold. I serve he who is most high, and I am governed by him and him alone. If I am called to atone for what I've done today, it will be by him, not by one such as you."

He waved his hand, and Nestor was tossed to the other end of the hallway. He held him fast against the wall with his mind while he walked over to the young lady on the floor.

"What is your name, child?" he asked.

"Danielle. Danielle Walker." Her voice was but a whisper, but it was all she could manage. Still suffering the effects of the poison in her system, she began convulsing again as two tears fell from her eyes and across her ear lobes.

"I'm sorry, child, I'm so very sorry."

He placed his hand on her chest and closed his eyes. He began drawing the poison out of her and into himself. As he did so, he also transferred his very essence into her as well, healing her body and undoing all the damage caused to it by Nestor. He poured so much of himself into her that he was greatly weakened and barely able to move at first, but this quickly passed, and he was himself again. Danielle felt better than she had ever felt in her life—stronger, more powerful, and in tune with everything around her. Then the angel stood up and faced Nestor, who was holding his face with his misshapen hand.

"It has been written, so I cannot smite thee, but nowhere does it say that I am unable to harm thee. Go now, lick your wounds, and let our paths never cross again, for truce or no, I will end you and pay the price."

Nestor stood up and glared at the girl, and then at the angel.

"I know who you are, 'Michael,' and I shall not forget what has happened here, and when our paths cross next, you will not find me as I am now, and no quarter will be given."

"And you should know, Niezztur, that I know of you as well; and should that time come, no quarter will be asked."

Nestor was taken aback at the correct pronunciation of his name. He backed up into the corner of the hallway, red eyes glowing as black blood fell to the floor from his still-open wounds, and as he did so, he seemed to shrink and shrink until he had disappeared into the shadows.

Michael turned his attention back to Danielle and said, "There is still yet something I must do to you. You cannot possess any memory of what has transpired this night, and so I must wipe it from your mind, but rest easy with this fact: I will never be far from you, and when you need me, I will be there."

He knelt and placed his hand on her forehead, and everything slowly went black. When she awakened, she was in her bed. She couldn't remember how she had gotten there. In fact, the last thing she was able to remember was walking home from the club and some strange man in a trench coat and hat saying something to her. She couldn't quite put her finger on it, but somehow, she felt different. She decided to go to the drugstore to buy a pregnancy test. She was a little late, and she wanted to make sure that she wasn't pregnant. She hadn't felt sick or anything like that, but she just wanted to make sure.

What could not have been known by anyone on that night was that an unborn baby boy would somehow absorb some of the poison that was not purged from her body, or that his very soul would be infused with the life essence and power of an angel.

But to each one is given the manifestation of the
Spirit for the common good.

—1 Corinthians 12:7 (NASB1995)

CHAPTER TEN

Realization

"Your true face," she said. He replied, "Yes, the
'face' that God sees when he talks to me."

In the years that followed, Danielle realized that her son was gifted. He would do things that would amaze her, like guess what she was thinking, or give her the answer to something she was trying to figure out. He was also incredibly fast and agile. One day, when Ezekiel was about five or six years old, she took him to the park to play. He was playing with some other boys on the monkey bars, and somehow, he fell or got pushed—who knows with little boys—but she was shocked to see him do a little twist in the air and land on his feet, almost like a cat. Then there was another time when she was looking out the window, waiting for him to get home from school. He must've been about twelve. Much to her surprise, he came racing around the corner followed by a group of boys, and then a few seconds later, a crowd of kids followed, shouting, "Fight! Fight!" She immediately rushed downstairs to come to her son's aid, thinking, *There's no way I'm gonna let those bullies beat up on my son. Not while there's breath in my body.* But when she got there, a voice in her head said, *He'll be all right, just watch.* And to her amazement, she did. She could hardly believe what she saw. Her son was like nothing she had ever seen before. The way he moved, his speed—it was so graceful. The other boys never stood a chance. One, two, three, four—it was over before it started. Four boys were on the floor licking their wounds, and the crowd was silent and in awe.

Later that night, while they were having dinner, she asked him what had been the cause of the fight. He lowered his head, put his fork down, and closed his eyes. He rubbed his face, starting from his temples, then across his eyes, down his nose, and finally resting on his jaw. He started to say something and then stopped, as if searching for the words, and then he spoke. "They weren't right," he said, "they were evil, and I saw them for what they were, and they didn't like it." He looked up at her, staring so intensely that he sent chills down her back.

"They will be back for me if I drop my guard and let them see my true face again."

"Your 'true face,'" she said.

"Yes, the 'face' that God sees when he talks to me."

She didn't know how, but she knew he was more than just a boy, and she also knew that he was here for a reason: a purpose that had yet to reveal itself. It was clear that he had a destiny to fulfill.

*These are murmurers, complainers, walking after
their own lusts; and their mouth speaketh great
swelling words, having men's persons in admiration
because of advantage.*

—JUDE 16

CHAPTER ELEVEN

Thomas Smyth

*Most people never really noticed Thomas—
even when he was right in front of them.*

THE ALARM CLOCK WENT OFF, AND THOMAS ROLLED OVER AND
hit the off button. The alarm was set for six thirty, but he didn't have
to get up until seven o'clock. He preferred waking up a bit early so
he could take his time getting ready. Thomas had a tendency to
worry about forgetting something or leaving something running,
so extra time in the morning gave him the chance to check all the
lights, locks, and windows, and allowed him to focus on the rest of
his day. He was paranoid and agoraphobic, with a touch of ADD.
So everything had to be in its proper place and had to be neat and
orderly, or it would nag at him and cause him to shut down. At this

point in his life, he had finally gotten to the point where he felt at least a little comfortable interacting with other people in a work setting—but just barely. A small man in his midforties, Thomas stood about five foot seven, with a potbelly. Most people never really noticed Thomas—even when he was right in front of them.

By four fifty, Thomas could barely contain himself. It seemed like it had taken forever for this day to end. Soon it would be five o'clock, and he'd be off to do his favorite thing in the world: cook. Thomas was a gifted cook who could put many a professional chef to shame. The key, he knew, was fresh ingredients. Everything had to be fresh; Thomas never cooked with processed food. He got up from his desk, closed his laptop, and placed it in his shoulder bag, along with the plastic storage case he'd brought his lunch in. He loved that case; it always warmed his food up just right. He closed his bag and threw the strap over his right shoulder, pressing out all the wrinkles in his jacket until everything was smooth. Then he pushed his chair under his desk and grabbed his mouse and clicked on the start button, and then on the shutdown icon on his computer. This small action always made him smile because it meant he'd gotten through one more day.

In the same way, let your light shine before others, so that they may see your good works and give glory to your Father who is in heaven.

—MATTHEW 5:16 (ESV)

CHAPTER TWELVE

Father Connors

Ezekiel looked at Father Connors again, but this time, much more intensely. Father Connors could almost feel him in his head. It tingled and cause goosebumps to rise on his arms and neck.

FIVE YEARS HAD PASSED, AND EZEKIEL WAS FINALLY LEAVING the prison. He was just a boy when he arrived at Folsom State Penitentiary, but he was much more than a man as he left. A few guards came to say goodbye as he was being processed for release. To his surprise, they seemed sad to see him go. He sensed that this was not because they felt he should stay there but because he had brought a calming spirit to the facility. Violence was almost unheard of now, and all of the gangs seemed to have put aside their differences and formed truces. When he would pray, it sounded like singing that resonated throughout the facility. He was special, and they knew it; they also knew that once he left, everything would likely change, and they had all been dreading that day. Even Warden Evens came down to see him off, something that almost never happened. He asked if Ezekiel had a place to go, gave him a few names of people to contact on the outside and his cell phone number, and told him to call him if he ever needed anything. Ezekiel had not realized that he'd had such a positive effect on so many people. As he walked through the last gate and out to the curb of the prison, he turned around and looked back. So much of his life had been spent behind those walls, and now he was finally free. He took a deep breath, turned around, and started walking toward the bus stop.

"Ezekiel, excuse me? That is your name, right? Ezekiel?"

Ezekiel turned and looked in the direction of the voice. "Who are you?" he asked.

"I'm Father Jacob Connors. Joshua sent me. He said that you would need a ride and a place to stay."

Ezekiel looked Father Connors up and down and then looked deep into his eyes. Father Connors felt uneasy and started to look away.

"Please don't do that. I need to see your eyes," Ezekiel said.

"What … why? What are you looking for?"

Ezekiel smiled. "Nothing; I'm sorry if I made you feel uncomfortable, it's just that I've been locked up for so long that I have gotten very used to sizing people up. You said Joshua sent you. Well, then, it's good to meet you." He held out his hand while he spoke.

Father Connors walked over to him and shook his hand. He noticed just then that he seemed to have an almost angelic presence. He was tall, well built, and unusually good-looking. He thought to himself that he must have had an extremely hard time in prison.

"Let me get that bag for you," Father Connors said. Ezekiel started to protest, but the man had already picked up his bag and was headed to his car.

"So, Ezekiel, do you mind if I call you EZ? What are your plans?"

"I'm not quite sure yet, but I have to find someone, a girl."

"Does this girl have a name?"

Ezekiel looked at Father Connors again, but this time much more intensely. Father Connors could almost feel him in his head. It tingled and cause goosebumps to rise on his arms and neck.

"Her name is Vera, and she's in trouble. I have to help her...protect her. She's special."

"Protect her from what, son? Are you sure you wanna be doing this? Why not just call the authorities and let them handle it? You go off trying to be a hero and you might get yourself a one-way ticket back inside."

"Let me ask you a question, Father, how did you come to know Joshua, and why did he send you to me?"

"Well, to tell you the truth, I never actually met him. I don't even know if he's real or not. It's kind of a long story, but I'll try to keep it short. I had reached a crossroads in my life, and I was struggling with my faith. I needed something concrete—something tangible that I could see and feel, so I could be sure that I hadn't wasted my life. While I was praying, a voice told me to come here and to pick you up. The voice told me to tell you that Joshua sent me, and you would come. It also told me that through you, my faith would be renewed."

Ezekiel was quiet. He was quite surprised. *Who does Joshua think I am that I could renew a man's faith—and a priest of all people too?*

"Did the voice tell you anything else? Anything about me at all?"

"No, but it's a long drive back to LA, so I figure we'll have a little time to get to know a little bit about each other on the way there," he replied. Then he smiled and looked over at Ezekiel.

"Sounds like a plan," said Ezekiel, and he smiled back. Then, after a slight pause, he started asking the priest questions about what had been going on in the world for the last five years. They talked for hours. Near Fresno, about halfway home, they stopped at a diner. They were both hungry, and neither of them would object to a bathroom break. They sat at a booth and ordered a couple of burgers and Cokes, still completely unaware of how important they would become to each other.

With my soul I have desired Thee in the night; yea,
with my spirit within me will I seek Thee early; for
when Thy judgments are in the earth, the inhabitants
of the world will learn righteousness.

—ISAIAH 26:9 (KJ21)

CHAPTER THIRTEEN

The Seven Judgments

They were warriors born and bred, and he guessed
that when they arrived on a scene, all the talking had
been done, and no more warning would be given.

IT WAS ALMOST NINE O'CLOCK, AND THEY WERE JUST A FEW
minutes away from Father Connors's church. They had made a few
pit stops on the way back, turning a six-hour drive into a ten-hour
one. In that time, they'd gotten to know a few things about each
other—that is, Ezekiel had gotten to learn a lot about Father
Connors without really saying much about himself. He thought it
best to hold onto details about himself for a bit, just until he got
to know the priest a little better. It surprised Ezekiel how much he

had to say about nothing. He wasn't usually so talkative, but he felt relaxed around Father Connors.

As they pulled up to the church, seven men were waiting out front, all dressed in black, each holding a black case. Father Connors thought to himself, *That's odd. I don't recall scheduling any church functions for this evening.* He turned to Ezekiel and said, "Hey, EZ, you get your bags, and I'll go see what this is all about."

"Don't bother, Father, they're here for me. Please wait here in the car until I tell you it's safe."

"Why? Who are they, and how do you know these men—are they friends of yours from prison?"

"No, Father, they are not. I don't know them, and they are not men. Please, stay in the car."

Father Connors turned to look at the men and then back at Ezekiel. He was about to say something, but the look on Ezekiel's face let him know that this was not up for debate. He nodded, and Ezekiel got out of the car and approached the men. They were all very tall and well-built. If they had not been wearing men's clothing, one might even have said they were pretty. As they faced each other, the men sized Ezekiel up, looking at him the same way he had done to Father Connors when they first met. Only Ezekiel didn't turn away.

Father Connors thought, *What is it with those looks? There's more to it than just sizing each other up. I have to remember to ask EZ about that later.*

"You stand as if ready to do battle, boy. Do you even know who we are?"

"Yes, I do," Ezekiel replied. "You are the keepers of the seven bowls of judgment. May I ask why you have come here?"

"Why, I would have thought that obvious. We would speak with you."

Ezekiel had seen a few angels before, but none such as these. The others had a humble, warm, and loving spirit, but these were different. They all seemed to have an air of condescending contempt about them, like they were too good to be speaking to the likes of someone like him. They were warriors born and bred, and he guessed that when they arrived on a scene, all the talking had been done, and no more warning would be given. The time for God's wrath would soon be felt, and they were his hands. Oddly enough, Ezekiel understood how they felt, and really, who was he that they, who had stood amidst God's glory, should have to humble themselves to speak with him?

"I am honored. How may I be of help to you?"

"Help us? You presume too much," said one of the angels. "We are here to warn you. Do not attempt to upset the balance of things to come or stay it from its current course, or we will end you. Our mission has been preordained, and as such, it is beyond tampering. The appointed time is near, and we walk the earth now. Soon we will open our cases and pour out its judgment upon the inhabitants of the earth, and woe be it to anyone who is deemed unclean in his eyes at that time."

"I am just one man, and you are angels. How could anything that I do interfere with or change your plans?"

Another angel step forward and said, "A man, yes, but not just any man. No mere man could bear the weight of us, much less endure a conversation as you do. You are something more, but do not let that lead you to believe that you are beyond our reach."

Ezekiel looked over toward Father Connors. He was sitting in the car, staring off into space as though in a trance. He looked across the street and then up and down the block. A couple of dogs were standing perfectly still, not moving a muscle, and people were sitting transfixed in their cars. A man stood motionless by the entrance to an apartment building, one foot elevated in midair. It suddenly occurred to Ezekiel what the second angel meant when he said that no mere man could bear the weight of conversation with them. This also put a few other things into perspective for him—thoughts he'd had about Revelations and the Rapture of the church. *These beings are able to alter our reality,* he thought.

They show up, and we just stop moving in a suspended state. They do what's needed, and when they're done, we carry on like nothing happened, not realizing that everything *has changed around us.* It occurred to him that they could also alter time. He couldn't help but smile at the thought of that. It was like someone had just pulled a blanket from his head and he could finally see clearly. The angels, unaware of the epiphany that Ezekiel was having, thought he wasn't taking them seriously and was smiling at them.

"Have a care, mortal, for thou hast much to learn before this day is done, and we will not endure mockery from a child."

"Enough," another angel said, walking past the first two.

"We have wasted far too much time talking to this boy and I will not stay my hand any longer. I shall lay him low and be done with it."

Ezekiel was surprised by this and realized that it was too late for him to try to explain why he had smiled. As the angel approached, he took a step forward, facing him. The angel seemed to glide as he swung what looked like a short blade, intending to cut him from his head to his shoulders.

Much to the entire group's surprise, Ezekiel caught his arm in mid-swing, disarming him and placing the blade at his neck instead. He held it there for a moment, poking the point of the blade into flesh. He wanted the angel to know that right at this instant, he had been beaten. Then he pushed him back, hard, causing him to stumble. Almost instantly, however, the angel recovered and was about to return the favor; then he stopped suddenly. He seemed to grimace with each step that he took toward Ezekiel. Whatever was causing the discomfort grew more intense the closer he got. This, too, suddenly made sense to Ezekiel, but he didn't smile at his realization of this as he had done earlier, in order to avoid any further misunderstanding. They did not have permission to act yet, and without it, they would be unable to harm him.

"It would seem that there is more to you than we gave you credit for, boy. It also seems that there is something to the whispers we have heard about you. But you should know that whatever you are doing to cause my brother discomfort shall be revisited upon you a thousand-fold."

"It's not me," said Ezekiel. "I've done nothing; it's just not your time. You may walk the earth now, but you may not have been given permission to harm all its inhabitants just yet, and as you said, you cannot alter what has been preordained. But since we are giving out warnings, here's something for you to think about. One, we serve the same God, and I am one hundred percent dedicated to doing whatever God deems necessary to get the job done, even if it means going up against you. But I doubt that could ever happen. God is not the author of confusion. And two, I am not bound to the same rules as you. I understand your concern, though, because I'm free-willed, and it's possible for me to upset your mission—you can't have that. Don't worry. I have a guardian, and he will guide me so I won't stumble. You may not know about me because our Father never gives us more than we need to know. All our eyes will be open at the appointed time. But you already know that. You should also know this: while it is true that what has been written cannot be altered, this does not mean that any of you will be the actual angels to pour out the judgments you carry. God is not predictable. There are multiple meanings to his word. Every time I read the scriptures; I see something new. Just something to think about."

It was almost like Ezekiel had struck them all a blow with his words. In all the years that they had endured the burden of carrying these judgments, none of them had ever thought that they might not be the ones to pour them out. He was also right about it not being their time to act. He was wise for a mortal, and brave. There was also something about him that the first angel recognized as well. Something in his eyes, his posture, and his manner reminded him of someone, someone he had not thought of in years.

"Mortal, your fate is yet undecided; pray that you never find yourself outside of his grace, or the next time we meet it may well be under different circumstances. But let us not be distracted from our true purpose any further. We came here tonight not to fight, but to give warning. You will be tested soon, and how you fare will determine when the judgments will be poured. You must ready yourself to the task at hand, and not be swayed, for it is not your life that will be lost if you fail, it is your soul, and the souls of everyone in your keep. Better to let us slay you now than for that to come to pass. It is still unclear to us how you can do what you do. And while you have sent more than a few of the fallen to Sheol, you might just as easily put one of us down as well, and that is an unacceptable alternative, which was our main reason for this visit. We had to see you and test your mettle. You do not bend when leaned upon, and that alone shows you are of noble character. God has gifted you with power, Ezekiel, a power that you have barely begun to understand. I see now that you have somehow surpassed that plain of mere mortal existence, and I doubt you got to this point on your own. But even with help, to have gotten as far as you have is nothing short of a miracle. So we are at an impasse for now. Know this: we feel that your presence here represents an undeniable threat to us.

The way you handle yourself here today proves that you are more than capable of being problematic if seduced by the dark one. We will be watching you, Ezekiel, and I will leave you with this advice. Your eyes see the truth of things as they are. Trust in them to guide you, and do not let your heart cause you to stray from the path you are now on. There is only death waiting for you there."

Ezekiel could tell that the angel was genuine in his concern and advice, though a bit condescending in its delivery. He didn't think he could help being that way, but he wanted to know more. Why did they feel it was easier to just kill him rather than to teach him, as Joshua had? It was almost as if they were afraid of him—well, not him, but more of what he might do.

"Before you take your leave of me, may I ask something of you?" The angel looked at him without expression and nodded yes. "May I know your name? Also, how will I know when I am being tested—how will I know if I have passed or failed?"

"I am Anafiel, chief of the crown judgment angels, and you are being tested now even as we speak. Should you succumb to the dark side of your nature, the earth's judgments shall be poured out on that day. Your test will be facing that which hunts you and not becoming its prey. And I know what hunts you; it threatens us all, but we were born to the task, and I know how we will fare; but you, well, that remains to be seen. Stay vigilant, young one, because there is only one outcome to this story, and it will come to pass with or without you."

"Who's hunting me? Where can I find him? What—"

"He'll find you. That's all I can say for now. Ask Joshua to tell you everything plain if you would know the truth, as he would be the one to tell it. Now, we have been here far too long and we must take our leave of you. I do not know you, Ezekiel, but I can see why he watches over you. There is something about you that has invigorated my spirit, which I find odd but pleasantly refreshing after all this time."

And just like that, they were gone. Ezekiel turned around full circle and watched as people began to wake from their premature slumbers and carry on as if nothing had happened. Father Connors was looking out the car window at him with curious eyes. He rolled down the window and asked, "Where are those men who were just there?"

Ezekiel walked back to the car and opened the door. "They are gone, Father, but they left me with quite a bit to think about."

Father Connors could feel strange energy radiating from Ezekiel, and he seemed to smell of honey, and lilac, and...maybe a little cinnamon too. It was subtle and overwhelming at the same time. A few tears fell from his eyes and rolled down his cheeks. He felt a little lightheaded, and his eyes began to close. He fell forward; Ezekiel caught him. "Father, Father! Are you all right?" He gently tapped his cheeks and gave him a few shakes. "Father, are you OK?" he asked. The priest's eyes opened and he began to feel more like himself again.

"What happened? Did I just pass out?"

"I'm not sure; I was talking to you and you just kind of went limp. It was weird. Sit back for a moment and catch your breath," said Ezekiel. "You are probably still feeling the effects of the angels."

Father Connors looked around and didn't notice anyone else who seemed to be lightheaded or drowsy. It was just him, and it had happened when EZ came toward him after speaking with those men. *Who is he, really, and what does God want me to do with him?* he thought.

Ezekiel got his bag from the trunk of the car and helped Father Connors into the church. He told him what had transpired and asked if it made any sense to him, because it didn't make much sense to Ezekiel. Oddly enough, it did. Father Connors also began to wonder if Ezekiel might be one of them.

Father Connors knew that a man is defined by the sum of his actions, not by what he says, but what he does. Claiming to walk with Christ and doing it are two quite different things. Most times it is impossible, simply because Christ was a supernatural, intrinsic being, body and soul. Father Connors figured that there was a lot more to Ezekiel than he had let on during their ride to the church, but he couldn't figure it out just yet. All he knew for sure was that for the first time in many years, he was ready to put his faith in something other than himself. He found himself wanting to pray—something he hadn't done in years either. Being a priest had become a mere job like any other. He was simply going through the motions. But now, something was different for him. Now he found himself wanting to believe again, as a spark of faith was rekindled within him.

He shall cover thee with His feathers, and under His
wings shalt thou trust; His truth shall be thy shield
and buckler. Thou shalt not be afraid of the terror by
night, nor of the arrow that flieth by day,

—Psalm 91:4–5 (KJ21)

CHAPTER FOURTEEN

The Dream

There were body parts everywhere and demons bathed
in blood, dancing and chanting to their dark lord.

HE COULD HEAR VOICES WHISPERING ALL AROUND HIM, BUT IT
was too dark to see anyone ... or anything, for that matter. *Ezekiel,*
Eeeeezzzekiel, the voices called out. He had learned a long time ago
not to answer them. Answering served as an invitation, and in this
place that was the last thing he wanted to do. Lord, no—no invita-
tions. None of these things are invited.

"Vera, where are you?" he called.

No one answered. He could make out something that sounded
like a muffled voice, and as he listened harder, he could hear

sniffling and crying. It was coming from upstairs, but that seemed like a million miles away.

"She's with us now, and not even you have the power to unbind her soul from our claim on her, but you are welcome to try. We would, however, consider a trade; your soul for hers. Give it to us willingly, and the girl goes free. Isn't that what you want?" one of the voices said.

He didn't answer. He knew the rules: *never talk directly with them, never let them know they have struck a chord with you, never let them know what you want or what scares you, or who's important to you, because that's what and who they will use against you in order to weaken you.*

The floor squeaked as he walked toward the steps. He felt weighed down and sluggish. He could see the white clouds of mist escaping his lips each time he exhaled. Every movement and action was labored and required a concentrated effort. His heart was pounding so hard inside his chest; it felt like he was having a heart attack.

As he reached the staircase, he could feel cold fingers pulling and pinching him. Their touch lingered and seemed to almost be under his skin. The voices were calling him more frequently and coming from all around him.

"Ezekiel! Ezekiel!"

Just then, he heard a scream. He instantly knew that it was Vera. He rushed up to the top of the stairs and ran to the door at the end of the hallway. It was an old door with broad, elaborate moldings and hand-carved cherubs and scenes of angels fighting demons—or maybe it was the other way around. He paused just before grabbing the large doorknob, which was fashioned like the head of a goat with horns. This all felt wrong to him. Everything about this place, the look of it, the smell of it, the taste of it—it was all wrong. Then he heard her scream again, and this time it was so close that it went through him. He grabbed the doorknob and twisted it. The door opened slowly to reveal a horror scene of debauchery and butchery the likes of which he had never imagined possible. And the godawful smell—it was sickening. There were body parts everywhere and demons bathed in blood, dancing and chanting to their dark lord. And in the center of the orgy of insanity was a large stone table. Vera was lying on it, and standing next to her was an extremely tall man. He was inhumanly thin, and his arms seemed to be too long for his body. He smiled a smile that was not humanly possible, exposing hundreds of fine sharp teeth. He slithered behind the table and picked Vera up by the waist. He cupped and caressed her right breast with his left hand, which looked strangely disfigured, and then suddenly, without warning, he bit her on the neck. She let out a small whimper, barely audible as blood made its way down her neck.

"Mmm, she tastes so good. I'm going to love ripping her aparts and devouring her souls."

He went to bite her again, but Ezekiel yelled out for him to stop.

"Ooooooh, you wants me to stop? Hen, hen, then come trades places with her. It's the only way. Otherwise, I'm going to rips her open right in front of you."

"No, no, don't do that," Ezekiel said. "I'll go with you. You win—just don't hurt her anymore."

The impossibly tall and thin man cackled, exposing his inhuman smile, Vera's blood still dripping from his lips. Ezekiel walked toward him. Then suddenly and without warning, the man was facing him, almost as if he had teleported right in front of him. He grabbed Ezekiel by the neck and lifted him off his feet. His long, lanky fingers wrapped around his neck.

"Only one thing left, Ezekiel. Surrenders your souls to me and the girls is frees."

With his free hand, he stuck his fingers into Ezekiel's chest, piercing his skin and cutting into his flesh. It felt like fiery blades searing into his soul, gutting him alive.

"Says the words, Ezekiel, and I will make it stop. I'll ends all your pain, and you'll finally be able to rest. Just says the words."

Tears were falling from Ezekiel's eyes, and blood began to bubble from his lips as he let loose a small cough. The smell of the demon was beyond imagination, and all he wanted was for the pain to end. He whispered, "Father, help me!"

Father Connors was in his room praying. It had been a while since he'd felt the pull of God on his heart and was brought to his knees. It was a good feeling. There was definitely something about Ezekiel that he couldn't begin to figure out, but there was also something about him that seemed to have watered the flowers of his faith. "*FATHER!*" a loud voice rang inside his head. He opened his eyes and looked around, trying to figure out who had called him.

"*FATHER, EZEKIEL NEEDS YOU NOW. HURRY!*" the voice shouted inside his head.

Father Connors got to his feet and rushed over to Ezekiel's room. He opened the door, and Ezekiel was in the middle of the room, floating—well, not exactly floating, but more like he was being held aloft. His body was arched backward, and blood was dripping from his eyes, mouth, and nose. Then, almost like magic, Father Connors could make out the shadow of a man—no, not a man, a thing—something not of this earth, that had a hold of him. It had Ezekiel, and it was pulling him closer to its mouth. The room smelled of death, and the air was thick and hot.

"*CALL TO HIM, FATHER, WAKE HIM UP NOW!*"

Father Connors quickly recovered from the shock of it all and yelled, "EEEZZZEEKIIIEEELLL!"

"*TELL HIM NOT TO GIVE UP,*" Joshua shouted. "*TELL HIM IF HE DOES, THE GIRL WILL STILL DIE! TELL HIM VERA WILL DIE!*"

Without hesitation, he called out to him. "EZEKIEL, You've got to wake up. The girl is going to die if you don't!"

Joshua continued shouting directions to Father Connors, "*TELL HIM IT LIES FATHER, IT'S A LIAR!*"

And Father Connors yelled, "It's lying, Ezekiel!"

Ezekiel could barely hear Father Connors's voice. It sounded like it was miles away from him. But he could hear the demon's voice clearly:

"Says the words, says the words and it will all be over!"

And he so wanted it to be over; the pain was so intense. He could feel the demon's fingers squeezing his heart and felt like it was going to burst.

Then he heard Father Connors's voice. It was very faint, but it was clear. "Ezekiel, if you don't wake up, the girl will die. Vera will die. *Wake up!* He's a liar. For the love of God, wake up. Think on Jesus and wake up."

Ezekiel shouted, "Jesus! JESUS!" This froze Nestor, and Ezekiel grabbed hold of the demon's hand and pulled it out from inside of him. As he did, its grip on his neck loosened as well. Father Connors recognized that Ezekiel was trying to free himself from whatever that shadow thing was. He rushed over and grabbed Ezekiel by the waist, giving a great big tug. And in that moment, while he was touching Ezekiel, he was transported into the dream realm with him. He was in that dark room, looking at the true face of the thing that held him. The putrid stench that permeated the room instantly overwhelmed him, and their eyes met: Father

Connors and the Shadow Man, except he wasn't a man at all. He was a demon, something that until this very moment, the priest had only read about and referred to as symbols of evil. He'd never truly believed they existed.

"Father, I can sees you . . . I can sees you plain."

Father Connors turned his head away from the demon, but his eyes somehow always caught his. They were penetrating. They seemed to look inside of him, unraveling his reality. An old song that his mother used to sing to him came to him. She would sing it to him before he went to bed after his prayer

"I got the blood as my shield to cover me. Ain't worried about no one trying to ha-arm me. I got the blood of the lamb to cover me. He is my light in the dark when I can't see. I got the blood of the lamb to cover me."

Ezekiel began to feel bits of foul air slip in and out of his lungs. He screamed, "No!" once again as he pulled the thing's hand completely out of his chest, and its grip on his neck was broken, as well as the hold on his soul. He fell into Father Connors's arms, and they both dropped to the floor. Father Connors could hear thunder outside, rumbling and shaking the very foundation of the church. The shadow demon turned and looked at Father Connors. Its eyes, still glowing a dark crimson red, pierced into him.

"I saw you, Fathers. I knows who you ares. Yes, I knows you now."

Then the demon just seemed to float back into the corner of the room and fade into the shadows. The eyes lingered for just a bit longer...hovering, looking in Father Connors's direction, and then they faded as well.

He looked back at Ezekiel and began to check if he was OK. *Oh, Lord, please be all right. Dear God, please let him be OK.* He straightened the young man's body out on the floor and placed his head on his chest to see if he could hear a heartbeat. It was faint, but it was there.

"Come on, Ezekiel, wake up—wake up now."

Ezekiel opened his eyes and said in a low dry voice, almost a whisper, "Thank you, Father, thank you. I was lost, and somehow you found me."

A tear rolled down from the corner of his eye and passed his ear onto his neck. It was cool, and it made Ezekiel smile, because he knew at that moment that he was still alive. And so was Vera.

<< >>

In the weeks that followed, Ezekiel and Father Connors prayed and studied. They read every bit of biblical text they could put their hands on: old folk tales, childhood stories, legends, and myths. And they prayed. Father Connors laughed out loud one day after a prayer. And Ezekiel looked at him, smiling, and asked what was so funny. Father Connors replied, "It's just that I think that in the last four weeks, I've prayed more with you than I have in my whole life. It's funny, because not too long ago I would get on my knees to pray, but I just couldn't find the words. But now I can't seem to do it enough. It's like taking a spiritual bath. I feel—" he paused a moment as his eyes darted back and forth, as if searching for the words he wanted in the air, and then he smiled and continued, "refreshed. And I have to tell you, EZ, I know it has a lot to do with you. I mean, even if that shadow thing hadn't terrified me, I know I would still feel the same. You saved me; you saved my soul. I really was a lost man."

Tears had begun to fall from his eyes, and he wiped them away. Ezekiel smiled and said, "Well then, Father, I am truly glad you came to my aid that night and for the renewal of your faith. For it is pleasing in the eyes of God."

It was Sunday, and Father Connors had prepared a simple but powerful sermon on the power of prayer. He asked if Ezekiel would come to services this time. Ezekiel had not been into socializing after what had happened a few weeks ago. He told Father Connors that he believed he had dropped his guard and that had made him open to that attack. But Father Connors could tell that he was feeling different today. He seemed stronger and recharged. And the funny thing was, so was he. Ezekiel started to decline but then changed his mind.

"Yes. Yes, I think I will sit in today, Father, thank you for asking."

Father Connors preached about the relationship between faith and prayer and how the two are intertwined with one another.

"Faith," he said, "is believing and trusting in something, or someone, and knowing in your heart that what you believe in is right. And when you pray, it's because you know that change can come from it. You don't *hope* that it will—you *know* that it will. Well, at least that's how it should be. But most of us only pray when we need something and hope that it will come to pass. But hope is not faith. However, here is why I know the Lord is good, because he'll answer that prayer just to let you know he's real, hoping you might have faith. Do you hear me?" He raised his hand to his ear as if listening for someone to say something. "You hear me, don't you?"

The parishioners responded, and Father Connors said, "Amen."

*Therefore it says, "When he ascended on high, he led
a host of captives, and he gave gifts to men."*
—EPHESIANS 4:8 (ESV)

CHAPTER FIFTEEN

The Blade

"Only he who is worthy may possess the finger of God."

HUNDREDS OF THOUSANDS OF YEARS AGO, WHEN THE EARTH
was new and men believed in polytheism, angels would visit the
earth and were revered. Every so often, those angels would be
inclined to reward man for his obedience to the Lord. A gift—a
hammer, a sword, a shield, or a talisman—would be given to a king
or a warrior to fight the enemies of God. Legends were born: the
Hammer of Thor or King Arthur's sword Excalibur. These weapons
possessed unimaginable power if held in the right hands. Over time,
as years passed, these weapons were lost, locked away, or became
artifacts in museums. However, many of these items were hidden
by the church because of their religious nature and power. But
every so often, a family would be entrusted to watch over one of
these treasures, and it would be passed down from one generation

to the next. This was how the blade had come to rest with Father James Mark Connors, a priest of one of the oldest churches in Los Angeles—perhaps one of the oldest in the country, a fact no one currently alive would know of or be able to confirm.

Father Connors could remember his father telling him stories about his family's history. How his family had fought at the battle of Jericho and watched the walls come down. Survived the volcano at Pompeii and witnessed the rise and fall of Rome. The stories would go on and on, and his father would always say that their family had played some special role in each event; he would point-edly allude to the fact that their family, ultimately, had helped to shape human history. Father Connors had always found that part hard to believe. He figured his father must've told him that to make the stories a little more interesting. Then one night, when he was about seventeen, he heard a kind of humming or ringing noise. The noise called out to him, and he followed it to a room in the church's basement. The ringing was louder now, and the pull it had on him was overwhelming. The room itself was simple enough at first glance. Inside was an old wooden desk that looked as though someone had carved it from one piece of wood. There were no visible seams or fitted pieces. The chair that sat behind the desk looked like it had also been carved from a single piece of the same type of wood. As he looked around, he realized that all the furni-ture in the room was like that. And there were strange writings on all the walls; it looked like Arabic. He didn't know how he knew the writing was Arabic—he just did. The humming sound was still ringing in his head, but now it sounded like voices praying. The words on the walls suddenly somehow made sense to him, and he found that he was able to read them: "*Only he who is worthy may possess the finger of God.*" These words were repeated over and over again throughout the room. He ran his fingers across other words on the walls, and it was like they were speaking to him. They said, *"The book: get the book, it is for him. Heed his call when it is your time, and tarry not, for time is short and he is near … heed the call and be renewed in the spirit, for he is near."*

None of it made sense at the time, but he couldn't help running his fingers over the words. As he did, he came across a seam in the wall, almost an invisible imperfection that couldn't be seen, only felt. He pushed on it and it gave ever so slightly, and a small drawer opened just underneath it. There was a book inside and a long box with more of the Arabic writings on it. It read, *"For he that is worthy to redeem the wicked and protect His chosen, the finger of God."* Father Connors picked up the box from the drawer and placed it on the desk. He took the book out and placed it on the desk as well. The book had a strange title that made absolutely no sense. *Ezekiel's Eyes.* He allowed his hands to glide over the box and felt power emanating from it. He opened the box and stared in amazement. It was a dagger, beautifully decorated with intricate carvings, created in impeccable detail. The hilt looked to be the body of an angel, and the blade itself was the angel's wings coming together to form a point. The dagger was about twelve inches long and one inch thick. He started to pick it up, and suddenly he was startled by the appearance of an ancient-looking black woman.

"I wouldn't do that iffin I was you. It ain't for you. You may be able to hear the blade singing, but holdin' it's an entirely different story."

"Who are you, and where did you come from?" he asked. He hadn't heard her come in. He wondered how she had gotten in here.

"Who I am isn't important at the moment, but I'm here for two reasons. The first is to tell you to keep that blade safe and secure. Don't speak about it to anyone less you want unwanted attention to be brought your way. It's a special blade for a special person. You will know who it's for when the time is right. Only he can wield the blade, as it is meant for him. And two, I will be needin' that book. It is to serve a later purpose."

Father Connors couldn't begin to explain why, but he felt completely at ease with this woman. It was unnatural, and yet he felt compelled to listen to her. He handed her the book and went to close the box and put the blade back in the drawer. He turned around to ask her what she was going to do with the book, but when he did, she was gone. He walked over to the door to see if he could catch her walking down the corridor, but there was no trace of her. He went back into the wooden room to return the blade to the hidden space behind the wall. But he couldn't resist the urge to see the blade one more time before putting it away. He opened the box and let his fingers glide across the hilt and over the blade. A tingling sensation in his right hand shot up his arm and down his spine. His fingers went numb, and everything went black. The next thing he remembered was waking up in a hospital room. The fingers on his right hand were still a bit numb, and his vision was blurred. He started to sit up but had to pause because he found that he was quite dizzy and unbalanced. His father was sitting in a chair beside his bed.

"Easy there, son, don't try to get up yet. You've been asleep for quite some time now. What's the last thing you remember?"

"Being in a wooden room in the basement. How did I get here?"

"I found you in the oak room—unconscious, with your hand on the blade, 'the finger of God' as we call it. How did you come to find that room, son? And how did you find the blade?"

"I don't know. It kinda called out to me. There was an old woman too. Did anyone see her? She said that I am to give the blade to someone, but she didn't say who. She said I would know who at the proper time. She also said she needed the book that was in the drawer with the blade. Then she just disappeared."

His father just sat there, rubbing his hand over his face. When he looked up, there were tears in his eyes.

"I thought I'd lost you, son. You were out for such a long time; nobody expected you to recover. And the doctors said even if you did, you wouldn't have normal brain function. Yet here I am talking with you now, like no time has passed."

He stood up and embraced his son, holding him so tight that Connors thought he was going to crack one of his ribs. That was when he realized that he had lost weight—a whole lot of weight. But how could this be? He had only been out for a couple of hours, or maybe a day, or so he thought. Then he found himself to be incredibly thirsty, and he asked his father for some water. His father released him from his embrace, which was a big relief on his ribs, and held him by the shoulders, just smiling at him.

"Sure, hold on, let me get some for you. Just rest and try to gather your strength. We have a lot to talk about."

By the time his father returned, there was a whole team of doctors standing over his bed examining him. Everyone kept repeating, "It's a miracle," as they stared at him in disbelief. As it turned out, he had been in a coma for four months. A month for every finger that had touched the blade, it seemed. This explained the weight loss and the dry throat, and all the other symptoms he was experiencing.

A few days later, he was released, and his father took him home and explained everything about the blade, the oak room, and the writing on the walls—where it had come from, why it was there. He also told him that most people were unworthy and that everyone who ever tried to hold the blade had died—until now.

Father Connors remembered that day like it was yesterday. According to his father, he was the only one who had ever survived after touching the blade. That was more than thirty years ago, but he could still feel the tingling and numbing sensation in his fingers. The funny thing was that before he'd met Ezekiel, he hadn't thought about that day for years. Now he was reliving this event like some sort of repressed memory coming to life in his mind.

Father Connors thought long and hard about what he had witnessed in the room that day with Ezekiel and the conversation that had followed. This was a spiritual battle that was unfolding right in front of him, something he could never have imagined in a million years. And Ezekiel was as special as they come, there was no doubt about that, but Father Connors knew he was going to need help in this battle. He wondered if that was why he had been sent to Ezekiel. He wondered if he was the foretold one—the one that was written about on the walls in that ancient text. This couldn't be a coincidence! He guessed that the only real way to know would be to test it out in some way. It was getting late, so he decided to sleep on it. Things always seemed to make more sense in the morning.

That night, he dreamed of angels preparing to go to war, and Ezekiel was among them. He wasn't sure, but it looked as if he had the blade at his side. Ezekiel lifted his head, looked directly at him, and spoke: "Thank you, Father, for everything you've done for me. But you've gone as far as you can for now. It's time for you to rest and let me take up arms for both of us. You've done your part, so rest now."

It was surreal, and yet it felt so real; he could still taste the smoke that was in the air in his mouth. And the weight of Ezekiel's words was infused with a touch of sorrow and a touch of regret. He sat up, still feeling a bit tired despite all the rest he just had. He went to the kitchen to get a cup of coffee and found Ezekiel sitting at the table, reading from the book he had given the old black woman so many years ago.

"Hey, EZ, where did you get that from?"

Ezekiel smiled and passed a cup of coffee to him. He told him the story of how he had acquired the book, and then Father Connors shared his own story about the old woman, the book, and finally the blade. Then he took Ezekiel down to the oak room and retrieved the box with the blade. He handed it to him, saying, "Here, I believe you're the one."

Ezekiel examined the box. It was heavier than he was expecting, and the exquisite detailing of the box was quite beautiful. He undid the latch and opened the box, revealing the blade inside. Father Connors could still hear it calling to him just like it had done so many years ago, only this time he knew better than to touch it. Ezekiel heard it too and went to reach for it, but Father Connors grabbed his hand just before he did.

"Are you sure, EZ? Everyone who has touched this blade except for me has died, and I was in a coma for a few months."

"I'm sure, Father. I can hear it singing to me. I believe it's meant for me."

Father Connors reluctantly released his hand, and Ezekiel reached into the box, ran his fingers over the blade, and then took it out of the box and held it, examining it in awe. He could feel the immense power and energy emitting from it; it flowed through him. The sensation was exhilarating. Father Connors was happy that Ezekiel was able to hold the blade, but then he wondered if this was a dream or a premonition of what was to come. What did it all mean?

*Fear thou not; for I am with thee: be not dismayed;
for I am thy God: I will strengthen thee; yea, I will
help thee; yea, I will uphold thee with the right hand
of my righteousness.*

—ISAIAH 41:10

CHAPTER SIXTEEN

Awakenings

**It's just not possible for all this evil to be in the
world and God not to be real as well.**

A FEW DAYS HAD PASSED SINCE FATHER CONNORS PULLED
Ezekiel down from Nestor's grip. His heart still beat a little faster
than normal when he thought about it. He had certainly never
seen anything like that in his life. He could still feel the eyes of that
thing—the demon—piercing through him. He had never known
evil like that truly existed. Sure, he was a priest, and he preached
about heaven and hell, but he always believed those places to be
metaphorical, not literal. His mind was ablaze with thoughts of
multidimensional beings. *Demons, really?* This was just too much
for him.

He said to Ezekiel, "EZ, do you mind if I ask you a few things? I've been struggling to process what I saw and a few other things in my life, and I'm beginning to think you're just the person to talk about this stuff with."

Ezekiel was sitting in an oversized red reclining chair. It was old and fraying a bit on the edges of the arms. The chair was so wide that two adults could have fit comfortably, yet somehow, Ezekiel made the chair seem small. Ezekiel could tell that Father Connors was shaken by the experience earlier. And if he was honest with himself, so was he. It had seemed like a dream, and yet he knew it was not. It had been one of his special dreams, which made it so much more. He looked at his wrists and saw the bruises from what was an all-too-genuine experience and thought, *I've got to get ready; I've got to get better.*

He turned his attention to Father Connors and said, "Um, yeah sure, Father, what's on your mind?"

"I've heard you tell me the stories of life in prison, and a few tidbits of your childhood, but who are you, really?" he asked. "Where are you from, and how did you get involved in all of this? I'm having an awfully hard time making sense of this. First there are angels outside of my church—if you can call them that—and then there are things in the mist with glowing eyes threatening me, and I'm just really confused about how this all came to be."

"Really, Father, after all of this, you still have doubts? I'm no one special. I just see things for what they are. For that reason, I have been chosen to be tormented by all the little things that go bump in the night. The problem with that is, everything hidden—good and evil alike—wants me removed, taken out, or dead. You think you've got problems just because something from out of the darkness looked at you? Well, welcome to my world. A world where I can't even let my guard down for a moment so I can sleep for fear that some demon will grab me and try to haul me off somewhere. Who am I? I'm a man who has been in prison for killing an innocent woman while I was trying to destroy the demon inside her. I spent the last five years of my life behind bars. I often think about the woman and pray for her soul. And just for the record, being locked up was hell, because if there's any place that evil truly lives, it is prison. Almost everyone in that place was possessed. You can't even imagine how hard it was for me to keep out of the spotlight of darkness. And how could I escape it when there's nowhere to run? Every day I had to fight murderers, rapists, and crazy people. You're looking for proof of your God? Well I *know* he's real. It's just not possible for all this evil to be in the world and for God not to be real as well. Who am I? That's what I was going to ask you. I thought you might be able to help me, especially since you—a man of the cloth—were sent to me, but it looks like I'm the one who is supposed to help you! I'm sorry, Father, if I sound angry; it's just that I am tired of this, and there's still so much to do. In truth, I think I've barely gotten started. I thought you would have known more about this stuff than I do!"

Ezekiel took a deep breath, rubbed his face, and then looked directly at Father Connors.

"Here's what I know, Father: my name is Ezekiel Aziar Reese. I believe that the spirit of the Lord lives inside me, and these things want me. I also believe it lives within you, and you and I are about to be tested—very soon. So, Father, any doubt you have needs to be resolved now, because there will be no room for questions or insecurity. Where we're headed, you will need to trust and believe that God is real and alive in you."

"But how can I? I'm not like you. I—"

"It's like this, Father," said Ezekiel as he reached into his pocket and walked toward him. He took Father Connors's hand and placed what he had removed from his pocket in the priest's palm.

Father Connors looked at it for a few minutes and asked, "What is this"?

"Mustard seeds," Ezekiel replied. Now, Father, where is your faith?"

*If we say we have fellowship with him while we walk
in darkness, we lie and do not practice the truth. But
if we walk in the light, as he is in the light, we have
fellowship with one another, and the blood of Jesus
his Son cleanses us from all sin.*

—1 JOHN 1:6–7 (ESV)

CHAPTER SEVENTEEN

Decisions, Decisions

*There's something in those shadows, she thought
to herself. A small voice escaped from her lips,
barely audible, "but I'll never go in them."*

VERA DECIDED IT WOULD BE NICE TO GO SOMEWHERE
different for a change. Maybe this would be just the thing for her
and Robbie. He had been acting strange lately, and whenever she
asked him what was wrong, he would say nothing, but she could
tell that something wasn't right. His aura seemed to grow dark
at times. Then, out of the blue, he invited her to go to a party
one of his friends was having in the city. She rarely went for that
sort of thing, but this time, she said yes, because the idea of it

seemed to give him a lift and brighten his spirit. Now, the day before the party, she was getting a little excited. So many people were talking about this party. It was a big event, and everyone who was anyone was going to be there. Robbie had neglected to mention that his friend who was throwing the party was one of the rich kids who attended their school. He and his family lived in a swanky downtown hotel, and he had rented out the ballroom for the party.

She had never really been part of the "in crowd" or associated with that circle, so all of this was very new to her, and even a bit intimidating, but she was happy to be going. It had been a while, but she was finally beginning to feel normal and good about herself. It was almost liberating. She only hoped that whatever had been bothering Robbie wouldn't bring him down tomorrow. Tomorrow was going to be special. They were going to dance and kiss and dance some more, and as she imagined their special night, she began to smile and giggled to herself.

When she told her mother about the party, her mother was shocked; she said with a smile, "You're going to a what? A party?" Then she started laughing joyfully. "Well, it's about time," she said. "Are you going with that Robbie fella?"

Theresa McNulty was very protective of her only child, Vera. She felt that Robbie was nice enough—a bit odd at times, but nice. He had always been respectful and had good manners; he always said please and thank you, and she'd never heard him slip up once and say a curse word—or anything disrespectful, for that matter. She smiled at Vera and winked.

"Mommmm," Vera whined.

Theresa, still smiling, asked, "So where is this party of yours going to be?"

"In the city, Mom, downtown."

"Downtown LA. Ooh la la," she replied. "I'm gonna need the phone number of the parent who is hosting," she said firmly.

"Oh, Mom," cried Vera.

"Oh, Mom nothing. Get me a number or you can't go."

"OK, Mom, I'll tell Robbie. It's a penthouse party. All the popular and cool kids are going to be there. I'm so excited! After all these years of being kind of socially awkward, I'm actually going to be rubbing elbows with the 'in crowd'!"

She smiled so widely it warmed Theresa's heart. It had been so long since she'd seen her daughter this happy. For a while there it had seemed like Vera was losing herself to some dark place in her mind. She reported hearing voices and claimed she could hear the thoughts of people around her. She had disturbing dreams in which she woke up screaming. Then sometimes she would be talking in her sleep in a language ... or what sounded like a language ... but Theresa couldn't make any sense of the words that were coming out of her daughter's mouth. She would just sit up with her eyes open, pointing at the wall, speaking gibberish. Then she would just stop and go back to sleep like nothing happened. Then one day she just stopped. It was around the time she'd started dating Robbie. At first, Theresa wasn't happy about Vera dating Robbie, but he had slowly grown on her. Although sometimes he seemed like he was someplace else too, which worried her. For the most part, he said and did all the right things, but she didn't trust him completely, and that's why she wanted a phone number.

Theresa had been doodling on a piece of paper while lost in thought about her daughter and Robbie. She glanced down at the paper she had been writing on and abruptly dropped her pen. She had written the name *Ezekiel* about fifty or sixty times in all different sizes and ways across the paper. What was even odder than that was that the first time she could remember ever hearing that name was when her daughter was having one of her waking dreams and called out, "Ezekiel!" She remembered it clearly because when she'd said it, her bedroom had rumbled and shook. It felt like an earthquake, and a strong breeze blew across the room and the door slammed shut as if something had left the room. She tried to convince herself that it was just the wind blowing through the window and nothing more. But deep in her heart, she didn't buy it. She tried asking Vera about that night and the dream, but she claimed she couldn't remember anything. Theresa didn't really believe that either. A mother just knew. She didn't want to bring it up; she figured Vera would tell her when she was ready. Theresa had forgotten about Vera's episodes until now. Was it an omen? Maybe—or was she just reading into things? She shook her head, glanced at the paper she was holding, and then folded it and put it back in her pocket. She said to herself, "You're just being silly," hoping that hearing the words out loud would help to comfort her and, for a moment, it did.

Well, she thought, *at least this Robbie fella has gotten my baby in a good mood, and I'll take that any day of the week.* Now she needed to get some of the particulars about this party and start planning. She started smiling and thought how nice it was for Vera to have something fun to look forward to: her baby's first teen party. The time just seemed to be flying by; she smiled again.

Vera went back to her room, spinning and dancing and holding her hand up in the air as if embracing a person she was dancing with. She hummed a tune to herself as she spun around. It was nice to have something positive and fun to think about for a change. So many weird things had happened to her. Hearing voices, strange dreams, and seeing odd shadows in the dark that almost seemed to move when she tried to focus on them. And now lately she couldn't seem to shake the feeling that she was being watched. *There's something in those shadows*, she thought to herself. A small voice escaped from her lips, barely audible, "but I'll never go in them."

Time was just too short to worry about all the things that were outside of Vera's control. She was going to live her life to the fullest while she could. It had been a few days since she'd heard Joshua's voice whispering in her mind. And she hadn't had any new dreams about that man Ezekiel either. *What a strange name,* she thought, *but he's so handsome.* Then she smiled and said out loud, "Ooooh, you bad girl!" and started laughing. Then she danced a little more and fell back onto her bed, a huge smile on her young face.

Naturally, Vera was completely unaware of the eerie figure on the rooftop across the street from her, peering into her bedroom. It watched her dancing with hatred and contempt. *Tomorrow,* it thought. *Tomorrow will be the day that he finally gets her. Tomorrow will be the day that she dies.* Its mouth parted slightly as a hideous smile made its way across its monstrous face and it began fading back into the shadows of the night.

But each person is tempted when he is lured and enticed by his own desire. Then desire when it has conceived gives birth to sin, and sin when it is fully grown brings forth death.

—JAMES 1:14–15 (ESV)

CHAPTER EIGHTEEN

Robbie

He hadn't realized it, but he'd been smiling like the Cheshire Cat from Alice in Wonderland. *He had a brilliant smile; it caused his dimples to sink deep into his cheeks, which didn't go unnoticed by Vera, who was now blushing.*

ONE DAY, THE CAPTAIN OF THE FOOTBALL TEAM, KEN, approached Robbie and said, "We've been watching you, Robbie, and you've got heart. You don't take stuff from no one. We could use someone like you on our team. Why don't you come to my party on Saturday, hang with me, and I'll introduce you to the rest of the team? Bring a date, but you might want to come solo, because there will be plenty of hotties there to pick from if you know what I mean."

Ken smiled and gave Robbie his address and a fist bump. "See you there," he said, and that was it. Just like that, Robbie was in. He was part of the "elite" group, the cool kids.

To say Robbie was a bit surprised when Ken had invited him to his party would be a bit of an understatement. He was blown away. He knew he had come a long way from that wimpy kid who was always getting picked on to now, a soon-to-be jock, with new friends and a hot girlfriend. But to be invited to this exclusive party seemed beyond what he could hope for. For the first time in quite a while, he was happy. There was a freeness about him he hadn't felt since the fight he'd been in two years ago. But this felt different somehow. It wasn't tainted with the air of hatred. It was light and refreshing—a feeling he used to get when his dad was still alive. He felt alive, and it was great. He was beaming. He thought this might be just what he needed to help bring him and Vera closer as a couple. He had been having mixed and confusing feelings about her over the past few weeks, and he could tell that she was feeling the same way. He wanted to take their relationship up a notch, but she kept saying she wasn't ready for that yet, and this had created a kind of unspoken tension between them. Without even realizing it, he had been putting distance between them, and he told himself that it was because of this, but that wasn't it at all. He liked her, but the voice in his head was always whispering in his ear, pushing and prodding him to pressure her into sex. It was like a little fly, always buzzing in his face, unrelenting. He could see himself acting like a jerk. It was him, but not really. It was hard to explain, but the voice in his head was causing him to act outside of his nature. But now, at least for the moment, he felt different, like his old self again, and it felt good. He wanted to tell her he was sorry for the way he had been acting, and maybe this party would help to break through her self-imposed walls and get them back to a good place. He wanted that. There was something about her he couldn't put into words, but she was special, and he hoped he hadn't pushed her away by trying to convince her to have sex before she was ready.

He met up with her after school on Friday and asked if she would go with him to the party tomorrow, and much to his delight, she said yes. His heart was racing a hundred miles a minute. He had almost forgotten just how beautiful she was if that was even possible. Her eyes were exquisite; they were hazel brown, but at times, when the light caught them just right, they looked green and seemed to almost glow. She had long, curly reddish-brown hair that adorned her head like a mane, and a golden-brown complexion that radiated light like the sun at dawn. When she smiled at him, it melted his heart away. She was going to the party with him, and he was so happy. He hadn't realized it, but he'd been smiling like the Cheshire Cat from *Alice in Wonderland*. Robbie had a great smile; it caused his dimples to sink deep into his cheeks, which didn't go unnoticed by Vera, who was now blushing. She took his hands, pulled him close to her, and kissed him on the lips.

"Call me later—I have to get home. My mom's waiting for me."

"OK," he said, a little wobbly from her kiss.

It had been a while since she had kissed him like that, and he could feel butterflies racing around inside of him. She kissed him again, turned, and walked away to meet up with her friends. She waved goodbye, and he watched her until she turned the corner out of habit. Then he looked at his watch. It was three thirty already. "Oh no," he said out loud. He would have just enough time to make it to work on time—just barely, but he would be cutting it close. He knew he couldn't afford to be late again. This would be the third time this month, and they had already given him a verbal warning. Luckily for him, he had to be at work by four and he was only about fifteen minutes away. Barring anything crazy, he figured he should make it to work with a few minutes to spare. He loved his job at Gold's Gym. He got to work out for free and got paid to do it. It was great.

<< >>

When Robbie walked through the doors to the gym at three fifty-five, his boss was there waiting. Looking down at his watch and then back at Robbie, he shook his head. The kid wasn't late yet, but this was a little too close for comfort. Robbie made his way to the locker room, changed quickly, and then headed out to the floor, where his first appointment was waiting for him. His name was Thomas Smyth.

"You ready to get your workout on, Tom?" Robbie asked.

"It's Thomas, and I was ready at 4:00. It's now 4:02. I expect you to be at your appointments on time, as I am for you. It's just rude to keep someone waiting."

"I'm sorry, Thomas. How about I give you an extra thirty minutes to make up for my tardiness. Is that all right with you?"

Thomas looked at him a bit oddly, and a weird, eerie kind of smile cracked the corner of his mouth. It made Robbie feel extremely uncomfortable. Still smiling as he looked Robbie up and down, he said, "An extra thirty minutes on the house . . . yes, that will be acceptable."

Robbie nodded and thought to himself, *What a freaking creep.* "OK, cool then. Let's get started."

As he began going over the workout routine with Thomas, his thoughts drifted back to Vera and the upcoming party.

*Ye are of your father the devil, and the lusts of
your father ye will do. He was a murderer from
the beginning, and abode not in the truth, because
there is no truth in him. When he speaketh a lie,
he speaketh of his own: for he is a liar, and the
father of it.*

—JOHN 8:44

CHAPTER NINETEEN

Nestor

*The voices of the night said that one of them was
he who has been foretold: the angel slayer.*

HE HAD BEEN PATIENT WITH THIS ONE. SHE WAS A SPECIAL ONE.
He hadn't encountered anyone like her in many years. At least not
since the world had changed. She would be his first key. Before she
could find her lock. She was a pure one, unknown to man—how
sweet it would be to taste her blood on his lips. The thought of it
was intoxicating. She had an intrinsic spirit as well. How else could
she have been able to call him out just outside the store?

Just thinking about that day angered him. *A mortal with such a gift,* he thought. How it will anger the Most-High when he takes her. The boy Robbie had been most helpful these past few months. Clouding her senses, allowing him to get closer and closer to her, undetected. This party would be the perfect time for him to collect from her the debt she owed him. After he had secured her, he planned to find this so-called foretold one and his charge, as they were called. Somehow, they had managed the impossible: finding and killing his children while remaining hidden from his sight. The voices of the night said that one of them was he who has been foretold: the angel slayer. He smiled at that. To have a mortal like that under his control would be priceless during these times, were he able to possess him. No power on earth could hold him to any truce. He would be unbound by any angelic law and thus free to do as he pleased, to whomever he pleased. He looked down at his misshapen hand and passed his thumb over the stubs of his missing fingers where they had been before Michael had taken them. Things would be quite different once he took this so-called foretold one's grace for his own. He smiled a bit as he thought about this and then recomposed himself.

Mustn't get too far ahead of himself, he thought. First things first. He would take the girl. Once he had her, then he could focus on the foretold one. He began gliding backward slowly from where he had been perched on the roof, watching Vera as she danced about in her room. Back into the shadows, he smiled as he thought of the taste of her and how he would savor her anguish as her soul became his and the light in her eyes faded. He would have his dance then, and she would be his.

He disappeared into the shadows, smiling his hideous smile.

"When I expected good, then evil came;
When I waited for light, then darkness came.
—Job 30:26 (NASB1995)

CHAPTER TWENTY

Party Time

She thought of her mom watching them before they
left, and suddenly a sharp chill ran up her spine.

It was ten minutes before six, and Robbie would be picking her up at six on the dot. Vera was putting the finishing touches on her makeup when she heard the doorbell ring. "It figures he'd get here early," she whispered to herself as she put on her lip gloss. She could hear her mother let Robbie into the apartment and she smiled as she heard her making a fuss over how handsome he looked. Robbie was quite handsome indeed, and these last couple of days, the way he'd been acting had endeared him to her. It was almost like he was a different person. Even his eyes seemed to be a brighter blue than they normally were.

As Vera made her way to the living room, Robbie could feel his heart beating harder. It got so bad it felt like it was going to jump out of his chest.

Vera could feel butterflies fluttering around in her stomach, and her palms were sweaty. This was a new feeling for her: exhilaration and nervousness all wrapped up into one. Then she saw Robbie, smiling such a smile that he seemed to glow. This was turning out to be one of the happiest moments of her life, she thought, and a tear fell from her eye and ran down her cheek.

She quickly took a tissue from her purse to dab her eyes before her makeup ran. She looked up at Robbie and smiled. He was just standing there, staring at her. What she didn't know was that Robbie was instantly taken aback when he saw her. He had never seen anything or anyone as beautiful as her, ever. He had always known she was pretty, but nothing like this. It was like he was seeing her for the very first time—and he was speechless.

He snapped out of his daze as he realized he was making her uncomfortable with his staring and gave a nervous smile, lowered his head a bit, and looked down at his feet for a second. But only for a second, that was all he could manage. He simply couldn't keep his eyes off her.

Her eyes were nothing less than hypnotizing . . . the most amazing sight he had ever seen. They seemed to glow when she smiled, which just made her even more alluring. He tried to tell her she was beautiful, but what came out of his mouth was a jumble of words that made little sense, except for the last one: "beautiful." Vera's mother smiled at that. She could tell that, right at that moment, the boy had fallen for her daughter.

Vera smiled, "Thank you, I think. You don't look half bad yourself."

She walked over to him and took his hand. As she did, his heart raced even harder, if that were possible. He was so proud to be going to the party with her. Everyone would be watching and wondering how he had gotten so lucky.

"So, Robbie," Theresa said, "get closer to Vera, would ya? I want to take a picture of the two of you together."

"Oh, Mom," Vera protested as she moved close to Robbie.

He instinctively put his arm around her waist. They both paused for a second and looked at each other, Vera blushing and Robbie beaming with pride.

"Smile, you two," Theresa said through a smile of her own. They took what seemed like dozens of pictures before Theresa allowed them to leave. "Make sure you have her back by eleven o'clock sharp, young man."

She put the phone number Robbie had given her in her pocket. She would only use it if they were not back by eleven.

"Oh, Mom, it's Saturday night, there's no school tomorrow."

"I said eleven and not a minute later, young lady. Is that clear?" She turned her head and directed her stare toward Robbie. "Is that clear, Robbie?"

"Yes ma'am," Robbie replied. "I'll have her home by eleven on the dot."

Theresa turned her gaze back to Vera and said, "Good, now go have a good time. Take lots of pictures."

Out in the hallway, Vera looked up at Robbie and said, "She can be so embarrassing sometimes."

"Aren't all parents, though?" Robbie replied, smiling back at her. "We're lucky my mom wasn't here, or we'd still be there taking pictures."

They both laughed at that. Then Robbie took her hand and looked deeply into her eyes. He paused for a moment and said, "You are so beautiful."

"Thank you," she replied, trying not to blush. They walked toward the elevator, both smiling at each other and making small talk.

Vera's mother watched from the doorway, smiling. She remembered when she was that age and had gone to her first dance. The elevator doorbell chimed, the door opened, and they got inside. As they did, Vera's mother closed the door to her apartment.

In the lobby, Robbie asked, "You ready for this?"

"Yeah, I'm happy you asked me to go. It's nice to see this side of you."

"Yeah, I know I've been obnoxious lately. I'm sorry about…you know, rushing you. I mean, we don't have to…you know. I'll wait till you are ready. I'm crazy about you, Vera, and I've got my head on straight now."

"Thanks for saying that, Robbie." Vera looked up at him sincerely and smiled. Now he was on his way to winning her heart.

They walked to Robbie's car and got in and they were off, still talking and laughing excitedly. It was funny how close she felt to Robbie right now; she was carefree. The butterflies had begun to calm down in her stomach, but she would still get hit with flashes of nerves every so often.

She thought of her mom watching them before they left, and suddenly a sharp chill ran up her spine. She looked at her watch— it was six fifteen. Vera made a mental note of the time and told herself to remember to ask her mom how she was feeling at exactly six fifteen, because she and her mom often got these weird feelings at the same time and then they would compare times. It made her toes tingle and her stomach do flip-flops. The feeling was so strong and overpowering she needed a moment to recompose herself. She put her hands on the dashboard of the car to steady herself. As she looked over at Robbie with a nervous smile, she took a deep breath.

"You OK?" Robbie asked, concerned.

"Yeah," she replied. "I guess I'm just a little more nervous about this party than I thought."

"We don't have to go, you know; especially if you're not feeling well."

He looked so worried when she looked up that it made her strangely at ease.

"No, I'll be all right, it's passing already."

They pulled up to the Standard Hotel. The valet approached the car and opened the door. "Welcome to the Standard. Will you be checking in?"

She smiled, and Robbie answered, "No, we are here for the Slyer party."

"Oh, of course, sir."

"We'll be back around ten o'clock for the car." Vera looked at him and smiled, remembering her mother's pretend threat to Robbie. Robbie wasn't about to find out if Theresa was serious or not. He was going to have Vera back home on time—maybe even a few minutes early. Vera thought he was so cute.

The valet gave Robbie a ticket, and he casually slipped him a ten-spot in his hand as he handed him the keys. He was feeling pretty good about the exchange as the two of them made their way up to the party.

And the Lord said, Simon, Simon, behold, Satan
hath desired to have you, that he may sift you as
wheat: But I have prayed for thee, that thy faith fail
not: and when thou art converted, strengthen thy
brethren.

—LUKE 22:31–32

CHAPTER TWENTY-ONE
Uninvited Guest

He lifted her off the floor within inches of his horrifying
face. His breath was hot and smelled of decaying flesh.

THERESA CLOSED THE DOOR, WALKED TO THE LIVING ROOM
sofa, and sat down. She picked up the photo album that was resting
on the coffee table and opened it. As she looked at a few pictures
of Vera when she was a baby and some more recent photos, she
started wondering where the time had gone. A big smile crept over
her face. *My daughter is all grown up.* Emotions of happiness and
sorrow welled up inside her as she continued to look at the pictures.
The doorbell rang, and Theresa figured Vera must've forgotten
something. She looked at her watch and checked the time. It was

six fifteen; she thought to herself that the kids were wasting all their date time as she walked toward the door.

She called out, "Now I know I said to be home on time, but I think you guys are going a bit overboard," as she headed toward the door.

She opened it, and a tall figure stood before her. It caught her completely off guard, and a slight gasp escaped her lips. She composed herself quickly and tried to say something, but the man stepped inside before she could get any words out. Somehow, he now seemed taller, if that was even possible, and his odor was unbearable. How had she not noticed that before now? How did he get inside so quickly? She had only just stepped back a second ago. She tried to tell him to get out, but before she could get the words out of her mouth, he grabbed her by the throat. He was inhumanly fast. She didn't even see his hand move. It was like one minute he was in the doorway and the next he was pulling her toward him. He lifted her off the floor within inches of his horrifying face. His breath was hot and smelled of decaying flesh. He had a steel-like grip. She tried to scream, but his hand held her voice at bay. Tears fell from her eyes, a combination of pain and fear. She'd heard stories about things like him. She had seen movies on TV featuring monsters like him. She knew instinctively what this thing was that had her. A demon. It began sniffing her like one would do a flower or old clothing that still had the scent of a loved one on it. The demon never released his grip or uttered a word, and then suddenly, without warning, it bit her on the arm. The pain was indescribable. She tried to scream, but the grip on her neck choked it back. Then it just let go of her. She fell backward onto the floor and kicked and pushed backward, kind of reverse crawling, until her back was up against the wall in the living room. That's when she noticed that this thing was chewing on something. She reached over to hold the spot on her arm where it had bitten her to stop the bleeding, only to grab hold of a bloody stump. She then looked at what was left of her arm in horror and then back at the thing that had done this to her. It had the rest of her arm in its mouth and was chewing on it. It smiled at her with its oversized jaw, which seemed entirely too big for its face. And with her blood dripping from its lips, it said,

"Delicious, if I do says so myself. I cans taste the fear in your bloods. It's exquisitely intoxicating."

His voice was not much more than a hiss and barely audible, yet somehow it felt like it was resonating throughout the room. "Why?" she cried. "Why me?"

"Because you made her. Because you are the mother. And, because I want to hurts her the way she hurts me. But most of all, because it's fun."

He smiled again; this time even bigger than before, revealing hundreds of sharp, needle-like teeth with bits of flesh in between them.

She started to say something else, but he leaped on top of her, biting her in the face. Then he bit her other arm off. She kicked and thrashed about on the floor. But she was gone. This only seemed to excite him more. He ripped off what was left of her clothing and proceeded to maliciously violate her, even though she was no longer aware. He wanted to make her suffer so he could savor every moment of it. But Theresa was no longer there. She had gone right after the bite to the face, and her guardian angel had carried her off to the Father. Nestor was so intent on punishing her that he didn't notice. When he was done, he left her mutilated corpse on the floor. It was then that he realized he had only ravished her body— her soul was gone. He had been cheated. Theresa had somehow managed to escape him. He let out a blood-curdling scream, hurled things around the apartment, and tore up the photo album. He was furious, but the night wasn't over. He wanted Vera to know about this; he wanted to devastate her beyond her ability to cope. Then, once she was broken, she would be easy to take. She would be his. And at that moment, he would make what he did to her mother seem like nothing. And he would have her soul. He smiled as he left the apartment, leaving the door slightly open so that her body could be found the way he left it. Maintaining his insidious smile, he faded into the darkness saying,

"I haves me a party to attend."

Then he vanished.

We know that God's children do not make a practice of sinning, for God's Son holds them securely, and the evil one cannot touch them.

—JOHN 5:18 (NLV)

CHAPTER TWENTY-TWO
The Party

She was quite stunning. She didn't normally wear makeup. It was almost as if they were seeing her for the first time.

VERA COULDN'T SHAKE THE FEELING THAT SOMETHING WAS wrong. It nagged at her in the back of her mind. Robbie had stepped away to get her something to drink to help settle her stomach. She just couldn't stop thinking about her mother for some reason.

"Penny for your thoughts." It was Robbie's friend Ken. He was all dressed up, looking spiffy and polished. He was also smiling at her in a complimentary way. Vera's makeup was on point; it brought out her beauty. He cupped his chin between his pointer finger and thumb with his head tilted to one side as he surveyed Vera from head-to-toe as he grinned broadly. Then he said, "Wow, Vera, I hardly recognized you. Damn, girl, you look good!"

He said it in a way that she was not used to hearing. It was like he'd just noticed her for the first time. It made Vera laugh because he was actually flirting with her. He realized how he must have sounded to her and started laughing as Robbie returned with a couple of sodas.

"Hey Rob, glad you could make it," said Ken.

"Thanks for having me. I see you've been chatting with Vera. Thank you for keeping her company for me."

He moved past him a bit and handed Vera a soda. Ken, looking surprised again, said, "Oh, wow, she's with you? I mean, of course she's with you. It's just that when you said you were bringing someone, I never would have guessed it was Vera. I mean, wow, that came out wrong. What I meant was, I didn't know that you two were a thing. I mean a couple."

He looked at the ground and cupped his face, then let it rise to push his hair back until it rested on the back of his head. He took a deep breath, hoping he wouldn't say anything else that would make him sound any dumber than he already did.

"Can I start over?" he asked. "Anyway, so glad you guys could make it. Come on over and meet everyone."

Ken put his arms over both of their shoulders and walked them through the crowd to a small group of people sitting at one of the tables in the back. It was mostly guys from the football team and girls from the cheer squad. *The in-crowd,* Vera thought. Once again, it seemed like everyone was staring at Vera—and they were. No one had ever really seen Vera all made up before. She was quite stunning. She didn't normally wear makeup. It was almost as if they were seeing her for the first time.

Vera knew why they were staring; it was obvious to her, but it didn't make it any less awkward. Robbie sensed it too, and he tried to break the mood by asking her to dance, which she quickly agreed to. When they got to the dance floor, they both remembered that neither one of them knew how to dance. Under normal conditions, this would have been quite funny, but as it turned out, they were the center of attention, and everyone was watching them. "This Is How We Do It" by Montel Jorden was playing. Luckily for both of them, the song was quite easy to move to, and they knew most of the words as well. Robbie smiled and laughed while he danced. This was a first for him as well. He was not used to being "that guy" at the party—or at any place with the pretty girl, for that matter. He noticed some of the other girls smiling and pointing, almost like they were flirting with him. Guys were giving him the thumbs up and nodding their heads in approval. After a few up-tempo songs had played, the DJ finally put on a slow song, "Can You Stand the Rain?" by Boyz II Men. Robbie placed his hand on Vera's waist, awkwardly at first, but as they began to sway with the music it became more natural and relaxed. She put her arms around his neck as he pulled her close to him. She smiled as he did, looking up into his deep blue eyes, and kissed him on the lips. She didn't know why she did it, she guessed it was because of the way he was trying to make her feel comfortable; she could tell he was feeling the same way she was. It was cute, so she kissed him, smiling at the thought of it. It was only a little peck—well at least at first. But then it somehow blossomed into a real kiss. Robbie became fully aroused at this and was a little embarrassed. He started to pull back, loosening his grip on her. But she held onto him. She could tell what was going on with him, but she didn't mind. It was natural, after all. Besides that, she wasn't ready to let him go just yet. She rested her head against his chest and listened to his heartbeat as they danced. The song finished, and the tempo of the music began to change again, and as it did, they began to make their way back to the table. As soon as they got back to the table, a couple of the girls met her, and one of them grabbed her hand. They were laughing and giggling. They smiled at the boys, and then one of them announced that the group was going to powder their noses. They were all giggling. The one who had Vera's hand pulled her along with them as they made their way to the ladies' room. Vera turned and smiled at Robbie as she was herded away with the crowd. He smiled back at her and waved.

"Peace I leave with you; My peace I give unto you, not as the world giveth, give I unto you. Let not your heart be troubled, neither let it be afraid.

—JOHN 14:27 (KJ21)

CHAPTER TWENTY-THREE

The Bathroom

Vera couldn't help thinking about the conversation. She may have been able to get the girls to change the sexually charged conversation, but she couldn't get it out of her mind.

"SO, MISSY, WHERE HAVE YOU BEEN HIDING, AND HOW LONG HAVE you and Robbie been an item?"

Vera smiled at the question. It sounded odd to hear someone refer to them being an item. Odd, but good.

"We've been dating for a while now. Nothing too serious, but I think things might change soon." She blushed and looked down, still smiling.

"Yeah, you think?" the other girl interjected. "I saw you on the dance floor. Everyone could see the sparks coming off the two of you."

They all laughed at that, but in a good way—the way people do when they are all in agreement.

"So, do you two have any plans after this?" the tall blond asked.

"Yeah, girl, are you going to take your relationship to the next level?" asked one of the other girls.

"No . . . I don't know," Vera replied a bit tentatively. She was feeling pretty uncomfortable with the direction of the conversation. The questions seemed intrusive; after all, she didn't know them all that well. So before anyone could throw another question at her, she said, "If you don't mind, can we just change the subject?"

They all got the hint and could see that Vera's body language had changed. This subject was off-limits with her. Vera was glad they got it and tried to lighten the mood a bit.

"I'm starving," she said, rubbing her stomach.

"Me too," one of the other girls said in agreement.

We should get back so the boys can get us something to eat. They were all looking in the mirrors, fixing their makeup and hair as they got ready to reemerge from the bathroom and rejoin the party.

Vera couldn't help thinking about the conversation. She may have been able to get the girls to change the sexually charged conversation, but she couldn't get it out of her mind. All these thoughts were very new and kind of exciting to her. Maybe it was time to raise the bar with Robbie, she thought, and she laughed quietly to herself. That dance had her head spinning, and she could tell that Robbie was feeling the same way too. The way he was poking her through his pants gave him away. She cracked a smile because she liked it, and she liked him a lot more than she had realized before this moment. She could feel the butterflies fluttering in her stomach and tingles rushing up and down her spine. She couldn't wait to get back to him now. The other girls were still talking, but she tuned them out. Her mind was on other things, and they all had to do with Robbie.

They all left the bathroom and headed back to the party. Suddenly they heard a commotion. As they got closer, they could see that it was Robbie and Tommy shouting at each other. Vera made her way over to Robbie just in time to hear him say, "And when I'm home hitting that later tonight, you'll be thinking about me while you're playing with yourself and looking at a picture of your mom."

Is that what he thinks about me? she thought. *Is this what all of them think about me?* It devastated her. She could feel her heartbreak as all eyes focused on her. She wanted to just disappear, but she couldn't move. At least not at first. Then she called out his name: "Robbie, how could you?" There was genuine sorrow in her tone.

Robbie turned to face her. He knew instantly from the tone of her voice and the look on her face that she had heard what he just said. He said her name, "Vera," shaking his head to negate what she was thinking while reaching for her. But she backed away from him. She couldn't hold back the tears that had fallen from her eyes and rolled down her cheeks. He called to her again, "Vera, wait! Let me explain!" But she had already turned from him, pushing her way through the crowded room toward the elevators. Part of her wanted to go back to hear what he had to say. There had to be a reason why he would say something like that about her in front of all those people. But she couldn't bring herself to do it. She was mortified and felt foolish for thinking about getting serious with him when this was what he thought of her. She had to get out of there. As she made it to the corridor outside the ballroom, she pressed the button repeatedly for the elevator. She could feel everyone's eyes on her, watching her every move, and it was almost unbearable. The elevator couldn't get there fast enough for her. She pressed the button a few more times. There was a chime, and the elevator doors opened. She quickly rushed in. As she turned around and looked up, she could see what appeared to be Robbie in the middle of some kind of conflict. She went to press the open button on the elevator to go to him, but the thought faded almost as quickly as it had come. With tears in her eyes, she let the doors close. When she finally reached the first floor, she rushed across the lobby and out the door.

being filled with all unrighteousness, fornication,
wickedness, covetousness, maliciousness, full of envy,
murder, strife, deceit, malignity. They are whisperers,
—Romans 1:29 (KJ21)

CHAPTER TWENTY-FOUR

Things Are Not Always as They Appear

Robbie snapped. He spun around, fist clinched, arm cocked,
and launched a punch directly into Tommy's mouth.

"So, Robbie, how'd you get so lucky? And whoa, where has she been hiding? I mean, damn, talk about a Cinderella story. Robbie, you're the man. She's probably easy too, I bet. I mean, she's gotta be starving for attention. Going from a boring little miss nobody to a hot little piece. She must put out. You know how those nerdy girls are, all proper when they're out in the open, but then turn into freaks when you get them alone." All the other boys laughed and high fived each other.

"What? What the F, Tommy. You're not serious, right?" Robbie asked, obviously bothered by his comments.

"Yeah man, I heard she let Ken hit it last week."

"Nahhhh man, keep me out of this. I never touched her," said Ken. He could see that Robbie was getting angry and wasn't trying to be the focus of his anger. Robbie was flushed with embarrassment. It was obvious that Tommy was picking a fight, but why, Robbie thought, confused. He wasn't afraid of Tommy, he just wanted to hang with the in crowd. But now all he wanted to do was punch Tommy in his stupid mouth for the things he was saying about Vera. But these were the cool kids. Everyone wants to be down with them. He didn't want to be on the outs with them before he even got in.

"Nah, it's not like that, Tommy, she's not like that at all. She's…" He paused for a second, looking down as he tried to think of the right words to say, when Tommy interrupted.

"Well, the only way to know for sure is to find out. She either is or she isn't. The real question is, are you man enough to find out. If not, then maybe you wanna step aside and let a real man step up to the plate."

Tommy wanted to make a name for himself. He was just as tall as Robbie and he worked out. If he could take this punk, he would be the man for sure. He stepped up to Robbie, folding his arms over his chest and posturing. Then he raised his hand and poked Robbie in the chest and asked him again.

"Well, are you gonna find out, or are you still that little punk that used to get his behind beat all the time?"

He started to circle Robbie with his arms open wide, his head tilted to the side with a smirk on his face as he taunted Robbie and said "What's it gonna be?" Robbie was furious. This freaking guy was a real jerk. He wanted to smash his face in, and he knew that for some reason, Tommy wanted to fight him. He didn't know why. If he took the bait, more than likely the other members of Tommy's crew would jump in and he'd lose. If he backed down, then everyone would think he was a punk like before and he'd end up losing all the respect he'd worked so hard to build up over the past year and a half. He couldn't let that happen. Then Tommy said, "The truth of the matter is, you're not man enough for her. I bet you're a virgin. I could tell by the way you were dancing with her."

He then gestured to Robbie's genitalia, insinuating that he was erect. Everyone laughed at that. Robbie's face revealed that Tommy had hit a nerve. He managed to fake a laugh.

"*F* you, Tommy. I get it, you're just jealous because one of the prettiest girls in school is here with me. When I was on the dance floor holding Vera close to me, all you could hold onto was yourself. And when I kicked Brian and Joey's butts on the stairwell, your punk behind probably lost a friend, or maybe one of those guys was your 'special' friend, and you're trying to defend his honor two years too late. Whatever the reason, you're a punk and you will always be a punk, and when I'm home hitting that later tonight, you'll be thinking about me while you're playing with yourself and looking at a picture of your mom."

At that last comment, everyone in earshot erupted into laughter. People were repeating different things that Robbie had said and pointing and laughing at Tommy.

In fact, everyone there was laughing—everyone except Vera. She had come back from the bathroom just in time to hear Robbie's last comment. Her heart was broken. She couldn't believe he would say something like that about her. What made it worse was that she had been considering being with him in that way. She wondered if he could sense it somehow and thought it would be OK to expose her and allow her to be the butt of his joke. She stood there with tears forming in her eyes. As they began to fall and roll down her cheeks, she called out to him. "Robbie, how could you say that about—" she paused for a moment as if the words were caught in her throat, "—about me." Her voice was barely a whisper. Robbie turned around in horror. He hadn't meant for her to hear that; in truth, he didn't even know why he'd said it. He was just so angry at Tommy and wanted to make him look stupid.

"Vera, it's not what it looks like; he was saying things about me, and I—"

She cut him off and said, "and so you thought it would be OK to say that stuff about me?" She turned around and started walking away from him.

"Vera, wait!" He reached out for her and caught her right arm, but she yanked it free of his grip violently and ran out of the party.

Robbie wasn't thinking clearly. It was as if he had lost himself in a stupid contest with someone who meant nothing to him. He wanted so badly to fit in with these kids because he thought they were so cool that instead of just rushing out after her; he found it more important to save face to impress them. It never dawned on him that the only reason Ken had invited him to his party was because he thought he could use him down the line in case Joey and his boys gave him or his friends any trouble. Robbie had beat everyone in Joey's gang, so he was useful. He could never have really been a part of Ken's inner circle. They were all rich kids. They were privy to a completely different life-style and would all be going away to Ivy League colleges when they left high school. Joey had been a pain to them as well, and if Joey thought Robbie was part of their group, he would think twice before he messed with any of them. Tommy was so angry that this little nobody had all his friends laughing at him, so he said, "Looks like you're going to be the one jerking off to my mother's picture, because your girl left your sorry behind." They all burst out laughing.

"Looks like you lost your girl, Robbie," one girl said derisively. The other girls snickered, and everyone roared with laughter.

Robbie was embarrassed, and then Tommy chimed in. "Yeah, I'm gonna go see what's up with your soon to be ex-girlfriend."

There were a few oohs and bits of laughter from Tommy's crew.

Robbie snapped. He spun around, fist clinched, arm cocked, and launched a punch directly into Tommy's mouth. Tommy fell backward onto a table, knocking it and a few drinks over onto the floor. Robbie went to hit him again, but before he could get to him, a couple of guys from the football team grabbed him and held him at bay so that Tommy could pull himself together. He stumbled to his feet. His mouth was full of blood from his busted lips. When Tommy finally straightened up, he spit out a tooth and cursed.

So, you want to *F* with me? OK, let's do this. Hold him down," he instructed two of the guys on his team. Tommy threw a punch, aiming for Robbie's nose. Robbie timed it right and managed to drop his head at just the right moment so that he ended up punching him on the top of his forehead, instantly breaking two of his fingers. To everyone else, it looked like Robbie had head-butted Tommy's fingers. Tommy jerked his hand back but before he could shout out in pain from his broken fingers, Robbie kicked him in the balls. Tommy just dropped without a word, holding his balls in his good hand. Then Robbie wrenched himself free from the kids holding him and kicked Tommy in the face. Tommy passed out. One of Tommy's friends tried to grab him, but he pulled free and punched the kid in the ribs. The kid dropped like a sack of potatoes. Robbie stood over them for a moment and then looked at the crowd of people that had gathered. Everyone had heard the rumor about how Robbie the punk knew how to fight now, and tonight he had confirmed that this was fact. Then, like a brick, it hit him: Vera. He turned around and sped across the room toward the elevators, hoping to catch her, but she was gone. He pressed the down button and almost immediately the elevator bell rang over the center elevator, announcing that it was there. He ran inside and repeatedly pressed the lobby button. It seemed to take an eternity for the elevator to reach the main floor. He rushed out into the lobby and then out the front doors, but no Vera. He asked the valet if he had seen the girl he'd come in with.

"Yeah, I saw her. She was crying and I asked her if she wanted me to call a cab for her, but she didn't answer, she just walked by me. When she got outside, she ran down the street."

"How long ago?" asked Robbie.

"About ten minutes ago."

"Did you see which way she went?"

The valet pointed in the direction that Vera had headed, and Robbie took off down the block. His head turned right to left as he scanned the area for her, but she was nowhere to be found. He stood at the corner for a long time and finally just looked down at his feet. *How did the night go so bad?* he kept asking himself. *How did this happen?*

He turned around and slowly started walking back to the hotel to pick up his car, all the while staring at his feet. He hadn't felt this bad since the time he lost his father. He kept asking himself how this had happened as he sat on the bench in the valet area waiting for his car to be brought around.

For we are strangers before thee, and sojourners, as
were all our fathers: our days on the earth are as a
shadow, and there is none abiding.

—1 CHRONICLES 29:15

CHAPTER TWENTY-FIVE

The Truth Is Never Hidden but Often Hard to Find

He was pulled backward off his feet and slammed
into a wall behind him. The pain in his shoulder
shot down his neck through his spine.

SEVERAL WEEKS HAD PASSED SINCE FATHER CONNORS HAD pulled Ezekiel out of the air from the arms of the demon. That experience had changed him. The priest had begun noticing weird things going on around him more and more when he was out walking in the street, and especially when he was with Ezekiel. He always seemed to feel as if they were being watched. Once, when he and Ezekiel were out, he tried to ask him about it, but Ezekiel stopped him.

"Not here, not now, Father. They're watching us. We have to seem as if we don't notice them. That's our strength, pretending that we don't know what's going on around us. The more they think we're oblivious to them, the stronger that makes us. If we tip our hand, then they'll have to be more creative. This way we can see them coming without them knowing we know who they are."

Father Connors did as instructed until they got back home to the church. Ezekiel explained to him in more detail that that was how he was able to stay alive in prison. Joshua had taught him how to spot evil without reacting to it and how to feel the climate of the world changing, when something big was about to happen, even when he wasn't sure what it was. He continued to explain that they would both have to be vigilant and forever on their guard.

He looked directly at Father Connors and said, "These things are not usually this obvious. They generally try to make their actions unseen. It's almost as if they're going out of their way to get our attention. From now on, Father, whenever we go out, we must be prepared and ready to defend ourselves. I'm going to start carrying the blade with me, and you're going to need a weapon as well. We're also going to have to train together. We need to hone our skills and be ready for anything at any moment."

"But why would they come after me, EZ? I understand why they would target you—you're, well, you're you. But me, I'm not special like you. I'm just a broken priest who's not worth—"

Ezekiel cut him off before he could finish. "Because God chose you, that's why. Because whether you know it or not, God has a purpose for you, and now that you are with me, the enemy will do anything to stop you and stay you from your course and your chosen destiny, whatever that may be. Your faith has made you a target, father. It's because they sense a growing strength brewing deep within you. You now have their attention as well."

Father Connors thought about this for a moment, unsure of what to say. He wanted to believe that there was a brewing strength somewhere within him. For some reason, that idea made him feel good. He looked at Ezekiel and said, "Training? What kind of training?"

"Some basic defense and attack moves. We also need to build up your endurance, strength, and reaction time."

Father Connors nodded and thought more about what Ezekiel had said.

A few weeks later, Ezekiel and Father Connors were out following up on what they thought was a lead to Vera. Ezekiel sensed Nestor was stalking her. He could feel it in his bones, and he was getting closer. If they were going to find her before him, they were going to have to find out what he knew, and that would require them catching and extracting the information from one of the lower demons. The plan was simple: they would follow one of the demons, catch it off-guard, and then squeeze it for any information they could about Nestor and the girl.

Father Connors wasn't sure this was the best idea, since all of these things were liars, but Ezekiel seemed pretty confident that he would be able to get some truth out of one or two of them and then piece the rest together. He kept saying: "Don't worry about that part father—they won't be able to lie to me."

He had been with Ezekiel on a few hunts now, and he knew that Ezekiel was fully capable of dispatching a demon, but he just felt that this was going to be a little different from pulling one out of a person. They would have to fear him more than they did Nestor, more than death itself, but from what Father Connors knew about demons from his religious instruction, he didn't see how this was possible. On the other hand, his religious instruction hadn't included anyone like Ezekiel, that was for sure.

The plan was, according to Ezekiel, to read between the lines and send as many of them as they could back to the pit. As the time went on, they captured half a dozen imps, each one saying something different. And then one night, one of them mentioned a potential meeting place that Saturday evening in downtown LA: an old landmark building, a bit run-down and in need of some attention. It was just the kind of place demons and creatures of the night might be found. After the creature spoke, a sound came from the shadows, distracting Ezekiel, and the thing sprung from his grip, leaped into the shadows, and disappeared. After that, Ezekiel and Father Connors began to survey the building and observe the different people as they would go in and out. Ezekiel was amazed. Not since his time in prison had he felt so strongly about a place. Then a man rounded the corner of the building and headed toward the door. He seemed nervous as he approached the entrance, and even though Father Connors and Ezekiel were well hidden, he turned and looked in their direction and said, "You coming?" Then he laughed as he entered the building.

"What the—? Did you see that? They know we're here, EZ. This doesn't feel right. We need to go and come back another time."

Ezekiel, however, almost as if in a trance, responded, "Yeah, I'm coming, you piece of crap," and took off running toward the building. Father Connors quickly took off behind him, trying to keep up.

"Wait up, EZ, slow down! This doesn't feel right; it feels like a trap." Father Connors's voice snapped Ezekiel out of his trance. He turned around.

"You're right, but I can't help feeling like this is the real thing. He might really know where she is, and I can't take the chance that they might get away. I have to follow him."

He opened the door, and they stepped inside. To their surprise, they saw the demon waiting for them by the door leading to the stairway. "You better hope you get to her before I do," it said. "Because we're about to have some kinda fun with her for sure."

Then it took off up the staircase, and without a second thought, Ezekiel took off after it. Father Connors tried to follow them, but he was having a hard time keeping up. He felt sluggish all of a sudden, and every step he took, Ezekiel took four. The distance between the two of them continued to grow as he made his way up the stairs behind that thing. It was all Father Connors could do just to catch his breath. He realized that it was air in this place—it was heavier and thicker for some reason. He found himself struggling to catch his breath. But it didn't seem to affect Ezekiel at all. Father Connors could tell Ezekiel was immune to the stresses he was experiencing as he watched him disappear up the staircase. Then suddenly he felt a hand on his shoulder. He started to turn his head to see what had grabbed him, but before he could get a look at what it was, he was pulled backward off his feet and slammed into a wall behind him. The pain in his shoulder shot down his neck through his spine.

His back was being pressed against the wall of the staircase, and his mouth was being covered. It was a vampi, or a vampire, as they are more commonly known. His fingers were icy and surprisingly soft. He never would have thought that possible. Actually, he had never even thought about it before now. Why would he? Until recently, he didn't even know these things were real. The vampi turned around and watched Ezekiel run up the stairs after the demon. Father Connors watched as well, as his muffled cries for help tried to escape through the bony pale fingers of the vampi. When Ezekiel was out of sight, the vampi turned to face Father Connors and smiled.

"Tis, tis, tis," he said while waving his index finger at Father Connors. "Looks like you're all by yourself, Father. I could've sworn I saw you come in here with somebody else, but I guess I was wrong. You really should've stayed out of this, Father; you're not built for this. And your boy there, well he's not built for it either and he's about to find out that if you play with fire eventually you get burned. But I digress, Father, where are my manners? I should be focusing on you." Then he smiled, baring his fangs, and winked at him.

Father Connors could feel his heart beating through his chest. *This is it,* he thought. The vampi grabbed him by the throat and picked him up off his feet, dangling him in the air and choking him slowly, savoring every minute of his kill.

"I can't tell you how much I'm enjoying this, Father. It's like Christmas come early."

Father Connors could feel himself slipping in and out of consciousness. He had lost all color in his face and was almost as pale as the vampi. This thing was so strong, and he knew that if he didn't do something soon, he was vamp food. He tried to say something, but his voice was less than a whisper. He tried again. "Let me go." It was barely audible, but the vampi heard him.

"What was that, Father?" he said, smiling. "I couldn't quite make that out."

He brought him down close to his ear. "Quickly, Father, I can hear your heart slowing down. Soon I'll be feasting on your lifeless corpse."

"Goodbye, devil." Father Connors's voice was still just a whisper, but it was crystal clear. The vampi looked at him, puzzled. Was he saying goodbye, or was he still holding onto some hope that he might escape? No matter, he was almost gone, and the vampi began thinking about joining the others on the roof once he'd dispatched the priest. His friend on the roof had genuine power emanating off him, and the vampi knew that killing him would sustain him and all of his group for days—maybe even a week. Then he heard it: a clicking sound that came from Father Connors's 357 snub-nose magnum when he cocked back the hammer. The barrel was pointed right under his chin. There was a loud bang and suddenly half of the vampi's face was missing. With the next shot, Father Connors took off the rest of his head. The vampi's headless corpse was still holding onto Father Connors's neck while blood sprayed from what was left of its neck and a few remaining pieces of its face.

Father Connors pried himself free and fell to the floor, gasping for air. He inhaled deeply, and as he filled his lungs with air, the color returned to his face. He began coughing and then threw up. The smell of the foul thing's blood was putrid, and he couldn't help himself. He got back to his feet and leaned against the wall for a moment to steady himself. He took a few more deep breaths and then started up the stairs. He didn't know how he was going to do it, but he had to help Ezekiel. The vampi had said that they were waiting for him up there. These damn things had set a trap for them. He knew something was wrong. It was all too easy. These things never told the truth. He rushed up to the roof as fast quickly as he could, laboring with his breath the whole way. It took him four minutes to reach the tenth floor, which was at the top of the building, but it felt like an eternity. He was out of breath and sweating profusely, but he couldn't let that stop him. Ezekiel was counting on his back-up and that's what he was going to do. He opened the door and rushed through, pointing his gun from side to side. There were bodies everywhere. Two by the door in front of him, another three on his right and two more on his left.

Ezekiel was fighting with the last one. His speed was blinding, and his moves were almost too fast for him the priest to follow, especially in the dark. He was so graceful as he fought that it almost seemed like he was dancing. There was something else too, but that couldn't be right—it looked to him like Ezekiel was glowing. He slammed the last one onto the rooftop with such force that the ground rumbled and vibrated under his feet. All Father Connors could do was stare at him in awe. How had he done all this in the time it took for him to get to the roof? It was nothing short of a miracle. But then he realized that him getting the drop on that vampire was a miracle too. He finally recognized the truth: it must just be that kind of night. He looked up to the sky and mouthed, "Thank you, Lord," and he was thankful.

A false witness will not go unpunished, and he who breathes out lies will perish.

                              —Proverbs 19:9 (ESV)

CHAPTER TWENTY-SIX

Vera and the Shadow

She could hear the muffled screams and popping crunching sounds of bones as they shattered between its teeth.

After running a few blocks, Vera finally felt fatigued and started walking. She was sure that Robbie was probably looking for her, but she didn't want to see him, not after what he had said. As she replayed it over again in her head, she began putting little things together...things that she hadn't picked up on before now. It was like this was all planned . . . the girls whisking her off to the bathroom, getting into her head, and getting her to open up about Robbie. She had already been upset, so when she overheard what Robbie said to Tommy, it overwhelmed her with emotion and she acted accordingly. She played it over in her head again, and this time she heard Tommy say all the things about Robbie being a virgin and a punk. She could remember feeling sorry—no, it was more like hurt for Robbie. But when Robbie had replied, it was like he was a different person. When he responded to Tommy, it was like he was back in that stairwell two years ago. She could feel the hatred coming off him in waves. There was something else too. He meant it. Everything he said was making a declaration of what was going to happen. There was no kindness in his words—or in him, for that matter. There was an underlying evil in his voice. He had somehow kept this hidden from her, but at the hotel she could sense the evil coming off of him. It wanted to consume her, and that was why she ran away. She kept walking while she was working things out in her mind and ended up on East Ninth Street. The flower district. It was deserted at that hour. She looked at her watch, surprised to see that an hour had passed from the time she left the hotel. She had been so lost in her thoughts; she hadn't noticed. Now that she was getting out of her head, she looked around and took in her surroundings. She also began noticing little things, like the shadows and sounds that seemed to be out of place. Without warning, it seemed like one of them moved, then another. She knew that couldn't be right. Her eyes must have been playing tricks on her in the dark. Maybe her eyes were still blurry from all the crying, she thought. But she knew better. There! Another one moved across the street, and she stood there for a moment to see if it would move again. Then she heard him. He had been in her head all this time, screaming at her to run away from this place, but she hadn't really paid attention until now. It was Joshua.

"Run, girl!" he said. "He's coming for you, now RUN!"

She looked up, and there he was: Nestor. He was across the street from her, beginning to emerge from the shadows. As she stared at him, she began to make out what looked like a smile on his face.

"RUUUUUNN NOW!" Joshua shouted again, and this time she took off. As she did, she turned around and looked over her shoulder to see if the thing in the shadows was still there, and to her horror, it seemed to be growing. It was getting taller and taller until it had grown to the size of one of the buildings around it. Then it started taking enormous steps toward her. She turned around and started running with all the speed she could muster. As she rounded the corner, she slipped a bit and one of her heels broke. She kept running, afraid to look back. She could almost feel the thing on top of her. She heard a voice in her head say, "Make a left here," and instinctively she followed the instruction of the voice in her head.

"Now turn right." She turned without thinking, and as she did, she looked behind her. The shadow thing was right behind her now and closing the distance between them quickly. It was too big for her to outrun. Every step it took was like twenty of hers. In a few moments, it would be on top of her. Just then, a homeless man startled her as he sat up from the cardboard blanket he was using to cover his body. She screamed out and almost tripped over him as he called out to her, "Hey, watch where you're going, Bi—" His voice trailed off. She turned around in time to see that shadow demon thing with the homeless man in its hand. It picked him up and threw him up over its head and caught him in its mouth, like a kid would do with a piece of popcorn. She could hear the muffled screams and popping crunching sounds of bones as they shattered between its teeth. Smiling all the while, it called out to her:

"You're next, girl."

It arched its head back to better swallow the remains of what used to be the man. She covered her mouth to keep herself from throwing up, but her body began heaving involuntarily. But she never stopped running, even as the remains of the mini egg rolls and pigs in a blanket exploded from her mouth, spilling onto her dress and shoes. Spit spewed from her lips as she made her way through a security door, which was left open. She ran down the hallway to the elevators. She frantically smashed the buttons, praying that the elevator doors would open and get her away from there. She could see the glass doors from across the corridor where she had just entered. She watched intensely and never stopped banging the elevator call button, hoping against hope that one of the doors would open soon. She could hear the electronic hum of machinery moving behind the closed doors as she continued to press the buttons. It felt like an eternity as she waited. A security guard appeared in the hall from the stairwell exit. He had heard all the banging and came to investigate. He rushed toward her. He could tell that she was distraught, borderline hysterical.

"Ma'am, please calm down. Tell me what's wrong, please. I'm here now. How can I help you?" But that was all he had time to say, as a giant hand grabbed him by the head and shoulders like he was a chess piece being moved across a board. She watched helplessly as it dragged him backward and out the glass door of the lobby entrance. She could see the demon's giant eye peeking through the entrance doors. It winked at her. Her heart stopped and then began pounding in her chest.

"Excuse me, darlings, I'll be rights with you in a sec."

Then it stood up and disappeared from the doorway for just a moment. There was a bloodcurdling scream, and then blood splattered across the glass doors and the screaming stopped. And then the demon was back. Its piercing eyes stared through the blood-stained glass. She could see it starting to stick its hand through the door and stretching across the lobby. Down the corridor, ever closer, toward her. She fell backward against the wall praying for the doors of the elevators to open. Its hand stopped just as it reached the threshold of the first elevator. She could see it shifting and changing as it reached for her. Almost like a cat's paw in a mouse hole trying to get hold of its prey—just outside its reach. For some crazy reason, just for a second, she felt a small relief watching the hand struggle to get to her and being just out of its reach. But then, to her horror, its arm began stretching like a rubber band, making its way closer and closer to her. She wanted to scream, but no sound escaped her lips.

"Almost gots you," she heard it say. "Almost there!"

Its hand stopped about an inch or two away from her face. Close enough for her to see and smell the blood on its fingers. She wanted to throw up again, but she couldn't move for fear of getting snagged by one of its fingernails and dragged away to be eaten. Then suddenly the hand, arm, and body started shrinking. The eyes outside of the door never released their gaze from her, and a moment later there was a tall, slender silhouette of what looked like a man, but the proportions were all wrong. It was just a little too thin and much too tall to be real. It began to walk toward her in such a way that it looked as if it were gliding across the floor. It stopped in front of her, looking down at her. It towered over her by what looked like two or three feet. It reached out and touched her cheeks, toying with her. She tried to turn her head, but its elongated fingers already had a grip on her face pinching her cheeks in between its thumb and pointer finger. It turned her head to face him as it looked her up and down, sizing her up—the way you do when you finally have something you have wanted for a long time, like a piece of cake. You take your time to savor the moment before you eat it. She could smell what could only be described as sewage. Its touch felt foul and cold. The demon smiled, revealing a mouth that had entirely too many teeth. She began to pray to herself, asking God to receive her soul and forgive her sins. This was it for

her, and she wanted God to know that she loved and trusted him
even now.

"He can't saves you now, little one. No one can. You're
mines now. Mines and mines alone."

"You're wrong," she said through clenched teeth. "You may
have my body, but not my soul. That belongs to God, and God
alone, and there's nothing you can do or say to change that."

The tone of her voice, even as a whisper, was strong and
powerful. The words themselves seemed to burn in his ears and he
grimaced. He thought it was incredible that even now, on this night
that belonged to him, she, a mere mortal, could have the power to
make him feel anything. This one was truly special: a chosen one. A
prize to be treasured. This, he knew, would make her taste twice as
sweet. He savored the moment as he wrapped his hands around her
neck with fingers so long they encircled her neck several times. She
could feel his grip tightening, and she lost her ability to swallow.
He arched his head back, opening his enormous mouth, and as he
did, saliva oozed out and dripped from his jaw, and he said:

"Let's see if you taste az good az your mothers did."

She thought, *What? Did he just say my* mother? She looked
into the thing's eyes and knew it was true. *Oh God,* she thought,
not Mom. Tears fell from her eyes at the realization of what had
happened to her mom. Her heart sank and was filled with anguish
and despair. This was the moment Nestor had been waiting for.
The loss of hope and moment of doubt. Now he would feast, and
she would be his. He leaned in, mouth agape, as he readied himself
to bite into her.

"Ding!" The elevator chimed, the doors opened, and Ezekiel
and Father Connors stepped off in time to see what was about
to happen.

"Nestor!" Ezekiel shouted while moving almost faster than the eye could track. He unsheathed the blade and lunged forward. He brought the blade down and caught Nestor across the side of his cheek, causing him to release the girl. The demon recoiled and stepped backward, holding his face. Screaming in an inhuman voice, he bounced from one wall to the other, cracking marble fixtures as he did. Almost instantly, he retreated backward toward the doorway, away from Ezekiel. He paused to look at the man who had cut him. He looked him up and down from head to toe and then back to his face. He wondered how this could have happened. Who was this man? Then anger and outrage exploded inside of him. He lunged at him wildly as his talon-like hands ripped through the grain of the porcelain tiles as he charged across the walls like an insect defying the laws of gravity.

Ezekiel stood his ground, in front of the girl, facing Nestor head-on with the blade in his hand. Acting on pure instinct, he leaped forward and lunged into Nestor's advance. He caught Nestor completely off balance. With a swift maneuver, Ezekiel eluded Nestor's attack and grabbed him by the neck, lifting him off the wall and slamming him onto the floor, creating a spider web crack in the marble floor. Nestor was completely shaken for a second time this night. Before he could process his indignation, he saw the blade coming down, piercing his shoulder and pinning him to the floor. He roared in what sounded like multiple voices, spewing obscenities in an unknown language. He thrashed and flailed about on the floor. Ezekiel rolled backward and up onto his feet. Father Connors now had Vera in his arms, and Ezekiel joined them. Not more than four or five seconds had passed from the time Ezekiel pinned Nestor to the floor to the time it took him to reach the two of them. When he turned back to face Nestor, the demon was gone. Only the blade remained stuck in the floor, stained with black blood.

Ezekiel scanned the hall and caught a faint image of Nestor's eyes in the doorway shadow.

"This day is yours, boy, but we will meet again. We will meet again indeed."

Then he faded completely into the darkness of the shadows.

He heard Joshua's voice in his head. "He's gone, but he will be back. He knows you now, and you hurt him. He will be coming for you, and he will want compensation in flesh."

And we know that for those who love God all things
work together for good, for those who are called
according to his purpose.

*—*Romans 8:28 (ESV)

CHAPTER TWENTY-SEVEN

The Elevator

The elevator came to a stop, and the door opened and
there she was: Vera. She was right in front of him.
But so was Nestor, the demon from his dreams.

Father Connors was a mix of emotions as he and Ezekiel
got onto the elevator. He was still trying to process the image
of Ezekiel charging through the air and fighting those creatures.
There were so many demons on that rooftop and just him, one
man alone with all of them. How had he put all of them down?
He was certain of one thing: Ezekiel was the one; God truly had
his hand on him. His heart was still racing, his body full of adrenaline, and he was terrified. What had he gotten himself into? He
couldn't fathom all that had happened the last few days. And
tonight had simply blown his mind. He wanted to be of more

help, but it was all he could do just to keep from being killed back on the staircase. EZ had just flown up the stairs effortlessly while he struggled. And when that vampire had grabbed him, he knew it was all over. Somehow, God had blessed him with the ability to escape his grip and fire his gun with precision. Had it not been for God's grace, he would have been vampire food for sure. Ezekiel was finishing up by the time he got to the roof, and what a finish it was. He ran out onto the roof, gun in hand, ready to blow away anything that moved, but after a few quick turns from right to left, he realized there was nothing left. There were about six or seven bodies down, and EZ had one in hand by the neck. He arrived just in time to see Ezekiel slam him onto the roof's surface, busting up the concrete as he did. The floor vibrated under his feet momentarily. He let go of the body and finally rose to his feet. He looked at Father Connors and noticed the bruises around his neck. The priest was bleeding and he knew he looked a little wobbly. Ezekiel sighed and asked, "You OK, Father? You don't look so good."

"Yeah, I'm OK now, but I sure could've used a little help a while ago. I almost..." He paused, swallowed deeply, cleared his throat, and then spoke. "I'm good. How about you, EZ?"

"I've seen better days; I can tell you that for sure. I'm sorry I took off like that, Father, I was just so caught up and blinded with anger. I shouldn't have left you like that. I don't know what I would have done if something had happened to you."

A half smile stole its way across the priest's face. Ezekiel returned a dry smile back at him.

"Are we good, Father?"

"Yeah, we're good, EZ. This is turning out to be a hell of a night though, I'll tell you that for nothing. We better get out of here before the cops or somebody come up here."

"True," Ezekiel said. "Surely someone has called the cops by now, with all the noise, and there would be no explaining our way out of this, not with all these bodies lying around."

They took another look at all the bodies. A couple of them had burst into flames and were turning to ash, but others were just people who had been possessed. When they were killed, their bodies remained.

"We need to go, EZ, right now. I think I hear voices. And we can't go back the same way we came up either. We have to find another way down."

"Yeah, that sounds like a plan, Father. Let's get over to the next building and go down that way."

They made their way to the rooftop next door and began their descent down the stairs when they heard what sounded like people making their way up toward them.

"What do you think, EZ, cops?"

"I'm not sure, but we can't get caught up here. Quick, Father, try the door on this floor, and I'll try the door on the next one."

They were both locked. They hurried to the next floor and tried that door, and it opened. They rushed through and closed the door behind them. A few seconds later they heard several people rushing by on their way up to the roof.

"Quick," Father Connors whispered, "that way," as he pointed to the elevator. The elevator door was open; they ran down the hallway and ducked inside. Father Connors pressed the lobby button and waited for the door to close. The elevator chimed, and the door closed. As soon as it did, they both let out a sigh of relief. *When will this night be over?* Father Connors thought. He went to wipe the sweat from his brow and noticed that his hand was shaking. He grabbed it with his other hand to steady it. Looking at the floor, he put his hands in his pockets. He looked up to see

Ezekiel looking at him. He did his best to reassure him, but he could tell by the look on his face that Ezekiel wasn't buying it.

"You gonna be OK, Father, once we get outta here?" Ezekiel asked.

He nodded but said nothing at first. Then he looked at Ezekiel and spoke in a voice that was barely a whisper. "How did you do that? Back on the roof. When I got there, all those men were dead. There wasn't enough time to do all that, and yet you did. It looked like you were flying, and just for a moment, you were glowing."

He looked down again for a second, and then back at Ezekiel, who was now looking at him intensely.

"I know I asked this before, and I hate to sound redundant, but who are you, man? Who are you really? Please don't get me wrong EZ, it's just there's so much I don't understand, and I just feel so useless. When we get back, we really need to talk about what we're doing, and where all of this is heading. I need to understand."

Ezekiel sighed and then nodded. He could tell that Father Connors was finally realizing the stakes of this game they were playing. The priest was unnerved and probably in shock. Tonight had already been more than just a little crazy, and all he wanted to do now was get back home and rest. That fight had taken a lot out of him and he felt exhausted.

"EZEKIEL, YOUR BLADE, QUICKLY!" a voice in his head shouted at him. It was Joshua, and there was a sense of panic and urgency in his voice. The sound of panic coming from Joshua was something very new to Ezekiel. "Ding!" The elevator came to a stop, the door opened, and there she was: Vera. She was right in front of him. But so was Nestor, the demon from his dreams. He had her pressed up against the wall, and it looked like he was about to bite her. Time seemed to slow down to a crawl. Without even realizing he was moving, Ezekiel was out the door, blade in hand.

He swung the blade up toward Nestor's face while simultaneously pulling Vera out of his grip. To Ezekiel's surprise, Nestor was startled. It seemed almost as if he was being pulled backward in some unnatural way as he recoiled from Ezekiel's assault.

Nestor's eyes were ablaze with fury and rage. This was a human; how could this be? How could a human even strike him, much less hurt him? This was the second time in less than a year that he had been made to suffer an affront to his person by a human. There was something not right with this boy who had struck him, and yet at the same time it was oddly familiar. The lights above them were flickering on and off. Some sparked and exploded. Shards of glass from the light bulbs fell to the floor tinkling and shattering as they hit the floor. Nestor held his cheek as thick black blood oozed from between his fingers. He bounced from one wall to the other until he reached the doorway of the building. Overcome with rage, he leaped forward, intending to rip Ezekiel apart and reclaim his prize, but his attack was thwarted by Ezekiel, and he found himself back at the doorway of the building wounded and confused. He looked at Father Connors and Ezekiel.

"This day is yours, boy, but we will meet again. We will meet again indeed."

Then he began to phase out of their reality and back into the realm of shadows. To everyone else, it seemed as if he merged with the shadows and then just disappeared.

"Jesus," Father Connors mouthed without uttering a sound. They all stared at the entrance door for a few seconds, mystified. "What was that, EZ? What in God's name was that?"

"It was him, Father. The man in the shade, the one who lurks in the shadows. And God has *nothing* to do with him. He's the thing that's been haunting my dreams."

Ezekiel was still holding Vera. He looked at her. She was shaking and muttering something incoherently. Her words were running over each other, which made everything she said sound like gibberish. The only words he was able to make out were, "my mother." Then her eyes rolled to the back of her head and her body went limp.

Father Connors was still looking toward the door where Nestor had been standing. His eyes were open wide and bloodshot, and his mouth agape. He looked at Ezekiel holding the girl. Still unable to speak, he thought, *He must be God sent, and God sent him to me.*

They didn't see any police in the hall and understood why the police hadn't seen Nestor. They were at the back exit of the building, and the police cars were around the corner. "We have to get out of here," Ezekiel whispered. "Quick. the police are around the corner. Let's cut through the alley before some of them decide to come back here."

Be sober-minded; be watchful. Your adversary the devil prowls around like a roaring lion, seeking someone to devour.

—1 PETER 5:8 (ESV)

CHAPTER TWENTY-EIGHT

Back at the Church

Vera's mind flashed back to the hallway. She couldn't get those eyes, or the feel of its touch, out of her head.

VERA WAS AWAKE FROM HER SLUMBER, AND TO HER DISMAY, SHE was by herself, or at least that was what she thought at first. Then she heard a voice:

"You awake now?"

It seemed to be coming from everywhere.

"Who are you?" she screamed. "What do you want from me?"

"Yous, I want yous . . . "

Again, the voice seemed to be coming from all around her. She looked around frantically, trying to get her bearings and figure out where she was and how she had gotten to this place. The last thing she remembered was running into a building and that thing chasing her.

"Who are you?" This time, the voice was much more focused. She was coming out of her daze. Father Connors was sitting across from her in a wooden chair with no arms. It looked hard and uncomfortable, and from the look on his face, she could tell he had been sitting there for a while.

"How are you feeling now? You were having a pretty rough go of it for the last hour or so."

"How long have I been here?" she asked "And where is this place?"

"You're in my church; you're safe now. I'm Father Connors, and you're Vera, I take it, right?"

She looked him up and down, scrutinizing him as she did. "How do you know my name?"

"It's a long story," Father Connors answered, "but we've been looking for you for a while now."

"We? Who's we? And why?"

Then she remembered the other man—the one who had rescued her. "Are you guys some kind of perverts or something?"

She knew they weren't; she could sense that kind of thing in people. She was just disappointed, angry, and scared. She wanted to go home, but she also wanted to know who he was, the man who suddenly appeared and saved her. They both seemed familiar—no, more like safe.

She seemed to drift off for a few seconds, but then she came back to the present. Father Connors thought she was just disoriented after everything she had just gone through.

"No, we're not perverts," he replied. "Ezekiel and I, we've—well, I guess I should say he's been looking for you for quite some time now. Although I must admit that at times, I wasn't sure you truly existed. Ezekiel, on the other hand, never had a doubt. But neither one of us expected to find you in the hallway of that building. Why was that thing after you? Do you know?"

Vera's mind flashed back to the hallway. She couldn't get those eyes, or the feel of its touch, out of her head. The stench of him. It was so bad she could still taste it. She sat up and clasped her head with both hands while looking down at her feet.

"No, I don't know why that thing was after me. Whatever it was chasing me. I just know that it's not of this earth. I know how that sounds, but it's true."

The words did not come easy for her. Her voice was gruff and shaky. A few tears welled up and escaped from the corners of her eyes as she spoke.

"All I know is that when it touched me," she paused, "it was like poison; it felt like it was draining my life's energy—no, my very soul—from me. Then he appeared, and when he, your friend, um—"

"Ezekiel," Father Connors said.

"Yes, Ezekiel, when he touched me and pulled me out of that thing's grip, I could feel his energy coursing through me. It was radiating all around him. It made me feel safe. It also made me feel somehow better. I don't know, it's hard to explain."

But Father Connors knew exactly what she was talking about. He had felt it too, many times now since meeting Ezekiel, and it never got old.

Ezekiel walked in, and they both looked up at him. Father Connors smiled and motioned for him to come in. Vera said nothing. She was still trying to clear her head and understand her connection to him. Try as she might, she couldn't take her eyes off Ezekiel. She felt drawn to him. He gave her a sense of belonging, of completion, like she should be with him.

"How are you feeling—better?" he asked.

She nodded, indicating she was okay.

"My name is Ezekiel, but you can call me EZ. You've already met Father Connors, and I know you've probably got a lot of questions for me. But first, if you don't mind, may I ask you, how did you come to be in that building last night? And do you know why that thing wanted to harm you?"

Vera started to speak, but her voice was so low it was barely audible. She cleared her throat and then began again. "My name is Vera."

"I know," Ezekiel said.

She looked up sharply at that. "How do you know me?" she asked

"I'll tell you everything in a moment, but first I need to know why you were there with him."

She looked down again before she replied. "I was at a party, and then I got mad and left." She didn't want to get into the details of why, and it didn't seem like Ezekiel was interested in the reason in any case. So she went on. "As I was walking home, that thing started chasing me. I ran into that building, and then you showed up and somehow chased it away. Now, why were you there? Oh yeah, thank you for saving me. I'm sure I would be dead if it weren't for you."

Ezekiel smiled at that last part. He couldn't help it, mainly because he knew she was right. Nestor certainly meant to kill her. He could sense his hatred for her. "Well, Vera," the way he said her name—no, scratch that, the way he spoke period—was so soothing, she thought. She was staring at his mouth as if trying to read the words in the air as they left his lips.

"It was just dumb luck that we were there at the same time. "

"I doubt it was luck, EZ," Father Connors said. "That was divine intervention if I've ever seen it."

Ezekiel gave a slight smile again. Vera, however, remained fixated on the sound of his voice and the way his words seemed to hang in the air. She still didn't speak.

"You asked how I know you. It's a bit hard to explain, and it's going to sound crazy, but I know you from my dreams. I've been seeing you in my mind's eye for long as I can remember. I know you like Cherry Coke from the fountain but not from the can. You like the way the ground smells after it rains on hot summer days and the sound of birds chirping early in the morning. I also know that you believe that sometimes even when things don't make sense, no matter how strange, you can see that they are true. Like the way you can see things about people, tell when they're lying, or sometimes you can hear someone's thoughts."

She was staring at him directly now. Not looking at his mouth or listening to the tone in his voice; she was fascinated. "How do you know this? I never told anyone about that, not even my mother."

"Because I'm like you, and I think my whole life has been leading up to this moment. But this is just the beginning. The creature that was chasing you is old. It has been around for thousands of years, and it's pure evil. I believe it was once an angel—not just any angel, but probably an archangel that fell in the great war in heaven. It's extraordinarily powerful, and it gets stronger with every day that passes. I think it has to do with the times we live in. Everything is upside down. Right is wrong; wrong is right. People make excuses for lies, wrong behavior, greed, larceny, blasphemy, and the exclusion of God. All of this has made it the perfect time for him to rise. The living plagues are among us now. We are truly in the last days. And for reasons that have not yet been made clear to me, God has seen fit to bring us all together. We probably need each other to defeat him.

"I don't question it; I simply go with it. It has always worked out better for me when I do. I've already learned some lessons the hard way, and it cost me five years of my life."

Ezekiel shook his head and grinned while rubbing his eyes. Vera smiled at him. He was very handsome and, just for the briefest of moments, she forgot herself and blushed.

Father Connors recognized the connection between the two of them instantly. The energy that was radiating from them was unreal. He could almost see and feel it in the air.

These two have both been touched by God, he thought. He fought back tears, but a few escaped and ran down his cheek. He sniffled and cleared his throat as he wiped his eyes. Then he said, "Vera." She turned sharply, like someone had physically pulled her gaze away from Ezekiel. "Where are your people?"

"My people? What do you mean?

"Your family, Vera, where are they? We need to let them know you are safe and get them here. That thing and its minions are out there, and they may go after them."

Her eyes opened wide as the memory of his words hit home. That thing, back in the hallway, it had said something about—"My mother!" She jumped to her feet, stumbling a bit at first as she tried to put on her shoes and hopped toward the door. "I must get to my mother." She was in a panic as the words played over and over in her mind.

What had the demon said? "Let's see if you taste as sweet as your mother did."

Horrified at the thought of that thing touching her mother, she slipped on her shoes as she scurried past the two men.

"Vera, wait for us. We are coming too, and we need to know exactly what it said to you."

The sound of Ezekiel's voice resonated a soothing effect, and it momentarily calmed her enough for her to slow down and speak coherently. "It said that it wanted to see if I tasted as good as my mother! That's what it said. But that thing doesn't know where I live, right? I've never seen it before. It must've just been saying that to hurt me, right?" Her voice cracked and her eyes welled up with tears as the words left her lips. Ezekiel didn't want to upset her further.

"Vera, this thing is a liar, but if it said that to you, I fear the worst for your mother."

"Well, I'm going now," said Vera. "I need to know that's she's OK. I have to let her know she's in danger."

"All right, but we will do this together. You must let us protect you," Ezekiel said. "Which means you must listen to me when I tell you something. That thing is out there, and we have made it extremely angry. It wants you, and the last thing your mother would want would be for you to go running straight into its arms. We have to be smart about this."

Father Connors held out a phone to her. "Call your mother first. Let her know you are on your way and not to open the door for anyone until you get there."

Ezekiel said, "It's still dark out; we should wait until first light before we go out. The night belongs to it. If we go out now, we must be careful. I can't risk losing you. Not after I've just found you. I just can't." His voice cracked, and he paused before he spoke again. "Call your mother, and then we will go together."

This was the first time in almost a year that Father Connors has seen anything upset Ezekiel. And it made him uneasy.

Vera took the phone. She didn't know why; she just felt compelled to listen to Ezekiel. "All right then. I'll call, and then we can all go together."

She dialed her mother's number. No answer. Then she hung up and called her mother's cell phone. Still no answer. She looked up, glassy-eyed, voice cracking, and said, "No one's picking up. I called both lines, but they both went to voicemail. We have to go now." She started toward the door, and Ezekiel and Father Connors followed her out.

Outside the church, Ezekiel asked Father Connors for his rosary. He gave it to him without asking why. Ezekiel cupped it in his hands and began to pray over it.

"Dear Lord, please continue to keep us safe under the umbrella of your grace and mercy. Please guard our steps and guide our actions. Allow us to make it to and from our destinations without harm or incident. And please protect us from the enemy who is actively pursuing your servants. Thank you for your strength and love. In Jesus's name, I pray. Amen." Then he handed the rosary to Vera. "No matter what we find, trust in God always."

She nodded but said nothing. The truth was she didn't know what to say. All of this was completely new to her, and she didn't have the time now to try and figure it out. For now, she just needed to get home to her mother. There was something special about the rosary he had handed her, she could tell. It was as if it was generating energy of some kind. It made her feel calm and safe, and that was just what she needed right now.

The righteous cry, and the LORD heareth, and delivereth them out of all their troubles.

—PSALM 34:17

CHAPTER TWENTY-NINE

Vera's House

At this point, Robbie felt a hole open in the pit of his stomach. Tears started to roll down his cheeks as he asked, "Is it Vera? Is she OK?"

ROBBIE WAS WAITING OUTSIDE OF VERA'S APARTMENT BUILDING. There were police cars and officers everywhere. Something bad had happened there, and Robbie was freaking out because he hadn't seen or heard from Vera since the party. He kept trying to get into the building, but the cops held him at bay. Then he thought to ask one of them if all of this had to do with apartment 5A or Vera McNulty. He was immediately ushered in past the barricade and taken to the lead detective on the scene.

"Detective Kelly, son, what do you know about the McNultys, and how are you connected to them?"

"Is Vera OK? Can I see her?"

"First answer my questions, son. Who are you and what's your relationship with the McNulty family?"

At this point, Robbie felt a hole open in the pit of his stomach. Tears started to roll down his cheeks as he asked, "Is it Vera? Is she OK? I was just with her last night."

"Where did you see her last? And can anyone confirm your whereabouts last night and that she was OK when she left you?"

"Um, yeah, we were at a party together. There was an entire room of people there that can confirm that. We kinda had a falling out. Then I got into it with some people at the party, which was the reason Vera left the party without me. I chased after her, but she had already gone. I thought I would give her some time to cool off and then come see her in the morning. That's why I'm here. Now, can you please tell me what is going on?"

"We are going to need you to come with us and give a formal statement. At present, we don't know Vera's whereabouts. However, based on what we have so far, this looks like a homicide."

Robbie looked up sharply. "Her mother? Oh no, this is awful. What happened? How?"

"We can't go into further details while this is an active investigation. For now, we're just going to head into the station and take that statement."

Come to me, all who labor and are heavy laden, and
I will give you rest.

—MATTHEW 11:28 (ESV)

CHAPTER THIRTY

Reunions

Her voice radiated power at that moment, and the
officer and Robbie both said "OK" in unison. It
was almost as if they had been hypnotized.

VERA LOOKED OVER AT EZEKIEL AND BACK AT THE ROSARY. THEN
she put it around her neck and tucked it under her dress. When
they got to Vera's street, they saw all the commotion in front of her
house. They already knew what it was, but no one said anything;
they just made their way through the crowd to Vera's apartment
building. Vera could see Robbie up ahead and pulled free from
Ezekiel's hand to rushed toward him. She called out to him and,
despite all the commotion, he heard her. He called out her name,
but he couldn't go to her because Detective Kelly was holding his
arm. Vera rushed up to him and asked Robbie, "What's going on?"

Ezekiel turned and said, "Father, go after her. I . . ." he paused for a second, and then said, "I'm a convicted felon. A murderer. No matter what I say, this just won't look good for me. So you must go with her and stay close to her for me. I will be close by."

Father Connors could tell that Ezekiel was nervous, but he just nodded and caught up to Vera.

"Vera!" Robbie shouted, looking in her direction and pulling free of the officer who had been holding him by the elbow leading him to the squad car. He rushed toward her. They embraced, holding each other for a long moment, and then Robbie whispered, "I'm sorry" in her ear. "I should never have said those things."

"Robbie, that's not important right now. Do you know why all these police are here?" Her heart was racing as she asked, hoping against hope. But before Robbie could answer, the officer that was walking him to the police car interrupted.

"Excuse me, miss, may I have your name, please?"

"It's Vera, Vera McNulty. I live here. What's going on? Why are all of you here? I have to get home; I need to see my mother."

"Miss McNulty, I'm going to need you to come with us down to the station house."

"Why?" she said, looking at the officer with fearful eyes. "Is it my mother?"

"Ms. McNulty, please, can you just come with us and we will explain everything down at the station?"

"I'm not going anywhere until I get to see my mother," she shouted.

Her voice radiated power at that moment, and the officer and Robbie both said "OK" in unison. It was almost as if they had been hypnotized. The officer led them through the crowd and into the apartment building. There seemed to be even more police officers inside. Some looked at them, while others avoided making eye contact. The officer led them to Vera's apartment and said, "Wait here." A few moments later, Detective Kelly came to the door.

"Ms. McNulty, I'm Detective Kelly. I understand you want to come inside right now, but this is an active crime scene. Only authorized personnel are being allowed in. Please let us do our jobs and go with my officer to the police station. I will be with you as soon as we have finished here."

"No. I WANT TO SEE MY MOTHER NOW!"

Her voice was like thunder, erupting in everyone's heads within earshot.

Without knowing why, detective Kelly walked her into the apartment. Instantly, she recognized Nestor's horrible scent and tears began welling up in her eyes. That thing had been there, and she knew immediately that her mother was dead. She noticed the blood trail on the floor leading to her mother's bedroom. She didn't want to go any further for fear of what she might see, but she had to know for sure. Vera opened the door to her mother's bedroom. The detectives in the room had not covered her mother's body yet. Vera looked at the mutilated remains that used to be her mother in horror. She thought, "This can't be my mother," and yet she knew it was. The limbs of her upper extremities had been torn off and tossed about the room. There were bite marks on her neck and torso. And her face was gone. Blood was everywhere, and the smell of it sickened her. She lowered her head and closed her eyes while covering her nose and mouth with her hands. Her legs felt like jelly, and she could feel herself sinking to the floor. How could anything do this to another living being? There was a pool of blood between her mother's legs, and Vera knew what that meant and what the demon had done to her. She began sobbing uncontrollably. She was filled with sorrow and anger. Her legs and knees were no longer stable and gave out. She slumped over and fell. Fortunately, Father Connors caught her before she hit the floor.

Detective Kelly and Robbie hadn't noticed Father Connors standing there until that moment. Neither one of them could remember if he had always been there or had just walked up. Had he been alongside Vera all this time and they just didn't notice until now?

"Who are you," Detective Kelly asked, "and why are you in the middle of my crime scene? None of you should be in here."

"I'm Father Connors, Detective, and I've been with Vera this whole time."

Robbie looked him up and down, very confused. He couldn't for the life of him remember seeing him before this moment.

"I was with her last night when she was attacked by some creep on the street."

"She was attacked last night?" Detective Kelly asked. He looked the priest up and down inquisitively. "All right. I'm going to need you to come down to the station and give a detailed statement, starting with your relationship with Vera and what your part is in all of this. In fact, I'm going to need all of you to come with me now."

Robbie helped Father Connors get Vera to her feet, and they were all ushered outside into two separate squad cars. Vera and Robbie were together in one car, and Father Connors rode in the other.

Ezekiel watched from a distance as the three of them were escorted from the premises and driven away. He was worried about Vera, but he felt good knowing Father Connors would be with her. But who was that other person who had gotten in the car with Vera? He noticed that one of the officers on the scene's badge read 15th, and he figured they were taking them to the nearest LAPD precinct. He rushed back to the car, got directions on his phone on how to get there, and drove off.

For we wrestle not against flesh and blood, but against principalities, against powers, against the rulers of the darkness of this world, against spiritual wickedness in high places.

—EPHESIANS 6:12

CHAPTER THIRTY-ONE

The House

It floated through the air and into Nestor's hand and eventually took the form of some hideous thing. A lower demon.

IN EVERY NEIGHBORHOOD, THERE ALWAYS SEEMS TO BE ONE scary house. Maybe it's because of ghost stories that someone might have told about the house, or maybe it's because of the people who live—or lived—there. Whatever the reason, that house is generally avoided. Well, 324 Figueroa Street was one of those houses. Oh, it looked normal enough from a distance. But if you took the time to look more closely, you would notice that no matter the time of day, somehow the sun never really seemed to shine on it. Dogs and cats would cross the street rather than simply walk past it. Even birds wouldn't fly over it. Standing in front of it would cause chills to run through your body. It was a gray building with stairs leading up to the front doorway and two windows on either side of the front door. But if you went inside, it was like crossing over into a different plane of existence—a place of pure evil. In fact, it was just the type of place that a creature like Nestor would be drawn to.

"WHO IS HE! WHERE DID HE COMES FROM?" Nestor roared. "HOW WAS HE ABLES TO STRIKES ME?"

He screamed out in frustration, disbelief, and anger. He was pacing from one side of the room to the other, smashing his fist into the walls as he did.

"She was in my hands, and then this boy showed up and somehow wrenched her away from me."

He touched his swollen cheek that was oozing and sore. How was this even possible, he wondered. No weapon forged by man could harm him, but that would mean that the blade that had cut him was not of this world. He asked himself the same questions over and over, getting angrier each time. Then the voices in the room whispered, "The foretold. The foretold. The foretold. He is the one who has been foretold."

Nestor spun around the room recklessly as the voices whispered. Furiously, he held out his hand toward one of the voices in the room, and one shadow pulled away from the wall and took shape. It floated through the air and into Nestor's hand, eventually taking the form of some hideous thing—a lower demon.

"Speaks plain," Nestor exclaimed, "or I promise you'll pray for a death that will never come as I peel the very fiber of your being away piece by piece over and over again for eternity. Now, what were you going on abouts?"

The demon looked at Nestor. It was a bit surprised but dared not express it. It tried to speak while wiry fingers pressed hard against its throat.

"The foretold—the child of David with the ability to lay hands on our kind and angels alike. Even you spoke of him before. It has been rumored that he was born dead but death could not hold him. Though he be mortal, it is said that he can walk among angels, and no shadows can exist in his light. He's bound by no restraints and governed by God's will alone. He is able to smite the unrighteous with a touch of his finger. He and another, a priest, have started a campaign of their own to send our kind to that final sleep before our time."

Nestor squeezed even harder now as he shouted,

"How is it I am just learning that he is here, in this place at this time? Surely one of you have seen or known of this foretold one's whereabouts before now? How could someone like this not be seen or felt by me? HE CUT ME! And how is it you knew that he was here, and I did not? HOW?"

Black blood now oozed down his arm and between his fingers as the head of the demon fell from his hand and to the floor. Waves of energy shot out from him like ripples in a pond ripping through everything in their path. Shadows in the room and on the wall exploded into smoke as they were hit.

"Finds him, this foretold one. Finds him NOW!"

There was another explosive wave of energy, and with that, all the rest of the shadows departed from the room. Nestor stood in the center of the empty room, motionless, as the very fabric of reality warped and shimmered. Nestor reached out and physically touched the minds of his minions and everyone he had ever possessed. He looked through their eyes, searching for the mortal who had cut him and the girl he had taken from him. No one on earth could take anything away from him, and there was no place on this earth that a mere mortal could hide and escape his wrath. Because this earth was his to walk to and fro and devour whomever he may.

"I want his blood, and I would have it this night!"

Suddenly, it hit him! He knew who the man was! He had held him in his hands and almost tasted his soul. Somehow, he had gotten away and remained hidden. But Nestor was determined to find him again.

"I'll find him and destroy him. I'll destroy him and that girl. The priest as well. That priest, he was with him when I saw him before, both times! I will have the priest for dessert."

He spoke the words, but for the first time in a millennium, he was unsure.

No weapon that is formed against thee shall prosper;
and every tongue that shall rise against thee in
judgment thou shalt condemn. This is the heritage of
the servants of the LORD, and their righteousness is
of me, saith the LORD.

—Isaiah 54:17

CHAPTER THIRTY-TWO

Eyes of the Shadow

They were all praying. Their voices, while
only whispers, were clear and beautiful.

VERA, ROBBIE, AND FATHER CONNORS WERE ALL BEING INTERviewed separately. While their stories seemed believable on the surface, Detective Kelly felt like there was something off about Father Connors. There was something else that the priest wasn't telling him. However, he was able to corroborate Vera's story about this mysterious man who had attacked her. At this point, it was looking like this might be the same person who attacked her mother.

Ezekiel waited outside the station for a bit. He wanted to go in, but he knew that wouldn't be a good idea. Ex-cons rarely make for good witnesses, and their motives are always questioned. For now, all he could do was wait. He decided to head back to the church and wait for them there. He realized that they might be at the police station for quite some time. He was in deep thought about what to do with Vera. He knew she was special. He had felt her power while he was outside her apartment earlier. This thing would surely come looking for her—and him, too, for that matter. Just then, he felt as if he was being watched. He looked up sharply and noticed two people staring in his direction. Then they turned their gaze to his left and back over to his right. They kept that up, even as Ezekiel walked past them. Even then, Ezekiel still felt like eyes were upon him. He looked up and noticed a woman in an apartment building looking down directly at him. He stared back at her, and then she shifted her gaze like the others had. He noticed a dark aura around her; he turned to look at the men who that had passed him and noticed they had dark auras around them as well. But it was more than that. Their auras were the same. This was impossible; everyone's energy signature or aura is different, and yet these were the same. Then it dawned on him. It was him. Somehow, he was using these people to look for him. *Only they don't seem to be able to see me.* He thought on that for a moment. Why couldn't they see him? Was this Joshua's doing?

"It's God, Ezekiel," Joshua whispered. "You are not meant to be seen by him until the right time. But do not toil or test His grace, or you could find yourself outside of it."

All right, so they can't see me for now by His grace, but can they see Vera or Father Connors? he wondered. He prayed, "Lord, watch over them, and please keep them safe." Then he quickly hurried back to the church. As he got there, he noticed four angels, one at each corner of the building. They were all praying. Their voices, while only whispers, were clear and beautiful to Ezekiel. He stood outside and watched them for a minute, in awe of their power and beauty. He could feel the energy they had created all around the church. He could feel the presence of God all around him, and he knew that Vera and Father Connors were safe. He walked into the church, sat down in the pew by the altar, and began praying as well. As he did, he could feel his prayers blending with the angels and was amazed. At the same moment, Vera felt a chill go down her spine in the police station. She suddenly had an overwhelming compulsion to get back to the church and back to Ezekiel. She looked around the room, feeling a little embarrassed. She noticed Robbie looking at her with an expression on his face that she could read clear as day.

"What is it?" he silently mouthed, and she just shook her head and mouthed, "It's nothing." She could tell he didn't believe her, but that would just have to do for now. She wondered why she was thinking about Ezekiel, and why she wished he was there with her now.

*Though I walk in the midst of trouble, thou wilt
revive me: thou shalt stretch forth thine hand against
the wrath of mine enemies, and thy right hand
shall save me*

—PSALM 138:7

CHAPTER THIRTY-THREE

The Police Station

*Her voice rattled the building and what can only be
described as a wave of energy expanded from her body and
throughout the station like a pebble being tossed in a pond.*

VERA WAS SITTING ON A WOODEN BENCH WITH ROBBIE AND
Father Connors. She couldn't help noticing how dated everything
looked around her. The walls looked stale and dingy. The interroga-
tion room she had been in earlier had smelled like a combination of
BO, bad cologne, and old coffee. She was happy to be out of there.
Now they were just waiting for the ride detective Kelly had said he
would arrange for them. That couldn't happen soon enough as far
as she was concerned. She couldn't explain it, but she just couldn't
shake this feeling that she had to get back to Ezekiel. And then a
chill ran down her spine. Goosebumps popped up on her arms and

legs, and the hairs on her neck were standing up. She suddenly had
the overwhelming feeling that she was being watched. She looked
around and noticed two people in the station looking in her direction with odd expressions on their faces. Then they turned their
gaze on someone else in the station. They kept shifting from one
side to the other, sweeping over the room. Somehow, she knew
it was him; it was Nestor looking for her. She looked at Father
Connors, who was looking back at her. He used his eyes to gesture
for her to look over in the direction of the men. She gave an under-
standing nod back. Then she looked over to Robbie to grab his
hands and noticed that he had the same look on his face as the
others. As he looked at her, it felt more like he was looking through
her—as if he couldn't see her at all. A tear fell from her eye and
down her cheek. She couldn't bear the thought of losing Robbie
to this monster. She reached out and grabbed hold of his hand.
He looked at her with a blank gaze. She stared deep into his eyes
cutting through the fog in his brain until she got to the source of
his current state, "Nestor." It felt to her like she was looking at him
with her own eyes.

"Theres you are," he said, beginning to smile. "I've beens
looking for—"

But she cut him off mid-sentence with a shout: "Release him!
Release him *now!*" Then he was gone from her sight, and Robbie
was looking at her. He was a bit confused, but he was himself again.

"Release who?" Robbie asked.

"You," she said with a hint of a smile. It quickly faded as her
attention turned back to the other people in the room who were
still in that dazed state, looking from one side of the room to the
other without seeing them. It was like they were sleepwalking. She
lowered her head, took a deep breath, and shouted, "RELEASE
THEM ALL!" Her voice rattled the building, and what can only

be described as a wave of energy expanded from her body and throughout the station like a pebble being tossed in a pond. All the windows in the building were blown out. The lights and phone lines all went out as well, but just for a moment. They all came back on a few seconds later. Vera was shocked when no one asked her why she had shouted out. As best as she could tell, no one even heard her. Everyone in the station had returned to normal. There were no more blank looks on anyone's face. The officers in the station concluded that there must have been an earthquake to explain the windows blowing out, along with the lights and phones cutting off. Everyone seemed to agree—everyone except Robbie and Father Connors, who were both staring at her in awe.

Three months had passed since the night in the police station. There were times when they would see a person with that blank look on their face looking around blindly. They would release them when they could, but most of the time, they would have to leave them in that state. Anonymity was their best ally, and they didn't want to make any unnecessary mistakes and draw any unwanted attention to themselves. Every action was well thought out and planned. Father Connors found that he was praying more and more these days. He wasn't sure if it was the influence that Ezekiel was having on him, all the past events, or a combination of it all. It was probably the latter, but in any case, he felt his relationship with God had greatly improved, and he couldn't be happier with that, despite the circumstances.

Ezekiel had been accompanying Vera back and forth to school. She was staying with him and Father Connors at the church now. Ezekiel had gone to her old place and cleaned everything up, but

Vera couldn't bring herself to go back to her place, much less stay there knowing what had happened in that apartment. Father Connors stepped up and became Vera's guardian, so she didn't have to get placed in the system.

Ezekiel and Vera's relationship grew almost immediately. The energy that came off the two of them when they were together was amazing. It was a palpable, tangible force that could be felt all around them. The two of them seemed to be unaware of it, but everyone else could see it plain as day—especially Robbie, and he didn't like it at all. He had watched their relationship grow, and while he knew in his heart that Ezekiel was not trying to steal his girl, he couldn't help being jealous of them. His and Vera's relationship had never quite been the same since the night of the party. He wished they had never gone; then maybe none of this would have happened, and Vera's mom might still be alive. He wished things could go back to the way they were before all this. Now the only time he was able to spend with her was at school, and they were approaching the end of the year. He didn't know where she was staying, even though he had walked her home from school many times, with Ezekiel as their escort. For some reason, he could never remember where he had dropped her off when he tried later. It was like he would lose time and find himself back in front of the school. For the life of him, he couldn't explain that, not to mention that he was getting tired of Ezekiel always being in the middle of things. Oh, he seemed friendly enough on the surface, but there was something about him that Robbie didn't like. At least, he thought, all of this was going to change soon. Tomorrow after school, he was going to take Vera out, maybe see a movie or get something to eat—anything other than what they had been doing. They needed this, and if Ezekiel tried to get in the way or interfere, well then, he would be dealt with. Enough was enough already with him. Robbie was so frustrated and angry about the situation that he hadn't real-ized he had been talking out loud to himself. People looked at him a bit oddly as they passed by. He felt a little silly and then looked at his watch to check the time. He sucked his teeth; it was time to head to work. He had to be there in an hour, and his first client was Thomas Smyth. That guy creeped him out. Maybe it was the way he was always biting his fingernails or the way he would look at him like he wanted to eat him or something ... or the way he spoke like he knew something you didn't know. Maybe it was all of that, maybe it was nothing, or maybe this seemingly harmless and nerdy little guy reminded him of how he used to be. But there was something else too—something hiding behind his eyes, some-thing dangerous. He recognized it because it was the same look he had in his own eyes, the same look he had when he'd fought Joey and Brian in the stairwell and when he'd heard that voice in his head. He thought on that for a bit while he hurried off to work, still checking his watch every so often to make sure he was on time.

What the wicked dreads will come upon him, but the desire of the righteous will be granted.

—PROVERBS 10:24 (ESV)

CHAPTER THIRTY-FOUR

Blind Rage

He began throwing things around the room, cursing and smashing everything he could get his hands on.

A FEW MINUTES PASSED, AND THEN HE SAW HER. *FOUND YOU*, HE thought, but something seemed off. It was as if it was him that was being watched instead of the other way around. No matter, he thought. He tried to focus on her, but everything around her was blurred. Then she was looking directly at him and vice versa. "There you are," he said, smiling, "I've been look—" but before he could finish his sentence, he started screaming and dropped to his knees, covering his eyes as he twisted his head back and forth. He could no longer see her. But before he could express his rage, he screamed out again in aguish, clasped his face and, begun rocking back and forth.

"So manys! She tooks them from me!"

He began throwing things around the room, cursing and smashing everything he could get his hands on. After a moment or two passed, he began to regain his composure. He looked up from the floor and out one of the dirty windows in the room. Black blood was dripping from his eyes.

"This is not overs, not evens a little. I wills finds you and when I do, I wills release yous from your life by peelings the very flesh from your bodys and devouring your souls."

*Therefore rejoice, ye heavens, and ye that dwell in
them! Woe to the inhabitants of the earth and of the
sea! for the devil has come down unto you, having
great wrath, because he knoweth that he hath but a
short time. And when the dragon saw that he was
cast unto the earth, he persecuted the woman which
brought forth the man child.*

—REVELATIONS 12:12–13

CHAPTER THIRTY-FIVE

Thomas Smyth— Decision

*Under normal circumstances, his boss would never
have agreed to something like this, but something was
whispering to him, almost compelling him to agree.*

WEEK TWELVE OF HIS TRAINING, AND HE WAS STILL NOT SEEING
the results he had hoped for. Oh, his arms and abs had a little more
tone to them, but it was nothing like he was led to believe when
he'd signed up for a trainer. What made him even angrier was that

his trainer, Robbie, had bulked up and shredded his body over the same period of time. Why wasn't he training *him* the same way he was training *himself*? That little pretty boy was cheating him. It wasn't right, and he was going to address it. Either Robbie was going to make it right, or he was.

Robbie came to the front desk and greeted him while he was in mid thought. "How's it going, Tom?"

"I told you before, my name is *Thomas*, not Tom."

"Sorry, I meant nothing by it. I just thought we were in a different place than we were a few months ago."

"How so? You're just my trainer, not my friend, and just an okay one at that. If I weren't paying for your services, would you still be training me?"

Robbie was silent. This was just what he needed today. "Hey, Thomas," he said with an air of sarcasm, "I don't know what's bothering you today, but that's not cool. If you just want to keep this professional, that's fine with me. But there's no need to be rude or disrespectful."

Thomas smirked at that and replied, "You know what? You're right. Let's just get to it and forget all about this for now."

Robbie shrugged and got started with Thomas's session, doing his best not to let his feeling of disgust show. At the end of the hour, Robbie collected his equipment and said goodbye, and then he went to his next appointment. He couldn't get away from the guy quickly enough for his liking. Thomas headed to the showers, thinking about how he could make Robbie pay. He needed to be taught a lesson so he would know his place. Something to take him down a peg or two, and then he would get him on the table. He smiled at that. It was time to put this plan into action.

After he had gotten cleaned up, Thomas made his way over to Robbie's manager's office and made a formal complaint, demanding compensation immediately as well as an apology from Robbie or his job. Under normal circumstances, his boss would never have agreed to something like this, but something was whispering to him, almost compelling him to agree.

Robbie was at the front desk checking guests in as they entered the gym when he was called into Mr. Miranda's office. This was a normal enough occurrence, so he didn't think anything about it. When he got there, however, he saw Thomas sitting in one of the chairs with his back to him.

"Come on in, Robbie, and close the door behind you".

Right away, he knew this was going to be bad. He did as directed, not sure of what was going on.

"You know Mr. Smyth, I take it?"

Robbie nodded yes but said nothing.

Mr. Miranda looked down at his hands as he placed them on top of his desk and crossed his fingers. Then he spoke again. "Well, it has come to my attention that you were rude and disrespectful to Mr. Smyth today during your session with him."

"That's not true, I—" Before Robbie could finish, his boss cut him off.

"I wasn't finished speaking yet. As I was saying, Mr. Smyth told me you snapped at him and continued to call him by some nickname that he told you to stop calling him by on multiple occasions. Is that true?"

Robbie was surprised and taken aback by all of this. He didn't even know how to respond or how to contain himself. He was livid. His face had turned red, and his fists were clenched. This little creep had really gone overboard with this nonsense, and his boss for some reason was not only taking Thomas's side, but he was coming at him hard. It was almost like he had been hypnotized or something.

"Well, Robbie? I'm waiting. Did you do these things Mr. Smyth is accusing you of or not?"

"Well, no, not exactly. I called him Tom, but I didn't mean anything by it. He got loud with me. I told him that was unnecessary, and from now on we would just keep things professional. Then we completed his session, and that was the end of it. It seemed like we were good, so I don't understand what all this is about."

"So, you did have an altercation with him then?"

"Well, I wouldn't call it an altercation. We just cleared a few things up, that's all."

"Well, it seems like it was a little more than that. Mr. Smyth is our customer and pays us—you—to provide a service, not call him out of his name or make him feel unappreciated. You owe him an apology."

"A what? An apology for what? You can't be serious."

"Yes, an apology, and if you want to continue working here, that's exactly what you'll do."

Thomas hadn't said a word during the entire interaction. He just sat quietly and watched as it all played out. But he couldn't help grinning. He had broken him down and put him in his place, and he knew it.

Robbie couldn't afford to lose this job, and his boss knew it. He looked over at Thomas with hatred. He could tell by the snide look on the man's face that he was loving this. At this point, Robbie was now a deep beet red, and he clenched his fist so tightly that his nails had cut into his skin. A thin sheet of perspiration had begun to form on his brow. His eyes had also begun to well up, causing him to rub them and wipe away the tears before they spilled out onto his cheeks and gave the appearance of him crying.

"Well, Robbie, we're waiting; what's it going to be?"

Robbie inhaled deeply and then let it out. Then a barely audible word escaped his lips through clenched teeth. "Sorry…"

"What was that? I couldn't hear you," Mr. Miranda said.

"I'm sorry." This time it was clear so everyone could hear.

"Will that do, Mr. Smyth?"

"Yes, that will do nicely," he said with a smile. "Thank you for addressing this issue promptly, Mr. Miranda. I'm sure Mr. Harrison has learned his lesson and will mind his manners going forward. Thank you, and have a good day."

He gathered up his belongings and made his way out of the office. As he was passing by Robbie, he winked. Robbie was so angry that tears began to run down his cheeks. He wiped them away quickly, but not before Thomas saw him do it. He didn't want to give off the appearance of weakness or defeat to his boss, who he also hated at this moment, but it was too late once the tears began to fall.

"I can see that you're sorry, Robbie, so I'm going to let this stand as a verbal warning, but I don't expect to have anything like this brought to my attention again. Are we clear?"

"It won't."

With that, he turned around and exited the office, fists still clenched, nails digging into his palms. All he could think about was getting his hands on Thomas and kicking his behind.

"You should, Robbies. Go finds him and kicks his behinds."

This was a familiar voice—one he had not heard for a while now. Not since the fight with Joey and Brian on the stairwell.

"He made fools of you. He humiliated you. Then he winked at you. He's just like all the rest of the bullies you've had to deals with. He just does his dirt differently. Kick his behinds. MAKES HIM PAY!"

Repeatedly, the voice went on in his head. It was all he could think about. He went back to the front desk and turned on his computer. He looked up Thomas's address, wrote it down on a piece of paper, and put it in his pocket.

"Kicks his behinds."

Oh, I will, he thought. *That's exactly what I'm going to do. I'm going to knock that smile off his smug little face.* He imagined different ways of smashing his face in and smiled each time he did. Something inside of him snapped, and he was openly talking with the voice in his head now and had every intention of listening to it. Thomas Smyth was going to learn what happened to people who cross Robbie. And he was going to learn it today.

*To me belongeth vengeance, and recompence; their
foot shall slide in due time: for the day of their
calamity is at hand, and the things that shall come
upon them make haste*

—D EUTERONOMY 32:35

CHAPTER THIRTY-SIX

The Setup

*It almost seemed like everything was happening
in slow motion. He tried to move out of the
way, but his body was not responding.*

A S T HOMAS LEFT THE GYM, HE WAS FILLED WITH A GLORIOUS
sense of satisfaction and accomplishment. He hadn't felt like this
for quite some time. The look on Robbie's face when he'd winked
at him was priceless. It took everything he had not to burst out
laughing. Now it would be time to work on part two of his plan.
There would be a confrontation between the two of them shortly.
He would just have to be ready for it, which would mean taking
control of and directing the course of events so that they play out
in his favor. A sinister smile emerged on his face as he remembered

how easily he had been able to manipulate the situation. He almost felt sorry for Robbie. Then he smiled again. *He'll probably try to confront me here at the gym at some point, and that simply won't work for me. I won't give him that opportunity. Instead, I'll set up a place of my choosing and make it seem like his idea, of course, which will make it easy for me to catch him off guard and take him down.* He thought about all the details of his plan on his ride home. He could leave nothing to chance. First things first, he would have to set up the room. And the table. Everything must be tidy. When he arrived home, he washed his hands and went to his bedroom, opened the top drawer, and pulled out a small black box. It was where he kept his supplies, and it was time to go to work. He opened the box. Inside were four syringes and a bottle of ketamine. He went back out to his dining room, placed the box on the table, pulled out a chair, and sat down. He opened the box and removed the ketamine. He filled up one syringe, then another, and so on, until they were all filled. He prepped each for use, depressing the plunger on the syringe just enough that a drop of its contents escaped the tip. Then he placed all the caps back over the syringes to make sure he didn't accidentally stick himself. He looked at the bottle of ketamine, also known as the "date rape drug," and smiled. He loved this stuff. It was tasteless and odorless, making it ideal for nonconfrontational sexual conquest. But with Robbie, it was going to be different. There was no way he would be able to get him to eat or drink anything from him. He would have to use the syringe on him directly. He had never tried this before with someone as big as Robbie, so he couldn't leave anything to chance. In his experience, fifty milligrams was usually enough to put a person into a state of euphoria, a dream-like state, but just to be safe, he had filled each syringe with seventy. He would have to place them strategically around his apartment where he could access them quickly.

This was going to be sweet, he thought. First he had humbled and owned him at his place of work, and next he would humble him once again on his table. Robbie was a bit older than he normally liked, but this was no matter. He would make an exception for Robbie. And when he was done with him, he might have to eat a bit of him too. The thought of it all excited him to the core. He began placing the syringes in different places around his apartment as he thought about how and what he was going to do to Robbie. He started to think about possible ways to get him over to his apartment. This was going to be tricky and had to be well thought out. Just then, his intercom buzzed. He walked over and pressed the talk button and asked who it was.

"Delivery for apartment 3D, Mr. Smyth."

"I didn't order anything. Who's it from?"

"Look, sir, I just deliver the packages. I don't know or care who it's from. The package doesn't require a signature, so I can just leave it here in front of your building. I was just giving you a courtesy call."

"All right, all right, just give me a moment. I'll be right down."

He wondered what this could be. He didn't recall ordering anything, and he didn't know who might be sending him something. Perhaps there was some kind of mix-up and the package was for someone else. *Oh well, someone's loss is my gain,* Thomas thought as he hurried to put his shoes on, grabbed his keys, and rushed to the door. When he opened the door, to his immense surprise, Robbie was standing in his doorway. He gasped and jumped in shock. To his horror, he saw Robbie drawing his fist back. It almost seemed like everything was happening in slow motion. He tried to move out of the way, but his body was not responding. He could see Robbie's fist coming toward his face, and all he could do was brace for impact. So many things rushed to his mind, but before he could make any sense of it, there was a sharp pain that felt like a brick smashing into his face. Everything went white, and he was temporarily blind. It almost seemed like he was floating. He was violently snapped back into reality with another blow to the head. Before he could recover from that, he could see, through blurred eyes, another punch smashing into his face. He fell backward, tripping over his own feet, his arms flailing about, trying to grab onto something to keep himself from falling, but he only found air as his head hit the floor with a thud. Robbie stepped inside his apartment and locked the door behind him as he did. He looked at Thomas on the floor, blood gushing from his nose and mouth. He sounded like he was gasping and choking on blood as he tried to figure out what was going on and regain his composure.

"Wink at me now, you little punk." As Robbie shouted the words, he launched a series of kicks that caught Thomas in the gut, which caused him to dry heave as his lungs searched for air that would not come. Tears poured freely from his eyes and he tried to speak.

"Stop, please…stop." His voice was barely louder than a whisper.

Robbie reached down and picked him up effortlessly by his jacket collar onto his feet. Thomas tried to turn and run, but as he did, Robbie put him in a chokehold, effectively cutting off his air supply.

"That's it, Robbies, chokes him, chokes him good."

Robbie now heard the voice in his head very clearly. It was no longer just a whisper but a roar. It consumed him, and he knew he would do whatever it told him to.

"Squeeze his neck, makes his head goes pop."

Robbie smiled as he tried to do exactly that. Thomas was on the verge of passing out. He was only five foot six inches to Robbie's six foot one. He could feel his feet dangling in the air as Robbie choked the life out of him. He couldn't believe he had allowed this fool to get the better of him. Then he heard a familiar voice in his head again, but this time it wasn't talking to him. It seemed like it was talking to Robbie, instructing him to choke Thomas—but that couldn't be right. That was his inner voice, so how could that be? He figured he must be delirious and hearing things. Then the voice spoke to him.

"Checks your pockets, Thomas."

Thomas fumbled around his pockets haphazardly, not knowing what for, and to his surprise, he found that he had placed the last syringe in his pocket just before he'd opened the door to go downstairs. He had forgotten all about it. Now if he could somehow get the cover off, he could stick Robbie and maybe survive this. However, the loss of oxygen threatened to overtake him. He was just about to give in and slip into unconsciousness when the voice spoke to him again.

"So I guess you're the ones who was humbled, Thomas. Looks like he's the ones who puts you in your place. Tells me, Thomas, do you hear laughter? Hen, hen, hen."

It was that laugh at the end that pissed Thomas off enough to make one final try. He managed to get the top off the syringe and swung his arm back, jabbing Robbie in the thigh a couple of times. However, he had only partially depressed the plunger on the syringe before he finally and reluctantly succumbed to his injuries and lack of air and passed out.

Robbie also heard the voice as it was talking to Thomas and wondered how that could be. He dropped him and jumped back when he felt the jab of the syringe—he didn't know what it was, but he knew that it hurt. When he looked down at his thigh, he saw the syringe sticking out of his leg. He was mortified and enraged even more than before. He pulled it out and began kicking Thomas's now unconscious body as he cursed him. Thomas had passed out, never knowing if his last-ditch attempt to get free from Robbie was a success. After the third or fourth kick, Robbie started to feel the effects of the ketamine. He began to feel a bit lightheaded, almost like he was floating. He looked at the syringe in his hand and then back at Thomas, cursed him again, and gave him another kick in the side for good measure. He was woozy now and leaned against the wall. He began to slide down until he was eventually sitting on the floor beside Thomas. Still holding the syringe, he slammed it into Thomas's backside and pressed the plunger, sending the rest of whatever was inside of it into Thomas. Then he slumped over, listening to his breath as his eyelids got heavier, until he eventually closed his eyes and slipped into unconsciousness right alongside Thomas. Just before he drifted off, he noticed a tall figure standing over him smiling a hideous smile.

"Wells done, Robbies, wells done."

That voice, he thought. *That's the voice in my head.* Now Robbie finally had a face to go along with that voice, and his last waking thought was that he wished he didn't.

For therein is the righteousness of God revealed from faith to faith; as it is written; "The just shall live by faith."

—ROMANS 1:17 (KJ21)

CHAPTER THIRTY-SEVEN

Discernment

This past year, with all that I have seen, if I ever had a doubt, and I did, it all left me when I saw that demon. Because if evil like that is real, then God has to be real too.

EZEKIEL WAS SITTING ON THE FLOOR WITH FATHER CONNORS, exhausted. They had been working on his meditation skills and expanding his consciousness and awareness. Father Connors was so impressed with Ezekiel's ability to see things that he often took for granted, and the young lady, Vera, was beginning to display the same skills more and more each day as well. It was natural for them, but he knew that it was a skill that he could learn as well, and over the past few weeks, he had been doing his best to acquire that skill. This turned out to be a major undertaking. Ezekiel had him on a strict diet and exercise routine, which included yoga, fasting, and meditation. Father Connors was fifty-six now, and after practicing this ritual for over a year, he was in the best shape of his life. These last few weeks had been particularly challenging. Ezekiel had been pushing the priest to his limits and beyond. His body had transformed. He was leaner and toned; he now had a visible six-pack and could bench press 350 pounds. He was also learning to get a feel for reading people's energies or auras. And Vera's boyfriend, Robbie, was rubbing him a certain way lately. It was nothing he could put his finger on just yet, just a feeling that would come and go. He chalked it up to Robbie having a bad day or being frustrated because he hadn't been able to spend any alone time with Vera. Father Connors didn't feel bad about that. The kids today needed to take things a little more slowly as far as he was concerned. Nevertheless, it was worth making a mental note concerning Robbie for now. At present, EZ was trying to teach him how to suppress his energy while reading others around him, which would give him an advantage over some of the bad things in the night. He was having a tough time with the suppressing part, though. It was proving especially difficult for him to grasp. He could tell that Ezekiel was spent and a little frustrated also. He had been a bit distracted lately, but he got the feeling that this had more to do with Vera than it did with him. It was clear to him that there was chemistry between those two. Talk about reading a person's energy. Those two were like stars in the middle of the night. It was crazy and bad at the same time. That kind of energy was felt by everybody, spiritual and nonspiritual alike. And for these spiritual types, it was like calling a moth to a flame. He could tell that it upset Ezekiel, and he figured this was because he felt he, of all people, should have better control of himself at this point, especially after all he had been through in prison. Hiding from all the evil in that place must have been unimaginably difficult for him, the priest knew. After that, this should be a piece of cake. But Father Connors knew something that Ezekiel didn't—or at least hadn't come to terms with yet. Ezekiel was in love and had been from the moment he'd laid eyes on Vera. It showed in his eyes whenever she was around him. It was clear that she made him happy, maybe happier than he had been in years. It is hard to put a lid on feelings like that. He smiled at that last thought, and Ezekiel caught his eye.

"What is it?" he asked, looking like he could use a reason to smile too.

"Nothing, I was just thinking about how good it'll be to have all of this behind us and maybe get some part of our lives back."

Ezekiel smiled and sighed. "I fear this is just the beginning of things to come for us, Father. Lately, I've been feeling more and more of the spiritual energy shifting around us, and evil is running rampant. People have been saying this for years, but I honestly believe that we are fast approaching the last days if we are not already in them. The signs are all around us. Even now, there are four angels on each corner of the church praying night and day to ward off evil from this place and keep us hidden. But more will have to be done now—and soon. Vera and I are becoming too big of a light for all to see, and we're not ready yet. In truth, I don't know that we ever really were."

"What are you saying, Ezekiel? Do you think we're going to lose? That God is going to lose?"

"No, nothing like that. I just don't think that any of us were ready to answer this call when we got it."

"And yet you still answered. Not only did you answer, but you called others in to serve God's cause, and here we are. I mean, look at me, Ezekiel. Just knowing you and your love for God, your faith in him, and how you trust in him to honor his word without question has changed me and strengthened my faith in God and all that he can do thousands of times over. I genuinely believe that all things are possible through God, and that's how I'm able to get up each day and face this test he has set before me. And make no mistake about it: this is a test. One that we can't afford to fail—and we won't. This past year, with all that I have seen, if I ever had a doubt, and I did, it all left me when I saw that demon. Because if evil like that is real, then God has to be real too."

Tears had fallen from his eyes as he spoke. "You just can't have one without the other, you see," he said, smiling and wiping the tears to the side of his face. "Plus, the Bible already tells you how this story will end." He looked up at Ezekiel, smiling brightly. His aura was glowing.

"Can't you see, Ezekiel? God has his hand on you, and wherever he would have you go, whatever he would have you do, I will do it with you and give my life if need be to help you get it done. Every day, I am humbled by his awesome grace and mercy, Amen, and—"

Suddenly, his body jerked, and a burst of air rushed through the church. Then he spoke in tongues, praising the Lord God. The angels outside the church began praising his name as well, and the music that was their prayers filled the church with the Lord's spirit. Ezekiel looked around the church, amazed to see that it was filled with hundreds of angels, all praying and giving thanks to God. He dropped to the floor, stretched out facedown, and did the same as well.

A few minutes passed, but it felt like an eternity. Father Connors seemed to be himself again. He was speaking normally, and all the angels were gone, but the spirit of the Lord was still abundantly present. Vera came running into the church from her room and found them still on their knees. She was bright-eyed and just as excited. It was the first time either of them had truly seen her smile since she had lost her mother.

"Did you hear them?" she asked. "They were singing . . . the angels. It was beautiful. Oh, please tell me you heard them!"

"Yes," Ezekiel replied, "I heard them, and they spoke to me as well. I know how to do it now. I've been trying to hold everything in when I should have been letting it flow and redirecting it into the earth. It's so simple. I can't believe I never thought of it before." Ezekiel was smiling as he spoke, which made the others smile as well. He started to get up and helped Father Connors up too. The priest was brimming with spiritual energy. Vera stepped to Ezekiel, took his hand, and kissed him on the cheek.

Never taking his eyes off her, he touched his cheek, smiling, and asked, "What was that for?"

"The angels told me that you were my protector, and I never really thanked you for saving me before. I don't pretend to know what's going on, but I do know that you are an important part of it. You too, Father. We have all been brought together here by God to accomplish something, and by his grace, we will do just that. I just don't know what it is yet," she said with a smile.

Ezekiel hadn't let go of her hand yet, and she noticed, but oddly enough she didn't think she wanted him to. Something was happening with her feelings toward him, and even though she knew better, especially with everything that was going on around them, she couldn't help feeling enamored of him.

"Hey, what about me? Do I get a kiss too, or am I just chopped liver over here?" Father Connors had his hands outstretched, waving them both in for a hug.

Vera smiled. "Of course you get one!"

She and Ezekiel, still holding hands, walked over to him. She kissed him on his cheek, which he was poking out and pointing his finger at. Then all three of them hugged each other and enjoyed the moment.

To every thing there is a season, and a time to every
purpose under the heaven:
                                                        —ECCLESIASTES 3:1 (KJ21)

CHAPTER THIRTY-EIGHT

How the Tables Have Turned

He smiled a bloody smile and then passed out. When he
came too, he found himself facedown, strapped to the table.

ROBBIE WOKE UP WITH A HEADACHE AND FELT NAUSEOUS. IT
took a moment before he recognized where he was. He sat up and
saw the still unconscious body of Thomas lying next to him. He
looked at his watch and was surprised to see that only about twenty
minutes had passed. It felt as if he had been out for hours. He
figured that he might have been if Thomas had finished injecting
him with everything in the syringe. He tried to stand up but was
having some difficulty focusing. He was dizzy, and his balance was
off. *What was in that syringe?* he thought as he finally got to his feet.
He stepped over Thomas and made his way over to the kitchen. He

leaned over the sink and threw up. He ran the water for a second and then cupped his hands under the water, rinsed out his mouth, and spit the water back into the sink. He took a moment to look around the apartment. It was nice and very spacious. The kitchen was modern and all the details looked expensive. Thomas's whole home was modern, in fact, with an open concept. The kitchen flowed into the dining area, which overlooked the living room as well. There was a fireplace in the living room, but from the looks of it, he didn't think it had ever been used.

Two French doors led to an outside patio with a couple of chairs and a table outside along with a small barbeque grill. It was just the right size for the space. There was a staircase off the living room area that went upstairs, and what looked like another couple of doors on the first level. Robbie went upstairs to check it out first. Two more bedrooms and bathrooms. Everything was immaculately maintained. Nothing seemed out of place, as far as he could tell. However, all the rooms—scratch that, the entire apartment—seemed cold and generic. There was no personality in the space at all. There were no pictures on the walls, for example, and everything was white—no colors, not even a plant. He went back downstairs and stood over Thomas's body, wondering what to do with him. He looked around for something to tie him up with but couldn't find anything, so he got a small knife from the kitchen, cut the cord of the lamp in the living room, and tied him up with that. Then he sat on the couch and put his head in his hands. He still felt a little dizzy and sick. He wondered why Thomas had had that stuff already in a needle. Was he somehow expecting Robbie to show up? He looked over at Thomas and grabbed the syringe, and then he placed it on the coffee table. He went to the bathroom and looked through his cabinets—nothing out of the ordinary. He opened a door he thought was a closet, but to his surprise, it was another room. As he stepped inside, chills ran up his spine. He had a bad feeling about this place. The room smelled of Pine Sol and bleach. There was a table in the middle of the room. It looked like it could be folded at certain points and reshaped into an X shape. *What could he possibly use this contraption for?* he thought. As he inspected the table a little more thoroughly, he noticed slits in all four of the corners. As he walked around the room, he heard a muffled whisper. At first, he thought it was Thomas coming around, but then he realized it was coming from what appeared to be a closet. He opened it cautiously, not knowing what to expect, but nothing could have prepared him for what he found. It was a little boy about nine or ten years old, bound and gagged. He had cuts all over his body, a few covered with bandages on his legs and buttocks. From the looks of him, he had to have been there for quite some time. He was emaciated and sickly. Robbie bent down and reached over to remove the gag from the boy, but he pulled back, cowering away from him and throwing his arms up to protect his head.

"I'm not going to hurt you," Robbie said. "You're safe now." Robbie held his hands up to show that he didn't mean any harm, hoping this would calm the boy down. He reached over to remove the gag again, and while the boy didn't whine or whimper, he still flinched a bit. "I'm just going to take this off," he said softly. The little boy seemed to get it and stopped moving away from him. As Robbie began pulling back the tape that had been used to gag him, he recoiled in shock, and tears instantly fell from his eyes. The boy's lips had been cut off, exposing his teeth and gums. He wondered what kind of monster could do this to another living person. Right then and there, Robbie's mind was made up. He was going to kill Thomas; there was no way he was getting out of this alive.

"What's your name, son?" Robbie asked in a soft voice.

The boy swallowed and responded with a low scratchy voice. "Sanny." He shook his head and cleared his throat and spoke again, a little slower to get it right this time, but it came out the same: "SANNY."

Robbie looked at him, a bit confused for a second, and then said "Oh, Sammy."

The boy nodded. Robbie suddenly realized that it must be incredibly hard for Sammy to speak now with no lips.

"I'm going to get you out of here and back home to your family, Sammy." He began untying the boy and noticed bloodstains on his underwear. His eyes filled again as he realized that Thomas was not just a torturing low-life kidnapper, but a sadistic pedophile as well, who had been doing God knows what with this boy for who knows how long. After he got him untied, he told Sammy to wait for him there while he went to get him something to put on. He came back with a shirt and some sweatpants from Thomas's room and helped him get dressed. Sammy was so weak that he couldn't even stand. Robbie picked him up and carried him upstairs to the extra bedroom. He made sure the boy couldn't see Thomas's still unconscious body on the floor as they passed by. Robbie wasn't sure how Sammy would react if he did, and he didn't want to find out.

"Wait here, Sammy, and be quiet, OK? I'll be back with the police." The boy nodded slowly and laid on the bed. He crawled into a little ball, shaking and shivering a bit. Robbie went back downstairs with a hatred and rage that he had never felt before inside him. Just then, Thomas let out a low moan and farted. He tried to move but soon realized that he had been tied up. His ribs and face were throbbing. His right eye was severely swollen, and he could barely see out of it. There was a sharp pain in his right side every time he took a breath, and he figured that Robbie must have broken one or two of his ribs at some point. He looked up and saw

Robbie walking down the stairs toward him. There was something different about him, something in his eyes that frightened Thomas.

"A little kid, TOM? How could you do that to that boy, TOM?" he shouted. "You deserve to die, TOM!"

Robbie's eyes were cold and dark. Thomas could see that Robbie fully intended to kill him, and he started crying. The sight of him crying sickened Robbie and only served to fill him with even more contempt, if that was even possible. He kicked him in the face as he screamed, "SHUT UP, TOM!"

He grabbed him by the collar of his shirt and dragged him across the floor to his torture room. He didn't know why he was bringing him in there; he only knew that he wanted him to know that he knew about him, what he'd done, and what he was.

"HOW MANY, TOM? How many kids have you done this to?" Robbie punched and kicked him each time he asked him how many. He fully intended to beat him to death, but he suddenly felt a sharp pinch in his back. He turned around and saw Sammy holding a syringe. Robbie felt like everything around him was moving on a wave, like water, and then he fell to the floor face first. He rolled over and saw Sammy, who now looked like more of an imp than a boy.

"I did good, right, I did good?" Drool flowed freely from his lipless mouth as he spoke.

"Yes, you did good," Thomas said, coughing and spitting out blood along with one of his teeth.

He dragged himself over to Robbie and spoke, his voice barely a whisper. "Forty-two," he said, still coughing as he spoke. "Forty-two kids before you, and you'll be my forty-third. I hope you're ready, because it's my turn now." He smiled a bloody smile, and then Robbie passed out.

When he came too, he found himself facedown, strapped to the table. Thomas was sitting in a chair in the corner, facing him.

His breathing was labored, and his face was a swollen, bloody mess. It was clear that he was badly in need of medical attention. Sammy was sitting on the floor next to him, resting his head in his lap like a puppy. Robbie assessed his situation and instantly realized what Thomas was planning for him: the same thing he had done to that boy, and countless others, no doubt. He probably would have been in the process of violating him right now if not for his present condition. Then he heard that familiar voice, as he had so many times in the past. But this time, it didn't sound like it was coming from inside his head. It sounded like it was right next to him. He turned from side to side but didn't see anyone. But he was now beginning to think he had seen something earlier when he had first gotten stuck with that syringe by Thomas.

"You can probablys gets loose. I don't thinks he had the strength to ties you down well enough to holds you. Looks at hims. Go ahead and gives it a try and sees. Or nots, and sees what he has in mind for yous."

Robbie looked over at Thomas, who was still sitting in the chair, and then he started pulling on the straps. His right hand slipped right out. His left hand, however, was fastened down pretty well. Sammy was trying to alert Thomas that Robbie was attempting to get free. Then he rushed at him like a crazed lunatic. He grabbed Robbie's free arm and tried to reattach it to the table. Thomas was now up on his feet and making his way over to the table. Robbie gave a few hard tugs on his left hand, attempting to get free while fighting off Sammy with his right. Where was this kid getting all this energy from? He'd had to carry him up the stairs before. There was a popping sound, and Robbie cried out as his left hand slid out from the restraint, leaving some skin from the top of his hand as it did. He had also dislocated his thumb, but he was free. He somehow managed to pull free of Sammy, who was now clawing

at his face and biting his arm. Robbie backhanded him with everything he had using his good hand, and Sammy dropped to the
floor, temporarily stunned. Thomas, to Robbie's surprise, had sat
back down. He was holding his side and gasping. It was almost
like he was drowning and trying to get air into his lungs. *Good,* he
thought, and he managed to pull his feet free and roll off the table.
He grabbed his left hand and pulled on his thumb, snapping it
back into place, but the pain was unreal. As he got to his feet, the
little boy had just leaped off the table and onto his back, clawing
and biting at Robbie's face. Robbie reached up and pulled him off,
slamming him down onto the floor. That's when he noticed that
there was something more about the little boy: he was possessed.
Robbie reached down and grabbed the boy by the neck, put him
in a sleeper hold, and began squeezing. At first, the boy thrashed
about wildly in Robbie's arms, but after a few moments, he moved
around less and less until he finally just went completely limp.
Robbie kept applying pressure even after the boy had stopped
moving. He wanted to make sure it was good and dead before he
let go. A minute passed, and Robbie finally let go, dropping the
body to the ground. He stepped over the body and started walking
toward Thomas.

"This is all your fault. It's all your doing, and now it's your turn
to pay for everything you've done." His voice was still no louder
than a whisper

Thomas replied, "And what about you, huh? You just killed
that boy. Don't you have to pay? Why is it OK for you and not me?
You're no better than me; you're worse, because you're pretending
to be something you're not. At least I am—" Robbie grabbed him
by the throat, cutting him off.

"I'm nothing like you, and in a moment, you won't even be here,
so who cares what you think? Goodbye, Thomas."

But just as Robbie began to squeeze down on Thomas's neck and end what was left of his life, he felt a hand on his shoulder.

"That will do's Robbies that will do's. I still have needs of Thomas, for now. But you, you have proved yourself to be a captain in my army."

Robbie turned to face the voice that for so long had only existed in his mind, or so he thought. It was a very tall, impossibly thin man. His extremities seemed longer than normal, especially his fingers. His skin was pale and gray, completely devoid of light, and his touch was cold. But what stood out was his smile. It was inhuman. His energy was compelling. Robbie felt it in his bones. He was a living nightmare. And he was who Robbie now served.

*That frustrateth the tokens of the liars, and maketh
diviners mad; that turneth wise men backward, and
maketh their knowledge foolish;*

—ISAIAH 44:25

CHAPTER THIRTY-NINE

Enemy/Friend

*It was his aura. It had changed. It was dark. It reminded
her of the time when he was on the staircase back in school.*

THREE MONTHS HAD PASSED SINCE THE UNLIKELY ALLIANCE
between Robbie and Thomas, much to Robbie's distain. He was
now working with him—as directed—though they both hated
each other. The thing was, they feared Nestor more, so they did as
they were told. It took an entire month before all the swelling went
down on Thomas's face. And he was now missing his two front
teeth. Robbie had also fractured Thomas's left arm and broken four
of his ribs. Some parts of his body were still black and blue from
the beating he had sustained. It still hurt when he inhaled deeply.
Thomas hated Robbie and wanted his pound of flesh, but knew
better than to try to get revenge, especially while his master had

plans for him. So for now, he would just have to wait and do as he was told.

Robbie didn't trust Thomas either, but he also knew that something good would come from working with him if Nestor told him to do so. After all, every time he had listened to Nestor in the past, good things had happened to him. Nestor promised him he would show him how to win the heart of his love back. He just needed to follow his directions.

Nestor told Thomas that he would make him a man to be feared and respected. Then he separately promised both Robbie and Thomas that he would allow them to finish the other one off once they served their purpose. This pleased each of them greatly— they both thought Nestor was just stringing the other one along like a fool.

Nestor saw how Robbie's insecurities regarding the girl had grown, and he played on that. Jealousy is a strong fuel for hatred. And hatred, doubt, coveting, and greed were the things that sustained him. Robbie and Thomas both supplied him with an ample amount of all of these. Nestor provided Robbie with a simple plan. Get the girl and bring her to him. Then they could finally be together, forever. For Thomas, the plan was even simpler. Help Robbie with everything he needed to subdue the girl so that he could get her to him, and he would reward him with a new plaything.

Over the past few months, Robbie had grown to hate Ezekiel. He was always there whenever he managed to get some time with Vera—the unwanted chaperone. Vera always invited him to join their conversations or meals, or whatever he had planned for them. He never got to spend any alone time with her. Whenever he would try, she would shy away from him. She barely kissed him on the cheek anymore, and he knew this change had to do with Ezekiel.

Robbie was outside the school waiting for Vera. He was hoping to meet up with her and hurry her away before Ezekiel showed up. Getting her to go with him was going to be hard enough without having Ezekiel interfering. He caught a glimpse of her as she walked out and called out to her. She looked up, saw it was Robbie, and smiled. She walked over and greeted him. He reached out and took her hand. It was warm and soft. It made him feel good. He didn't know why, but it did. "Come on," he said, "I need to show you something, but it's only for you."

She pulled back on her hand a little to slow him down. "Robbie, wait, Ezekiel is coming to pick me up. I should wait for him to get here and let him know I'm with you."

"There's no time. Besides, he would only get in the way. Unless that's what you want. What's the deal with you two? Why is he constantly around you? How come you always seem to have time for him and none for me? Do you like him?"

Until that moment, Vera had never really allowed herself to think about this out loud, but as Robbie said it, she knew it was true. She didn't know how to answer without hurting Robbie's feelings. But it was too late. He could tell from the look in her eyes and her flushed complexion that it was true. He was livid. He squeezed her hand and jerked her toward him. And in a low voice, he spoke to her between clenched teeth.

"We need to talk."

He pulled her along a bit for a few blocks and into an alleyway; then he let go of her.

"How could you do this, Vera, after everything I've done for you?"

There was something different about Robbie that Vera was just noticing. It was his aura. It had changed. It was dark. It reminded her of the time when he was on the staircase back in school fighting those boys. Back when she'd heard that voice … just then it hit her. That had been his voice: Nestor's. How had she missed this before now? She looked up at him with a mix of emotions.

"Robbie, you're scaring me." She took a few steps back, but he grabbed her and pulled her close to him.

"Have you been with him? Is that why he's always with you? Well, maybe you would feel that way about me if I were with you all the time too. Maybe I should show you what you've been missing."

Vera was shocked into silence. She didn't even know how to begin to respond to him. But she could tell he was deadly serious about showing her what he meant. She tried to push him away, but it wasn't until that moment that she realized just how strong Robbie was. He picked her up and pressed her back against the wall behind a dumpster in the alley.

"Yeah, maybe I should give it to you right here."

He tried to kiss her, but she twisted her face from side to side, trying to avoid his lips. He grabbed her face to hold it still and pressed his lips against hers, hard. She thought quickly and stopped fighting him, pretending to kiss him back and hoping to throw him off a bit. It worked. He relaxed his grip on her slightly and stopped to look into her eyes. When he pulled his face away from hers, she spit in his face and kneed him in the balls. Robbie cried out in pain and anger. He let go of her and grasped his balls with one of his hands, shoving her hard into the wall with the other. Vera felt all the air leave her lungs like a deflating balloon as she hit the wall. She slid down until her butt came to rest on the floor like a rag doll.

"You whore!" Robbie cried out. "You were supposed to love me! Well, if I can't have you, then no one will."

He started toward her but was suddenly pulled backward and thrown into the fence on the other side of the alleyway. It rattled loudly as Robbie bounced off it and onto the ground.

"I don't know what's gotten into you, but that's enough!" It was Ezekiel. Robbie quickly recovered and got to his feet.

"Oh, you're gonna pay," he said. "You're gonna pay with blood."

He charged Ezekiel and hit him with his shoulder right in his midsection, intending to wind him and knock him off his feet. This, however, was not the first time Ezekiel had been charged, as Robbie quickly learned. Ezekiel used an old prison trick on Robbie and yanked his shirt over his head, trapping his arms and obscuring his vision. Then with one punch to Robbie's solar plexus, the fight, if you could call it that, was over. There was a popping sound, and Robbie dropped to the floor on his knees. His eyes were open, but he couldn't see, much less breathe.

He broke my rib, Robbie thought. *Right in front of Vera, he broke my rib.* He tried to speak, but his breath had not yet returned to his body. All he could do was hold his side and wait to be able to breathe again. Ezekiel walked away from Robbie, leaving him on the ground and checked on Vera.

"Are you OK? Did he hurt you?"

"How did you know I was here?" Vera said in a frightened voice.

Ezekiel answered her as he helped her to her feet, "I was a few blocks away on my way to you when I saw you leave with Robbie. I didn't want to intrude, so I hung back a bit to give you some space. Had I known this was what he had in mind, I would have stopped him much sooner."

"I don't know what came over him. It's like he was a different person. He was so angry and hurt. I'm just glad you came along when you did. Ezekiel! Look out!" she shouted abruptly.

Ezekiel ducked and spun around in one perfectly timed motion, catching Robbie in the jaw with a right hook, which caused his feet to swing out up over his head from the force of the blow. He hit the ground, hard, on his back. Robbie didn't need to go to the hospital to know that his jaw was broken. The pain in his mouth told him that. Ezekiel picked Robbie up by his shirt collar with his left hand and was about to punch him in the face again with his right when Vera stopped him. "Ezekiel, please don't."

He turned to look at Vera, still holding Robbie, and asked her, "Why?"

But before she could answer, he felt a sharp pinch on the back of his neck. He turned around quickly to see who or what had stuck him. And to his surprise, it was a small man holding a needle.

"Who are you? What was that?" he asked.

His vision became blurry. Then Robbie produced a switchblade from his pocket and stabbed Ezekiel twice in the gut. At first, Ezekiel thought he had stuck him with another needle, but as he let go of him and looked down at his stomach and saw all the blood and the knife in Robbie's hand, he realized that he had been stabbed.

He stumbled and then fell backward onto his butt, holding his stomach. Robbie, however, leaped forward, pushing Ezekiel onto his back and pinning his arms down with his knees. He plunged the knife into his chest repeatedly until Vera knocked him off.

"What have you done?" she screamed, looking at Robbie's blood-soaked body in disbelief.

But before she could say anything else, she felt a sharp pain in her neck, and then everything went black. Her body folded like an accordion as she fell, hitting her head on the ground and passing out. Thomas was standing over her with a syringe in his hand, smiling and sucking his teeth.

"Now, now, that's no way for a young lady to behave. But the master will get you fixed up right as rain when I get you back to him."

"Don't touch her," Robbie said through a strained jaw that was now swelling. "She's mine, Thomas."

"You don't look like you're in any shape to be barking orders, Robbie. You don't look like you're doing much better than the big guy on the floor. Although I must admit, even after the beating he put on you, you sure got the drop on him and put him down for good. Ain't no coming back from this."

"I said, get away from her. She's mine, and I'll bring her before him, the master." Robbie stood up and wiped his face, smearing blood across his cheeks as he did.

"Get the van and help me get her inside. We have to get out of here before anyone comes."

Thomas looked at Robbie for a moment, sizing him up. He really wanted to take the girl and leave him there, but even in Robbie's present condition, he knew he was still no match for him and would probably end up lying dead on the floor next to the big guy over there. He smiled and shrugged. "Sure, Robbie, I'll get the van." A few moments later, he was back with the van. They put Vera inside and drove off.

Ezekiel watched helplessly as all this transpired. He was slipping in and out of consciousness, and just before he passed out, he saw through blurred eyes a figure running toward him.

"Ezekiel, no! Hold on, son, hold on!" Father Connors had gotten there just in time to see the van pull off. He called 911, gave his location, and waited for the paramedics to arrive. He kneeled on the ground next to Ezekiel and propped his head up to rest on his knees. "Hang on, son, help is on the way."

Therefore if any man be in Christ, he is a new creature: old things are passed away; behold, all things are become new.

—2 CORINTHIANS 5:17

CHAPTER FORTY

The Cost of a Life

Death is a normal part of man's life, and yours has run its course.

FATHER CONNORS RODE WITH EZEKIEL IN THE AMBULANCE. HE watched helplessly as the paramedics worked frantically to stop the bleeding. None of this made sense to Father Connors. *How could this have happened?* he thought. *There's no way someone could just stab Ezekiel and not be dead on the floor next to him.* It just wasn't possible. Not after all the things he had witnessed him do. "Hang on, EZ, we're almost there."

When they pulled up to the hospital, they rushed inside and took Ezekiel right to the operating room. Doctors were waiting to attend to him. Father Connors had to wait in reception.

He waited a few hours, asking anyone who walked through the swinging doors if there was any word about his friend's condition. He eventually sat down and rested his head in his hands.

"Excuse me, are you Father Connors?" a deep voice asked. "We met back at the station house a few months ago. It is Father Connors, right?"

It was Detective Kelly. The hospital had notified the police due to the violent nature of Ezekiel's injuries.

"Um, yes, hello, Detective. You have a good memory."

"Do you mind if I ask you a few questions, Father?"

"If it could wait, Detective, I would appreciate it. This isn't a good time."

"Yes, well, that's just it, Father. You seem to be having a run of bad luck with your friends either turning up dead or near dead. It just seems too odd to be a coincidence. So no, this really can't wait. I'm going to need you to tell me what happened to your friend in there."

Father Connors stood up abruptly, looking down on Detective Kelly, who was only now noting the differences in their heights and constitutions, and took a step back.

"Look here, Kelly, that's my son in there, and before you say another word to me, I would suggest you don't. I told you, it's not a good time."

Before Detective Kelly could respond to that, a doctor came through the swinging doors and approached them.

"What's the word, Doc, is he going to make it?" Father Connors asked.

The doctor paused slightly and then cleared his throat.

"His injuries were too severe. He suffered one collapsed lung, and his pulmonary valve and right ventricle in his heart were punctured. Not to mention the damage caused to his liver and small intestines from the stab wounds he sustained in his abdominal area. Honestly, we're not even sure how he's still alive right now. It's by his sheer will alone. At this point, we've done all we can to make him comfortable, but I think you might want to go in to see him now."

The news hit Father Connors like a brick to the head. His legs went weak, and he fell back in his chair. He felt as if the room was spinning around him. Nauseous and dizzy, he needed a minute to catch his breath.

"Do you think he'll be able to answer a few questions, Doc? We'd like to get some idea of who did this to him," Detective Kelly asked.

"As I said earlier, he's heavily sedated. We're just doing what we can to keep him comfortable. I'm not sure he'd be any good to you in his present condition."

Father Connors spoke up. His voice was a scratchy whisper. "Can I see him now?"

"Yes, Father, come with me."

Father Connors could feel the energy in the air changing around him as they approached Ezekiel's room. It was as if the very air around him had taken on weight. When he walked through the doors, his legs and arms felt extremely heavy, and it was hard for him to breathe normally. He noticed a tall man standing over Ezekiel on his right side and Joshua on the left. Father Connors turned to look at the doctor to see if he could see Joshua too, but the doctor was still back at the door in suspended animation. He turned back around to Joshua, who was now looking at him kindly. The other man, however, only seemed interested in Ezekiel.

"You have come a long way in the short time you've been with Ezekiel, Father. That you are still conscious and able to move about is proof of that. It is good to see that you have been reborn in the spirit."

"Joshua, who is this man, and why is he looking at Ezekiel like that?"

"He is no man. He is Azrael, and he has come for Ezekiel. Yet even now, he resists."

"Azrael, the angel of death?

"Yes, Father, now say no more, as he is communing with Ezekiel now, and his fate is being decided."

Father Connors stood by Joshua, reached over, held Ezekiel's hand, and said, "Keep fighting, EZ, keep fighting."

Then Azrael spoke. "Not since Jacob has anyone stayed my hand this long, but it is all for naught. For though you are highly favored, you are still subject to the laws of nature. Death is a normal part of man's life, and yours has run its course. Come with me now, Ezekiel. Let go of your mortal claim to your life here, and come with me to glory."

"I can't; I'm not ready. I still have things to do. People are counting on me."

"There's nothing you can say that I have not heard before. It is just your time, and if you will not come willingly, then I will take you. If I am present, then a life is required. And while it makes no difference to me who I might take, nothing save God can stay me from my task. Now, tarry no longer, as I have others I need to attend this day."

Azrael reached over. He placed his hand on Ezekiel's forehead and then slowly began to move his hand back. As he did, Ezekiel's soul began to rise from his body. Father Connors was horrified and in awe at the same time. His soul was so bright and beautiful the entire room was engulfed in an intrinsic light. It was warm and filled with what could only be described as love. Pure love.

Even Azrael paused for a moment, for truly, this soul was special.

Joshua gently placed his hand on Azrael's, momentarily halting the process.

"Is there nothing that can be done, Azrael?"

"I'm sorry, Joshua, but though he may be favored, my presence here means that a life is required."

"Then take me in his place," Father Connors blurted out. "If you have to take someone, then take me in his stead. He has people counting on him. Possibly the whole world. He can do things that most of us cannot because he belongs to both of our worlds. Surely you can feel this too. You can clearly see, he is truly a light to this world, and you just said that it doesn't matter to you who you take—just that a life is required. Well then, that settles it. Take me in his place."

Azrael turned around at that and faced Father Connors. The conviction of his words and the pureness of his heart was over-whelming. "I have had this request made of me countless times by grieving loved ones over the years, but yours comes from a place of inherent knowledge of what must be—no, of what needs to be done—and I feel compelled to comply. Father, if this be your wish, then so be it. I will take you to Glory in his stead. No greater sacrifice could be asked or made of you or anyone else for that matter. The scales of life and death will be evenly balanced for a trade such as this."

Joshua cleared his throat and then spoke. "I too would trade places with him if it were possible. Both of these men have and would continue to do the good work if allowed. Work that we are not yet permitted to do at this time."

"Great though he may be, he is still just mortal, and you are far more than that," Azrael responded. "That you would sacrifice your-self for a mortal does him a credit beyond measure. But not even I could sanction such an arrangement. It would have to be ordained by he who is above all."

Almost as if on cue, Ezekiel's soul returned to his body, but the room seemed even brighter now. Then they heard a voice that rang like thunderous music. "Let your light so shine before men, that they may see your good works, and glorify your Father which is in heaven."

It was a quote from Matthew 5:16, and they knew it was God who had given it to them. All of them prostrated themselves before the Lord and began praising his name. The light faded, and it was just the three of them in the room again with Ezekiel. Father Connors was beyond speech; tears of joy fell from his eyes. He was not alone in this. Joshua and Azrael both shed tears as well. Not since the time of the disciples had such an event taken place. Then Ezekiel sat up in his bed, born anew. His body was completely healed, and he thanked God for his mercy. For on that day, they had all witnessed the power of God himself and were jubilant.

Joshua said, "Behold, I believe you have your answer, Azrael. And nothing could have been more pleasing than the sight of my Lord and all his glory. My Lord also spoke with me and repurposed me as well. I must go with you home now, Azrael. My task here has run its course. Ezekiel, I have been your guardian all your life, and a part of me will always be with you."

He leaned over him and hugged him, and as he did, energy flowed from him into Ezekiel.

"I do not know how this is possible, but if God allows it, then I gift you this power gladly and joyfully that it might help you on your journey. Remember what I have taught you and the life lessons you have learned. You are meant to do incredible things. I'm sorry that I can't go with you any further for now, but as long as you keep God first in your heart, everything else will fall into place."

Joshua walked over to Azrael's side, turned to Ezekiel, and said, "Because of you, my faith in man has been restored. I will see you again soon, I'm sure, in this life or the next."

Then they vanished. Father Connors looked at Ezekiel with a smile and then hugged him tightly. "I thought I lost you, EZ, I thought I lost you." Just then, the doctor walked in with Detective Kelly.

It's like I said, Detective, I don't believe he will be in any condition to answer any questions.

Father Connors started to say something to Ezekiel, but before he could, he said, "I know, Father, I got this."

The doctor was astonished. He couldn't even form a coherent sentence. Detective Kelly looked confused and asked, "So, is this the guy that's knocking on death's door? He looks pretty healthy to me. Were you guys just messing with me to cover something up? Where's the guy that was reported stabbed?"

Ezekiel said, "Father, we must get out of here. They have Vera, and there's no time to waste. Where are my clothes? We need to go now."

The doctor and Detective Kelly spoke in unison. "You're not going anywhere." They looked at each other and then approached Ezekiel.

"I don't have time for this!" Ezekiel said. "Sleep." Both men instantly dropped to the floor.

Father Connors looked at Ezekiel in awe. "How did you do—"

Ezekiel cut him off as he spoke. "I'll explain on the way."

"Where? Where are we going, EZ?"

"Back to the church, and then to get Vera. We end this tonight."

*Finally, my brethren, be strong in the Lord, and in
the power of his might. Put on the whole armour of
God, that ye may be able to stand against the wiles of
the devil. For we wrestle not against flesh and blood,
but against principalities, against powers, against
the rulers of the darkness of this world, against
spiritual wickedness in high places. Wherefore take
unto you the whole armour of God, that ye may be
able to withstand in the evil day, and having done all,
to stand.*

—EPHESIANS 6:10–13

CHAPTER FORTY-ONE

Spiritual Armor

*They both knew that it was a possibility that they
might not make it back from this, and it was important
to be right with God before they embarked.*

WHEN THEY ARRIVED AT THE CHURCH, FATHER CONNORS
stopped at the gate in awe of the two figures he saw standing on
either side of the church.

Ezekiel had told him that there were angels posted around the church, but he had never been able to see them before today.

"Come, Father, time is short and there is much to do. We're going to need all the help we can get tonight. How soon can you have some other members of the clergy join us here? We are going to need prayer warriors praying for all of us."

"I can probably have people here within the hour."

"Good. The next thing may seem a bit odd considering all that we've been through, but I'm going to need you to formally baptize me."

"What? You're kidding, right?"

"No, I was never formally baptized. My mother told me she did it. She fasted and prayed all day to cleanse her spirit, and then she dipped me underwater when she was bathing me. I think it would be a good idea if a man of the cloth did it. And I can't think of anyone I'd rather do it but you."

For the second time that day, Father Connors was shocked—first at the hospital, and again at this request. He never would have guessed this in a million years. "Yes, of course, EZ."

Father Connors made some calls to his people and explained what was needed. Then he prepared the baptismal area for Ezekiel. When Ezekiel arrived, Father Connors was in the water tank waiting for him. Ezekiel was wearing all white. He stepped into the tank and stood before Father Connors. They both smiled at each other, wishing that they had more time to take in the beauty of this moment, but of course time was short. Father Connors dipped his finger into the water and marked a cross on Ezekiel's forehead.

"Son, do you believe that Jesus Christ is our Lord and Savior who died for our sins? Do you believe that only through the Lord Jesus Christ can you enter the kingdom of heaven? Do you believe this in your heart, and have you confessed this with your mouth?"

Ezekiel answered, "Yes, I believe that Jesus Christ is Lord with all my heart and soul."

Father Connors then placed one of his hands on the back of Ezekiel's neck, and the other on the top of his forehead. He gently lowered him into the water, and as he did, he noticed that the church was filled with angels who had come to bear witness to this moment.

"Then I now baptize you in the name of the Father, Son, and the Holy Ghost, in Jesus' name, Amen."

When he brought Ezekiel up from the water, Father Connors heard the angels sing praises to God. Then he asked Ezekiel to do the same for him, as he didn't know anyone more suited to the task. Ezekiel smiled and then baptized him. And once again, the angels sang praises unto God.

A short time later, both men had changed and prepared their gear for the night's mission. They both knew that it was a possibility that they might not make it back from this, and it was important to be right with God and to make sure their spiritual armor was on before they embarked, which was why each had baptized the other. Father Connors's people had arrived—two yellow school buses full of nuns and priests who specialized in spiritual warfare.

They were given instructions to pray through the night for Father Connors, Ezekiel, and Vera, that they might face this evil and defeat it. Ezekiel and Father Connors both noticed that there were angels in the church praying with them. They gathered their gear and left to find and save Vera. This was the day of recompense, and Nestor's tab was due. Today, either Nestor or Ezekiel would die.

Rest in the LORD, and wait patiently for him; fret
not thyself because of him who prospereth in his way,
because of the man who bringeth wicked devices to
pass. Cease from anger and forsake wrath; fret not
thyself in any wise to do evil. For evildoers shall be
cut off; but those that wait upon the LORD, they
shall inherit the earth.

—PSALM 37:7–9 (KJ21)

CHAPTER FORTY-TWO

Dumb Luck or Providence

It was just dumb luck I noticed them walking down the
block as we were in the van waiting to grab the girl.

VERA WOKE UP ON A TABLE, BLINDFOLDED AND GAGGED. SHE
could tell it was dark in the room because there wasn't much light
seeping in through her blindfold. There was a damp, mildewy smell
to the room and something else. Something rancid and vile. It was
the smell of death and despair. She could hear voices all around

her, whispering in languages she didn't understand. Incredibly, it almost sounded like praying, but no praying she'd ever heard before. She tried to sit up and realized that they had also bound her. Then Robbie and Thomas walked in.

"I think she's awake now. You were right, Robbie, she's beautiful. And now that you don't want her, I'm sure the master will gift her to me. Especially after the gifts I have for him."

Robbie grabbed Thomas by the neck and backed him up against the wall. "Listen to me, because I'm only going to say this once: she's off-limits, is that clear? I'm only working with you because the master said if I did what he asked, he would bring her back to me. So after he gets whatever information he needs from her, she's mine. And if you come anywhere near her, I will KILL you. Are we clear?"

Thomas tried to speak, but Robbie's grip on his neck was too tight for him to get any words out, so he just nodded his head.

"Good."

Then he let him go, and Thomas slithered to the floor, inhaling deeply as he did.

"Now go play with your little trophies, pervert," Robbie added.

Thomas slowly rose back to his feet, coughing a bit and staring at Robbie with his eyes set deep in his head. He was rubbing his throat. He was beyond furious, and his only thought was, *That's the last time.* Without realizing it, he had said the words aloud in a very scratchy voice.

"What was that?" Robbie asked.

Thomas looked at him. "That's the last time you put your hands on me, Robbie. I've had to suffer bullies all my life, and I'm done. The next time you put your hands on me, one of the two of us will die. I'm not taking any more of this. Not from you or from anyone else."

The reference to bullying surprised Robbie. Had he somehow become like the people he used to despise? If so, how ironic that it would be a creepy low-life like Thomas who pointed it out to him. But that didn't matter—it was only Thomas, who was a dirty pedophile; who cared what he thought or said? As he took a step toward Thomas, Nestor suddenly appeared.

"I hears you haves brought me a present, Robbies?"

"Me too," Thomas interjected, not wanting to be excluded from his part of the credit.

"Wheres is she?"

"She's tied to the table. We gagged and blindfolded her too, just as you asked. And after you get what you need from her, you'll make her love me like you said you would, right?"

"Was that's what I said? No, I believes what I said was, I would makes its so you could be togethers forevers. Sounds better that way, right?"

Then Nestor winked at Robbie.

"Same difference, as long as we are together like before."

He walked Nestor over to the table where Vera was tied up and showed her to him. Nestor was so excited he could barely contain himself. It was her. She was here, and she was his.

"I'ms not quite sure how you did it, but I'ms absolutely thrilled. Looks at me, I have goosebumps. How did you gets her? Wasn't she with the chosen one, as they call him?"

"Well, no, not at first. I picked her up from school and was walking her to the spot where Thomas and I had the car parked. Then her so-called self-proclaimed bodyguard showed up and tried to interfere with our plans. I had to kill him."

Nestor turned sharply and faced Robbie.

"Kills who, boy? The one called Ezekiel? The foretold one?"

"I don't know anything about the foretold one stuff, but yeah, I killed Ezekiel. I left him on the floor bleeding out. He's gone."

"The foretold one? How could you have done what Is could not so many nights agos?"

"He was distracted, just for a second, but that was all I needed. I stabbed him after Thomas stuck him with one of his needles, and then I stabbed him again a few more times. I don't know how many; I lost count."

"You killed the foretold one?"

This time, Nestor was smiling as he said it. *How ironic,* he thought. With all he was able to do, he was still just mortal, and it was a mortal who fell him. How wonderfully unexpected. He let out a hideous laugh that seemed to have multiple voices attached to it. He only wished he could have been there to see it.

"Wells done, Robbies, wells done. You killed the angel killer and brought me the girl. This day could not be mores fortuitous."

"Don't forget about me, what I did. I helped as well," Thomas exclaimed, not wanting to be excluded from the praise.

"Oh, I haves not forgottens about you, Thomas. I owe you thanks on this day as wells."

Thomas smiled at that, feeling recognized. Then Nestor turned his attention to Vera.

"You haves been quite troublesome, I must admits, but now all of that's about to change. We ares finally gonna sees what makes you so special."

He leaned over and whispered in her ear so only she could hear.

"Thens I'm gonna eat ya. Shhhhhh, don't tells Robbies, he thinks I only wants to ask you a few questions, then you can runs off and be together. He's kinda right, though. I'm gonna eats hims too. So, I guess you wills be togethers after all."

He looked up at Robbie, who was just now beginning to think that he might have messed up by bringing her there.

Then Thomas walked out of the room and came back with a little boy and a woman. "Look what I found over by the schoolyard while I was waiting to grab the girl," he said. They were both unconscious—Thomas's stock in trade. Nestor smiled and said:

"Aww, Thomas, you shouldn't haves."

He glided across the floor to inspect the offerings, and to his surprise and delight, he found that it was Hector and his mother, Lydia.

"Thomas, I must says that you haves truly outdone yourself todays. How could you have knowns?"

Thomas explained, "A while back, I was walking down the street when this little boy burst through the door of this little candy shop holding a bag of candy. He pushed the door open recklessly, and it hit me in the face. Well, there was no way I was going to let that stand. So I followed the boy back to his school, where he met up with another little boy. They talked for a while and then started walking down the block. I followed, hoping I would get the opportunity to grab them up. But I knew I couldn't do it where anyone could see, so I planned to follow them back to their house and knock them out with the syringe that I always keep on me and then come back later with my car and take them back to my place. But then they ran down this alleyway and right into you, my master. I stood there in awe, watching while you swallowed the first boy whole. As you brought the second boy up to your mouth, some rude woman crashed into me as she rushed past, knocking me to the ground. My glasses fell off my face, and in the time it took for me to pick them up and put them back on, you were gone. It was just the woman, who I later learned was the boys' mother, and the one boy remained left. I was so angry. She just shoved me and didn't even apologize, just like her wretched little boy had done earlier. I didn't know how or when, but I knew I was going to make both of them pay for bumping into me and for making me miss the rest of what happened in that alley. I watched them for months after that, but the timing was never right. They kept to a very public route, and neither of them was ever alone. It was just dumb luck I noticed them walking down the block as we were in the van waiting to grab the girl. They heard the commotion in the alley with Robbie and Vera, and the woman was about to call the police. While she was looking in her purse for her cell phone, I just walked up behind both of them and stuck them both. The van was already in the alley, so it was a piece of cake getting them into it without being seen. That's why I was a little late getting there to help Robbie."

Nestor stood there with an increasingly growing smile as he processed Thomas's story and found that it truly impressed him. It was almost impossible to surprise him, and yet Thomas had done so.

"Oh, Thomas, you haves outdone yourself," Nestor said while gently caressing his cheek. "I wills not forgets this."

He looked at Hector and Lydia.

"We haves unfinished business, yous and I. I told yous I'd be seeing yous." Lydia, barely conscious, said in a weak almost whisper of a voice, "Get away from him, you monster. You took my Rico, but I'll be damned if you think I'll let you take my Hector, too. Not while there's still breath in my body."

Then she faded off back into unconsciousness. Nestor just smiled at that because he knew that she already knew the truth. They were both dead already. All this bravado was for the sake of her son. He held up Hector's head to see the hopelessness in his eyes, but the look in the boy's eyes was not fear or anger—it was hope. He was hoping for another miracle like the one that had saved him not too long ago. But none would come. This place had been warded against angels. No one would come to save him or his mother this day.

"Ties them up and puts them in the corner by the table, Thomas. The time is growing near, and I must prepares. Tonight will be a fulls moon, and my powers wills increase two-folds. At that times, I wills rewards you and Robbie both for your deeds of this day."

Then he vanished.

Thomas did as directed, talking to himself as he worked. Robbie pulled up a chair and sat beside Vera, stroking her hand and speaking to her softly, "It will all be over soon, and then we can leave this place and be together. Everything is going to be fine; you'll see."

But he wondered if it was her he was talking to or himself, as a feeling of dread now began rising within him.

*The people which sat in darkness saw great light; and
to them which sat in the region and shadow of death
light is sprung up.*

—MATTHEW 4:16

CHAPTER FORTY-THREE
Behind the Door

*He grabbed her up to face him and looked deep into her
eyes. There was no fear, only hate—pure, undiluted hate.*

10:30 p.m.

THOMAS WAS TALKING TO HIMSELF AND PACING BACK AND
forth between Vera, Hector, and Lydia. He had managed to make
Nestor smile, and he knew he had bought some favor with him.

"The master will soon reward me with one of you for everything I've done. And I know just what to do to make him love me
even more. Slow roast ya. I can almost taste it now. That sweet meat,
so tender, will just fall away from the bone and melt in his mouth.
He's never had anything like that before, so I'm gonna cook you
two up special just for him, and that's when he'll make me like
him. And then I'll make them all pay for laughing at me. I'll make

Joanie pay too, that cock tease." He looked over at Vera and shouted, "You're all cock teasers, but now who's laughing, whore? Me, that's who, and I can't wait to slice the meat from your bones for what you've done."

Vera tried to speak, but the gag made her words indistinguishable, so Thomas removed it so he could hear what she had to say. "For what I've done?" Vera replied. "You're out of your freaking mind; I don't even know you. I've never done anything wrong to anyone, especially to you. Let us go, PLEASE! I promise I won't tell on you if you let us go. Don't do this—you know in your heart that this is wrong. At least let the boy go."

He grabbed her by the throat, bringing his face as close to hers as he could, pressing his forehead against her, and whispered, "Shut your filthy whore mouth or I'll put something in it, and I bet you'd like that, wouldn't you, whore?"

Tears began to fall from Vera's eyes; not because she was scared, but because she was angry and hurt. If she hadn't stopped Ezekiel when she did, Robbie would never have gotten the drop on him and killed him in that alley. If she had just stayed put like she was supposed to and hadn't gone with Robbie in the first place, she wouldn't even be here now, helpless and tied to a table with this maniac screaming in her face in a room full of demons. Robbie rose from the chair he was sitting in and grabbed Thomas by his shirt collar, jerking him back hard. He fell to the ground, scraping his hands on the floor.

"Don't you even think about touching her, Thomas, or so help me you'll wish I'd finished you off back in your apartment. She's mine, and I swear to God if you so much as look at her funny again, I'll kill you."

"Yours, you say? You're a fool, Robbie. The girl knows it, all these creatures in here know it, and somewhere deep inside of you, you know it too. Do you really think the master is going to give you this girl after everything he's done to get her? What kind of table do you think he had us tie her to, you freaking moron? It's a sacrificial table. She's a sacrifice. Do you even know where you are, or who we serve? He's a devil, or something close to it. that's who we serve, so all your threats don't really hold much weight with me in comparison to that. We're all gonna die in here, so as long as the master allows me to live, I'm going to say and do whatever the hell I want. And if he lets me take a piece of her for my troubles and service, then I will, and there's nothing you can do to stop it."

"Mr. Smyth, a word if I mays."

Thomas was startled and caught a little off guard at the sound of Nestor's voice, and when he turned around to find him standing directly in front of him, he almost fell over. "I didn't hear you walking up to me—you startled me."

Nestor smiled.

"You didn't hears me walkings over to you because I didn't want you to, but evens if I had, I don't thinks you would haves been ables to hears me over your rantings. So, Mr. Smyths, what is its that has gottens you so worked up?"

He caressed his face as he spoke, trying to seem genuinely concerned. His fingernails cut Thomas, causing a light trickle of blood to beat a path down to his cheek and off his chin to the floor.

"Oh, I'm sorrys, Thomas, but you knows sometimes things like that happens with these nails of mines."

He licked his fingers, looking at Thomas. Then he turned his focus toward Vera, the boy, and his mother. Still smiling, he looked at the blood drops that had fallen on the floor. The blood almost appeared to come alive as it moved toward him and onto his foot and absorbed into him.

"I'm sorry, master, I didn't mean to disturb you. It's just this little tease, she—"

Nestor grabbed Thomas by the mouth with his three-fingered hand, placing one finger over his lips to shush him.

"Language, Thomas, language. She is my guest, and she's easily worth threes or fours hundreds of you, so I'd watch hows I'd speaks to hers if I were you."

He released him and slivered over to Vera. He leaned over her, running his hand over her leg, across her stomach, in between her breasts, and then resting on her cheek. He took care not to cut her as he had Thomas.

"Are yous all right, my dear? Did the little mans scares yous? Would you likes me to kills him for you? I wills if you wants me to."

He looked up from the table and stared at Thomas, smiling.

Lydia, now awake, sniffled a bit and whispered, "Yes, kill him." It was barely audible, but Nestor heard it, and just like that, he was in front of them.

"You'd likes that wouldn't yous, Lydia, for me to kills the little man?"

Nestor, who seemed to just appear in front of her, startled Lydia. She hadn't realized anyone could hear her whispers. She knew this demon had no intention of letting any of them leave this place. He had already taken her baby boy, Rico, and now he had brought them there to finish what he started so many months ago. She never knew that she could hate a thing as much as she hated him. If she could kill him with her eyes, Nestor would have died a thousand deaths. In this place, hatred was an aphrodisiac, and Nestor was drawn to it. He picked her up to face him and looked deep into her eyes. There was no fear, only hate—pure, undiluted hate.

"I'd love it if you'd kill that little creep, and the boy helping him too."

Robbie looked up at her at that comment.

"The only thing I'd like more would be to kill *you* for taking my Rico."

The hatred flowed from her in waves, and Nestor could no longer contain himself. He opened his enormous mouth, which expanded to accommodate her size. She knew there was nothing she could do. Just before Nestor bit down into her, she spit in his face. "I hope you choke on me."

He arched his head back and snapped it down on her, biting off her head and part of her left shoulder. Her left arm was held onto her body by a few pieces of skin, which fell to the floor. Blood sprayed everywhere from one of the severed arteries where Nestor had bitten her. Some of it hit Thomas in the face. Then he tossed her still moving but lifeless body to the floor. Upon seeing this, Hector cried out, "Noooo, Mommm, no!" It was too much for him. First Rico, and now this thing had taken his mother. He was enraged and horrified and the same time. He pulled at his restraints desperately, trying to get free to avenge his mother, but he could not. So he cried, because it was all he could do.

"Absolutely intoxicatings. I wish everyone tasted as sweets. Did you sees that, Thomas? She wanted yous dead, and now she's dead. Who else wants Thomas dead?" he asked as he cackled.

Thomas could see pieces of flesh stuck in between his teeth, and he threw up. He was terrified and unable to move or speak; a dark circle formed in his crotch area as warm liquid spilled from his bladder. His bowels slipped as well, and tears rolled down his cheeks, mixing with the blood that was splattered across his face.

Vera also cried out, "No!" but she knew it was too late. She heard Lydia's soul cry out the moment Nestor took her. He hadn't just consumed her flesh; he had eaten her soul. This was a special treat for Nestor, because she was an innocent. He had been seduced by her anger and hatred and had taken her. Vera let out a scream of frustration, and one window in the room exploded.

"Gag her quickly," Nestor commanded Robby.

Her arms and legs pulled against the ropes that restrained her, and she tried to sink into herself but couldn't. She couldn't stop thinking about the little boy's mother—losing not just her life but her soul. This was the demon's plan for all of them, to be sure, but she knew that he had something else planned for her. She would be a beacon that he would use to draw souls to him, and she would also form a shield that he would conceal himself with until it was too late. She knew he would never let her go. Theirs would be an unholy marriage of light and dark, and her only hope for freedom rested on the shoulders of a man she believed to be dead.

Thomas, still in shock from what had just happened, wiped the blood off his face and cleared his throat. He wanted to say something, but he thought it best to remain silent. Over the past ten years, he had killed and eaten his fair share of innocent people, and he'd thought nothing about it. But he had never seen or even heard of anything like this before. He finally understood who he was in servitude to, and it was also at that moment that he realized he truly was damned. Two tears rolled down his blood-stained cheeks, leaving a trail behind like running mascara.

Nestor looked at Thomas inquisitively and then frowned.

"You stinks, Thomas. Go cleans yourself up, and don't thinks anymore. Leaves that to those who cans. Your jobs is to do what you're told, not to thinks, is that understood?"

"Yes, master."

His voice was barely a whisper. His head was held low and he was staring at the floor, clearly no longer quite so full of himself. Nestor had successfully broken him.

"Good, now go brings me the boy. I'm stills hungry."

He smiled and looked back over at Vera.

"I haven't forgotten about you, missy. I'll be over in just a minutes."

Then he looked back at Thomas, who was dragging the boy over to him. He grabbed the little boy by the arm and walked him over by Vera's table, directly in front of her.

"I wants you to see this."

He picked the boy up and licked his face. The boy was screaming and kicking his legs in the air, still calling out for his mother. This made Nestor smile even more.

"Don't worry, child, you'll be with her soon."

At that moment, just for a second, Hector's fear was replaced with hate, and that's what Nestor was waiting for. He opened his mouth wide and then held the boy up over his head, getting ready to swallow him whole.

Vera gave a muffled scream through her gag, which filled him with joy and caused goosebumps to form on his skin. He got a little shiver and shook it off. He was so excited that he giggled. Vera turned her head and closed her eyes. She would not watch; he couldn't make her watch this. She wouldn't.

"Hold her heads, Thomas, and opens her eyes, I wants her to see."

Thomas took a step toward the table, and Nestor screeched, "No, not you. You stay where you are. You, Robbie. You hold her." Robbie did as he was told. He held her head in his hands, and she felt him peel her eyelids open so she could see.

"Yes, good, watch."

He tilted his head back and began lowering the boy into his mouth. Suddenly, the building began shaking. All the walls seemed to shimmer and ripple like water, and then they exploded and burst into flames. Then a few of the demons in the room began bursting into flames as well—first one, then another, filling the room with black suet and sulfur. The floor rocked violently, and a great wind came out of nowhere, tossing Robbie and Thomas back and forth around the room. It blew the boy out of Nestor's grip, and the shaking floor caused him to shift his body weight to catch his balance. An enormous crack came from the door through the length of the room, right under Nestor's feet. Nestor levitated to avoid falling through. The front door opened, and a bright white light burst into the room. A figure stepped through the doorway but could not be made out from within the light.

"When you go out to battle against your enemies and see horses and chariots and people more numerous than you, do not be afraid of them; for the LORD your God, who brought you up from the land of Egypt, is with you.

—DEUTERONOMY 20:1 (NASB1995)

CHAPTER FORTY-FOUR

Ezekiel and Father Connors

Do you think he'll treat you differently once you're one of us?

10 p.m.

THEY HAD CHOSEN A DARK NIGHT FOR THIS VENTURE—NOT the color of the sky, though it seemed darker than usual, but the atmosphere overall. This place that Ezekiel had been drawn to was evil. You didn't have to be a supernatural being to know it either. There was a weight to it—a texture, if you will. Father Connors couldn't shake a feeling of foreboding.

He knew that Ezekiel had struck gold with this place, and until now, he didn't even know a place could feel so unwelcoming. Shivers ran up and down his spine every time he looked at the building. It was a three-story flophouse in downtown LA; the area was commonly referred to as Skid Row. He had passed by this place thousands of times but never noticed it. He'd never even realized it was there until the other day when he had been driving by and Ezekiel had made him stop. He'd told the priest that they needed to go to this building if they wanted to find Vera. The difference in the building's appearance now, in the dark, was literally night and day. A shadow slithered by across the wall and into a window. Then he swore he saw a pair of glassy white eyes reflecting the light of the red moon back at him from a different window as he got out of the car.

"Ezekiel did you—"

"Yes, I saw it."

Goosebumps popped up all over Father Connors's arms, and his heart started beating faster as the adrenaline kicked in. "So how do you want to do this, EZ? I'll follow your lead." His heart was beating so hard he swore Ezekiel must've been able to hear it.

"First, we must cover the ground around this building with salt. That is to make sure nothing gets in or out. At least nothing in the spirit, that is."

Father Connors looked up at him sharply and asked, "What do you mean 'in the spirit,' EZ? I thought this was all spiritual."

"Not quite, Father. There are other things that lurk in the night, and they're dangerously understated in everything we've been taught. When we get inside, I need you to stand in the corner by the door. If anything comes through the door, shoot it. If anything tries to get out that door, shoot it, and for God's sake, if anything comes at you, shoot it. And if you must get out of there, don't wait for me. I don't know what we're going to find inside, but whatever it is, they will outnumber us."

Father Connors nodded. He checked his shotgun, packing extra buckshot that was filled with salt and silver, specially made by Ezekiel, into his pockets. He had a feeling that he was going to need it all.

Ezekiel felt nervous. It wasn't obvious to look at him, but he was. He had done nothing like this before, and never with anyone else's help. He was grateful to have Father Connors with him, but he also feared for his safety. He hoped they would both come through this none the worse for wear, but he knew deep down that was not possible. Something like what they were about to embark upon changes a person. Ezekiel knew that the priest would never be the man he had been after this.

Father Connors did his best to seem brave as he slung his shotgun over his shoulder, checked his pack one more time, and started walking toward the entrance.

They could both hear whispers from the shadows calling out to them.

"Father, join us, we've been waiting for you . . . we've always been waiting for you. You will not leave this place alive. Tonight, we will feast on your soul, priest. We've already done away with your charge, Ezekiel. Haven't you heard? We gutted him like a pig. He's gone, Father, and soon you will be with him."

"E—"

"Don't say anything, Father, Ezekiel interrupted. "Either they can't see me or they don't recognize me. Whatever the reason, let's not show our hand until it is absolutely necessary."

"But how can that be? You're right here with me—unless you're not you anymore . . ."

Ezekiel turned and faced Father Connors. "I promise you, Father, I am me. I'm just different now. They think I'm dead because they bore witness to my death at Robbie's hands. They did not, however, witness my rebirth at the very hand of God. When Azrael touched me, I died, and then God touched me and brought me back. Both events changed me. I don't fully understand it yet, but I know that I'm different." He placed his hand on Father Connors's shoulder to comfort him and, as he did, Father Connors felt energy and power coursing through Ezekiel and flowing into himself. He felt better than he had in years. No aches or pains . . . no fear. His heart slowed down to normal, and he seemed more attuned to his surroundings. Like Ezekiel, the priest realized that he too was different.

"Come, Father, let us say a quick prayer before we enter. Dear Lord, please give us the strength of mind and fortitude to carry out this task now set before us and forgive us now our shortcomings and transgressions or anything that we may have done that was wrong in your eyes. Amen."

"Boy, you weren't playing when you said quick. So, you ready for this?"

"As ready as I'm gonna get, I guess, let's do it."

They made their way up the stairs and into the building, and when Ezekiel stepped over the threshold, the building began to shake slightly, making the walls and floors seem to be buzz with life. The whispers and voices grew louder and more frequent. Nothing could have prepared them for what happened next. Two images appeared from the shadows and leaped onto Ezekiel. They were completely black and devoid of any color, except in the eyes. The eyes were blood red, and they seemed to glow. Father Connors backed up into the corner and watched in horror and awe as the two shadows enveloped and seemingly consumed Ezekiel in their darkness. They picked him up off the floor and slammed him from one wall to the next. And then, somehow, Ezekiel seemed to grab hold of them. They screamed in a tongue unknown to man as what looked like red veins began to appear, giving shape to the formless figures within the blackness that enveloped him. They were demons. The black feathers of their wings began to spark and burst into flames as they dug their talons past his corporeal flesh grasping for his core, hoping to rip out his soul—a spiritual gutting. But Ezekiel held on to them by their necks, and the veins grew even wider still. It reminded Father Connors of lava as it flows down a volcano; the two demons looked like a glowing patchwork of black outlined in crimson. The smell of sulfur filled the air, and their bodies simultaneously ignited and burst into flames. As they did, Ezekiel fell from the ceiling, landing in what almost looked like a track and field running position, still holding the smoldering remains of what was left of the demons' bodies. Before Father Connors even had time to take in and process what he had just seen, a vampire grabbed him from behind and whispered in his ear.

"Let's see what you can do, Father."

His touch was cold and clammy, but his strength was incredible. Father Connors could barely move; he felt the vampire's hot breath on the side of his neck.

"Tell me, Father, do you think he will treat you differently once you are one of us?"

He licked the priest's neck, marking the spot he was preparing to bite. Father Connors slammed his head back, hitting the foul thing in its nose and causing it to loosen its grip just enough for him to bring up his shotgun and shove it into its open mouth just as it was about to deliver its life-changing venom and rob him of his life's blood. There was no time to think or second-guess himself—he just pulled the trigger. Blood and brain matter splattered all over the wall, and some got on the back of his head. His right ear was bleeding, and everything sounded muffled. He turned to look at the headless corpse, which was still twitching, and said, "No, I think he would do to me pretty much what I did to you. Feel better now." He looked over at Ezekiel, shocked to see that he was almost on top of him. The boy was so fast.

"Are you all right, Father? I thought I lost you for a minute there."

"You thought you lost me? Shoot, it'll take more than one skinny vampire to do old Father Connors in, and besides that, I wasn't the one who was floating up in the air a minute ago, you better watch your six too, EZ."

Just for the briefest of moments, Ezekiel smiled. Then he heard whispers in the distance: "Leave us the priest, and you can go." "Leave the priest." Over and over the voices said the same thing.

"Father, can you hear that?"

"Hear what, EZ?"

He realized then that they were talking in the high speech, or angel's tongue. "This was a mistake; I shouldn't have brought you here with me. They are going to come at you hard because of me. I should have known better."

"EZ, listen to me. They were going to be coming for me, whether or not I was with you here today. I've never been closer to God than I have been these past few months, and so much of that I owe to you. I—"

But before he could finish his sentence, Father Connors was snatched up into the air, feet kicking and arms flailing about. He could smell the foul breath of the thing that had hold of him, which caused him to gag and throw up. His entire body felt as if hot needles were being poked in and out of him. He could hear voices all around him cursing, laughing, and taunting. Then he felt as if he were outside of himself; he had no control of his body, and then they were inside him. He opened his mouth to scream, but no words escaped his lips. He could see and hear things around him, but he was no longer in control of himself. It was like being in that dream state just before you wake up. You try to get up, but your body doesn't respond. Ezekiel looked on in horror. He had never witnessed anyone taken or possessed before. He always dealt with people after the fact, and it had never been anyone close to him.

"He's ours now; soon you will be ours as well."

Without realizing he was moving, Ezekiel leaped into the air, grabbing hold of Father Connors's foot, and yanked him from the hands of the demons. They fell to the floor. Ezekiel placed his hand on Father Connors's chest. He said two words, "LEAVE HIM."

The priest's body arched and shook as black shadows poured from his body like blood from an open wound. Seven shapes took form in a semicircle around Ezekiel. He waved his hand, and they were all pressed fast against the side of the wall, unable to move. Father Connors inhaled deeply, as if he could suddenly breathe again after being underwater.

"Thank you, EZ." He coughed loudly for a moment and then thanked him again. "Those things just pushed them-selves inside of me. They were trying to take my soul, but they couldn't. It burned them. They said if they could not take me, they would rip me apart."

Ezekiel looked furiously at the wall where the demons were pinned. "By your own words shall be your punishment so that you will know his power." The air around the demons rippled, and they screamed. The wall cracked and splintered behind them, and they exploded into pieces, but they were not dead. "This is how you will remain until the time of judgment," Ezekiel said, "and your pieces will be cast among the flames, where you will burn for eternity.

And all who have borne witness can now testify to the power of the one true God."

He then helped Father Connors to his feet. The priest looked at his friend and said, "You know, I think just saying you're 'different' is a bit of an understatement, son." Then he smiled.

"Can you stand on your own, Father? There is still much to do."

"I'm good; let's get to it."

They made their way up the stairs to the second floor. While they tried to move silently, their footsteps echoed on the metal steps. There would be no sneaking up on anyone, Father Connors thought, with all of this noise. When they got to the second floor, Father Connors felt like they had just passed through some kind of void. The air was different, heavier. The ground was brittle. It cracked and popped as they walked across it. Everything moved around them like waves in the ocean. Father Connors had to place his hand on the wall to steady himself. He felt seasick. He noticed Ezekiel had done the same. Then two of the biggest cockroaches Father Connors had ever seen in his life ran across his hand on the wall and bit him. He pulled his hand off the wall—shaking it all the while to make sure nothing was still on him. Then he noticed more roaches running all around and disappearing into the floor. Actually, they weren't quite disappearing, but more like blending. He turned on the flashlight attached to his shotgun to get a better look and let out a startled shout. The floor wasn't making the popping sound, as he had thought earlier; it was the roaches being crushed underfoot. They covered the floor, and they were crawling all over their feet and pants. He began swatting them off wildly. He hated roaches. They freaked him out. It was like he could feel them crawling all over him. The smell of them filled his nostrils. He was jumping around erratically, trying to get them off of him. Then he slipped, lost his footing, and fell to the floor, squishing more of the bugs as he did. The wet, gray mucus-like substance oozed over his hands and fingers from the roaches that were caught under his hand. The ones not crushed began biting him. Now they had crawled up his arm and onto his chest. Father Connors dropped his gun, and the light shined awkwardly against the wall as he began grabbing the bugs and swatting them off frantically. He could hear them saying, "Inside him, inside him."

They tried to crawl into his mouth, pushing their way past his lips, or into his nose and ears. He instinctively clenched his teeth, accidentally biting one foul thing in half as he did. He gagged immediately, trying to spit it out and threw the rest of its still moving body to the floor. The half in his mouth fought to stay in, trying to crawl down his throat. He had to stick his fingers in his mouth to pull the thing free from him. The putrid, bitter ooze that was its blood caused Father Connors to throw up involuntarily seconds after it was free of his mouth.

Then he heard Ezekiel say, "Enough." And they were off of him, all floating in the air. It was almost like they had never been on him. Almost. Father Connors's hands and legs still bore the marks from the bites. Ezekiel, however, was unmarked by the encounter. He mentally gathered and pushed them all into one corner of the room as they screeched in protest. One by one the insects began merging into one another until they formed one grotesque roach-like being.

"We know you, boy, don't we? You are he who was foretold, aren't you? Still alive we see; it seems that the reports of your demise were a bit overstated."

"It would seem so," Ezekiel said as he reached into his backpack, pulled out a bottle of holy water, and began splashing the thing with it. Hundreds of voices all speaking as one cried out as burning, hissing sounds came from the areas struck by the water. Sparks flashed and popped all over its body. It took a wild swing at Ezekiel with its insect-like arm, desperately trying to connect with his head, but Ezekiel unsheathed his blade and cut it off in mid-swing. When the severed arm hit the floor, it instantly reverted into roaches that scattered about the floor and into the shadows. Then he threw the blade at the demon's head, pinning it to the wall. It looked like it wanted to say something, but the words wouldn't come; it just burst into flames and fell apart into a pile of smoldering ash. Ezekiel walked over to Father Connors and helped him to his feet.

"Are you all right?"

"I've been better, I can tell you that for sure," Father Connors said as he spat on the floor and tried to rid his mouth of the taste of the roach.

"Listen, Father, we've crossed between two planes of reality. I know you felt it. Words and thoughts can be made manifest. You must control your fears and be mindful of your words lest they be made real. You get me?"

Father Connors nodded but he wasn't sure how he was going to be able to control his thoughts. He wanted to ask Ezekiel how, but he was afraid he might cause something else to appear.

"Focus on your cross and what it represents," Ezekiel said, almost on cue, as if reading his mind. Father Connors nodded again, dusted himself off one more time—he still felt like bugs were on him—picked up his shotgun, and readied himself. Ezekiel, however, seemed to be in his element. This was something he had prepared for all his life. He had worked on keeping his thoughts clear and his mind focused since he was a child, and he had perfected this skill with Joshua's help during his time in prison. He told Father Connors to stay close as he continued to lead him down the hallway.

*Yea though I walk through the valley of the shadow
of death, I will fear no evil; for thou art with me; Thy
rod and thy staff they comfort me.*

—PSALM 23:4 (KJ21)

CHAPTER FORTY-FIVE

Separation

*Then he raised his hands, and long sharp teeth began
to protrude from the center of each of his palms.*

FATHER CONNORS WAS ANGRY. THESE THINGS WERE SINGLING him out for a few reasons. First and foremost, he knew it was because they figured he would be an easy win for them. They were not in the least bit threatened by him. Second, they knew he was important to Ezekiel, so they had decided to get to him by hurting the priest. Third and most importantly, they did not believe in his faith in his God. It was almost as if they didn't know that Father Connors had been caught up in the spirit not too long ago. How could they see him and not Ezekiel … at least at first? How could this be, he wondered. He was saved too. He knew it must be as God willed it, but he still couldn't help being angry about it. He knew one thing for sure: before this night was over, these things and all who dwelled within these walls would know the name Connors and would recognize that his faith in God was not weak.

"We have to get to the end of this hallway and then up to the next level, Father. I can feel her. Vera. She's in great distress, but she is still alive."

"If I didn't know any better, I would think you'd been here before, with the way you seem to know your way around this place."

"It's not that, Father. It's like Vera and I are magnets being drawn to one another. It's nothing I could put a finger on, exactly, but somehow I always know where she is. Except before, the feeling was always kind of vague, and now it's clear, like a beacon."

"Can you see anything else, or just Vera? Because a heads up would be great with some of these bad boys."

"No, this place has been warded. The fact that we have gotten this far is by the grace of God alone. We just have to be on our guard."

Ezekiel reached into his pocket, pulled something out, and put it in Father Connors's pocket. "What was that?" the priest asked.

"Just something to keep you safe when you need it most."

Father Connors nodded, and they continued down the corridor. There were four doors in the hallway: two on the right and two on the left. They tried the door handles on each door as they passed by. The first three were locked, but the fourth was open, and they entered the room. It was empty and dirty, so they cleared it and exited, closing the door behind them as they left. As they started toward the third flight of stairs, a black shadow-like hand reached through the wall and grabbed hold of Father Connors's jacket, jerking him back toward the wall. His body hit the wall, hard, and he tried to pull himself free but was unable. There was a second tug, and suddenly he was through the wall and back into the room. Ezekiel turned around just in time to see Father Connors pass through the solid wall. He raced to the place where Father Connors had been standing and placed his hands on the wall, searching for the spot where he could pass through as well, but the wall was solid. He then rushed to the door and turned the handle—it was locked. He tried to force his way in, but the door would not give. Then, from behind him, he heard a voice.

"I wouldn't worry too much about him, boy. You should be more concerned with what's about to happen to you."

Ezekiel turned around to see two lower vampires and one Alpha. They had appeared from nowhere and moved with super-human speed. The two lower vampires pinned Ezekiel to the wall, restraining both of his arms. The Alpha walked over to him, smiling. "We could not approach you earlier while the priest was here. He somehow seems to have gotten stronger from when he first entered this place just minutes ago. But you, however, we can't sense anything foreboding from you. So here we are."

"That you sense nothing from me is probably a good thing, because I honestly don't want to hurt you. I just want to get to my friend. For the sake of time, I'm willing to let you three go on your way, and I promise that the next time we meet, I will give you a quick and merciful death. However, if you make me fight you now, you'll pray for a death that will not come."

This response from Ezekiel was not what they were expecting. The Alpha stopped in his tracks to reexamine his prey, trying to ascertain if there was something he had missed. He shook his head and smiled. Then he raised his hands, and long, sharp teeth protruded from the center of each of his palms.

"I'll say this for you, boy, you talk the talk. Take comfort in knowing that you made me smile, a feat that is not easily accomplished by one such as you or your kind. As fun as this has been, all good things must eventually come to an end. I'll let the priest know how brave you were right up to the end as I siphoned your life's energy from your body."

But before he could place his hands on Ezekiel to make good on his promise, Ezekiel lifted both feet off the ground and kicked the vampire in the chest and into the wall across the hallway. Then, with surprising speed, he pulled his arms free of the other two minor vampires as if they were coated in oil. He pulled out his blade and with one sweeping motion decapitated both of them before they had time to react to him being free. The Alpha extracted himself from the wall and leaped into the air, swooping down on Ezekiel. But his actions had already been anticipated. With a circular strike, Ezekiel separated all four of his limbs from his body. The vampire's torso fell to the floor face first. He was screaming muffled obscenities while his arms and legs flopped about the floor like fish out of water. Ezekiel rolled the Alpha over onto his back and asked in a sarcastic tone, "What are you sensing from me now, vampire, anything yet? Or do I still feel like your next meal? You should have walked away when you were able."

The vampire started to say something, but Ezekiel rolled him back over onto his face. He pulled some duct tape from his backpack, tore off a long piece, and wrapped it around the Alpha's head, covering his mouth and rendering him silent. "When this is all over, I'll come back and we can talk about me putting you out of your misery or me putting you in a box and burying you someplace where you probably won't be found for a century or two. Until then, like Tupac used to say, 'Keep your head up.'"

Ezekiel went back to the door and continued trying to break through it with his shoulder. After a few minutes passed, Ezekiel turned around. He rested his back against the wall, lowered his head into his hands, and exhaled deeply. He was sad and angry at the same time. Over the past two years, Father Connors had become like a father to him. And now one of these things had just taken him away. He was almost beside himself with emotions. He didn't want to leave, but he knew that he had to. He walked back over to his backpack and put it on, kicking the vampire in the face one time for good measure. Then he started to make his way up the third staircase. He prayed that God would give him the strength to do what must be done and that he would be able to hold Nestor to account for his deeds. That he would be able to get justice for Father Connors, his friend and mentor.

Ye are of God, little children, and have overcome them: because greater is he that is in you, than he that is in the world.

—1 JOHN 4:4

CHAPTER FORTY-SIX

Room for Seconds

"We have your friends, and soon you will be joining them."

.

FILLED WITH RAGE, EZEKIEL RACED UP THE STAIRS INTO THE dark, not knowing what direction he was going but driven forward. In his mind, he could hear the screams of his friends as they were being tortured. He could only imagine what was being done, because the voices no longer sounded human but more like animals caught in a cage.

When he finally reached the top of the staircase, he saw that it led to a long and dark corridor. There were three doors on his right and one door at the end of the hallway, facing him. He could see shadows moving around underneath the last door. They were very clear; in fact, it was almost like they were being projected onto the floor. Suddenly, the shadows stretched and grew. They took the form of hideous misshapen hands with elongated fingers. When the shadow reached his foot, it stopped. Ezekiel thought to himself that while that was weird, it wasn't close to being enough to scare him, much less keep him from going down the hallway to look for his friends. Then, without warning, the shadow grabbed his leg. He could feel nails digging into his calves, and he tried to pull away, but the pain was so intense that it was all he could do just to keep standing. Spots of blood seeped through his jeans where the shadow had grabbed him. He could hear voices whispering, "We have you like we have your friends." They echoed back and forth throughout the corridor. "Soon we will have their souls, and yours will follow." Now it seemed like less of an echo, and more like hundreds of different voices all around him calling out. "We have your friends, and soon you will be joining them."

Ezekiel knelt, trying to grab hold of the thing that was digging into his leg, but there was nothing there to grab hold of. Then the shadow began pulling him toward the door at the end of the corridor. He lost his footing and fell backward onto the floor, all the while holding on to his leg and hoping to find whatever had a hold on him and get free. The pain was now, way beyond anything he had ever imagined. It felt as if his very flesh was being peeled back from the bone, and then hot grease was being poured over it. He could hear his flesh sizzling and popping like chicken in a deep fryer as the thing that had him tightened its grip. He cried out in pain and tears fell freely from his eyes as the thing continued dragging him toward the door. He began praying as he struggled through the pain.

"Dear God, please give me the strength to fight this thing. Lord, do not let it take me; do not let me fall at the foot of the enemy after all of this."

"Grab the shadow, EZ," a whisper-like voice called out to him, and just for a moment, he thought it was Joshua. Then he heard the voice again: "Grab the shadow quickly while you can."

Ezekiel leaned forward and looked at the shadow holding his leg on the ground, He grabbed at the shadow where the wrist ought to have been. To his amazement, he latched onto something. He squeezed hard with everything he had within him, and the hand opened, releasing his leg. He immediately felt instant relief, like when you burn your hand cooking and then stick it under the faucet and run cold water over it.

The voices began calling out to him again, but this time they weren't whispering. They howled, and the walls and the ground around him began to shake and rattle. It was just then that Ezekiel realized why the shadow thing that had grabbed him was so strong. It wasn't just a single entity but a host or legion of them that had combined themselves into one being for one purpose, and one purpose only: to capture him and win his soul.

But now, it was he who had them in his grip, and the tides had just turned in his favor. He thought about Joshua sacrificing himself so that he could live, and Father Connors and Vera, who were somewhere in this building and were depending upon him to save them. He began pulling up on the shadow's hand, growing stronger and stronger with each passing moment. His body began to glow, lighting up the corridor, and scores of winged creatures became visible on the walls all around him. They cried out to him, "Mercy, mercy! We're sorry, so sorry. We thought you were human; we didn't know it was you Mich—"

"I shall grant you the same mercy you gave me—mercy befitting the likes of you. You will be welcomed in the very pits of shoal, where you will wait until the time of your judgment." The creatures began to burst into flames. A great wind blew, and all the windows in the hallway and on the second floor blew out, as a large crack formed and made its way from his feet all the way down the middle of the floor to the door in front of him. Then the walls began to warp inward and imploded, bursting into flames as well. Dust and smoke filled the air all around him. What was left of the wall was burning, and the smell of sulfur filled the air. With his body still glowing, he reached down and held his leg, which was shredded and burnt. It began to heal, undoing all the damage that had been done to it earlier. Then he looked up at the door in front of him and began walking toward it. He knew that this was where he would find Vera and possibly Father Connors. But most importantly, this was where he would find Nestor, and tonight he would bring all of this to an end. Tonight, Nestor would die.

*But the Lord is faithful. He will establish you and
guard you against the evil one.*

　　　　　　　—2 Thessalonians 3:3 (ESV)

CHAPTER FORTY-SEVEN
Alone in the Dark

*"Yea though I walk through the valley of the shadow
of death, I shall fear no evil. Because I have my
shotgun and bullets blessed by God to comfort me."*

A strong force pulled Father Connors back and he hit
the wall. Then a second tug on his jacket pulled him through the
wall, and he was back in the room he and Ezekiel had just cleared.

"So, you thought you had escaped us, Father."

The voice seemed to be coming from everywhere. Father
Connors quickly got to his feet, shining the flashlight that was
attached to his shotgun around the room.

"Over here, Father . . . no, over here," voices whispered in his
ears on either side of him. It threw him off a bit, and he spun
around wildly. Suddenly, right in front of him there stood a demon.

It grabbed him by the neck and picked him up off the floor, holding him there while it examined him.

"You would call yourself a demon slayer, Father?" Then it laughed and tossed him across the length of the room into the wall. "I have good and bad news for you, Father. The good news is that you've grown too strong in your faith for me alone to possess you. The bad news is that I'm just going to kill you instead, but I'm going to do it real slow." It dragged that last part out for a second or two to accentuate its point, and then it smiled again.

Father Connors managed to get back on his feet while the demon was monologuing. When it was finished, he spoke. "Are you done, or do you still have more to say about how badly you're going to hurt me? Because I've got better things to do than listen to you go on and on about it. Whatever you're going to do, do it, and let's get this over with already."

His voice and posture showed that he was at peace with his situation. He was not afraid, as the demon had hoped; he stood ready to face him. The demon was enraged and flew toward him. It was going to make him pray for death while it ripped him to pieces. The demon grabbed Father Connors and backed him into the wall, hard. It made a loud thud.

"I think I'll start with an arm, Father, and then a leg."

"Sounds like a good plan to me," Father Connors replied as he shoved the mouth of his shotgun into the armpit of the monster and pulled the trigger. The demon fell back, surprised. Its right arm was still holding onto Father Connors, but it was no longer attached to its body. Then Father Connors shot it in the kneecap, severing the lower part of its leg and sending it to the ground, howling.

"How? Those are just bullets! This is not possible!"

Father Connors's mind flashed back to a time when he and Ezekiel were back at the church in the basement. They had gathered about a thousand silver crosses of various sizes and prayed over them for hours while they soaked in blessed holy water. They melted them down, made pellets out of them, and filled shotgun cartridges for the better part of that week. Then they prayed and fasted and prayed some more, essentially consecrating the shotgun cartridges. Ezekiel had also written a number on each of the cartridges: 53787. When he asked him why, he simply said it was to make them powerful before our enemies. And it wasn't until this moment that the priest realized what this meant and how deeply profound it was. The numbers had multiple meanings when matched up against a phone keypad. They spelled out the name "Jesus," and there was power in his name. But they also added up to thirty, the same number of pieces of silver that Judas had received for his betrayal, and consequently, the exact number of pellets they had put in each shotgun cartridge.

Father Connors refocused his attention on the maimed demon and replied, "Bullets, yes, but specially made and blessed for this task, praise God, and by his power, I will dispatch you back to the pits of hell."

Then he fired his shotgun two more times, taking off the rest of the demon's limbs as it had originally intended to do to him.

"*Yea though I walk through the valley of the shadow of death, I will fear no evil. Because I have my shotgun and bullets blessed by God to comfort me.* You'll forgive me my embellishment, but it seemed to fit given our current situation."

Then Father Connors aimed at the demon's head and, with no hesitation, pulled the trigger. The thing was dead. He then walked back to the wall he had been pulled through, slung his shotgun over his shoulder, and placed both hands on the wall. He began praying, and as he did, the wall rippled like water. He closed his eyes, took a deep breath, and stepped forward, passing through

it. He was back on the other side. He noticed the bodies of the
vampires on the ground. *Holy moly,* he thought, *this must have been
some fight.* He paused a moment to reload his shotgun and began
to cautiously make his way over to the stairway. He knew that this
was where he would find EZ, and he hoped he could catch up to
him and be of some help in whatever way God would let him. Then
he heard an explosion, and the building rocked. All the windows
on the floor exploded, and a gust of wind hit him so hard he had
to steady himself with the banister on the staircase and take a knee.
Something had just gone down, but he couldn't tell whether it was
good or bad. He only knew that he had to get to Ezekiel and Vera,
and quickly. He raced up the stairs, and as he did, he could hear
voices crying out. The stairwell seemed to get longer right in front
of him as he ran upward; it was like a scene out of some bad horror
film. Demons began jumping out at him from the shadows, but he
shot them down as they did. He got to the top of the stairs and
saw Ezekiel. He was seated on the floor and holding his leg, which
looked to be bleeding. A strong wind was blowing, and the noise
in the hallway was deafening. Father Connors tried to shout over
it, hoping Ezekiel would hear him: "Grab the shadow EZ, grab the
shadow quickly while you can!" He didn't know why he said it. It
was almost as if there was a voice speaking through him. He refocused his attention on the demons that kept popping up out of the
surrounding shadows. He hoped he wouldn't run out of rounds,
but if this kept up, he knew he wouldn't have enough. He was going
to have to try something else, and soon.

He could hear what seemed like hundreds, maybe thousands, of voices, all crying out in pain. Father Connors looked
back toward Ezekiel, who was now on his feet, holding the arms
of a giant shadow creature. He was glowing, and the room was in
flames. Then it was gone with a howl, and so were all the rest of the

demons. He watched as Ezekiel bent down and held his leg for a bit, and then he stood up and started walking toward the door at the end of the hallway. He looked like a new man. He was still glowing, and if he didn't know any better, he would say he looked angelic. He called out to him before he got to the door. "Hey EZ, wait up."

Ezekiel stopped and turned around, almost as if he was expecting a trap or a trick. But when he saw that it was Father Connors, he almost fell over. It was just too much to hope for. His eyes welled up, and a couple of tears fell from his eyes before he could wipe them away. He ran over and hugged the priest tightly, picking him up off his feet. The energy coming from him was warm and soothing, like that feeling you get when you sit in a hot tub and the water covers you over. He put him down and assessed his condition. The priest had a few cuts and bruises on his hands and face, and his clothes were disheveled, but he appeared to be in good shape. Ezekiel also noticed that there was something different about him. Something had changed with him as well. He was finally "awake."

He spoke. "Father, I'm so glad to see you. I tried to get back into the room, but the door was locked and I couldn't break through it. What happened in there?"

"I could ask you the same thing. I saw the bodies of the vampires on the floor when I finally got out of that room. I would like to talk more with you about all of this, especially the numbers we wrote on the bullets, but for now, I think we'd better stay focused on our mission. If we make it out of here in one piece, we can share war stories over a beer."

"That's a deal," Ezekiel responded with a slight smile. They both checked their gear. Father Connors reloaded his shotgun, and then they proceeded toward the door at the end of the hallway. As they got closer to the door, Ezekiel began to glow brighter and brighter.

It was like staring into the sun, except Father Connors found that he didn't need to cover his eyes. Ezekiel reached for the doorknob. It was shaped like a ram's head. As he touched it, a wind began to build from out of nowhere. The building itself began to shake and rattle. It was akin to being in an earthquake. The door resisted him, and the head of the ram tried to bite his fingers as he held it. The door frame had also begun glowing, and cracks began to form in the door itself. This door was warded, and whatever was behind it was powerful. Both men knew it had to be Nestor.

Father Connors readied his gun and prayed silently. The door warped and bubbled and then finally imploded. Ezekiel was so bright at this point that Father Connors could no longer make him out. As Ezekiel stood in the doorway, lower demons began exploding from his light. Parts of the room burst into flames as well, and the smell of sulfur filled the air. He saw Vera tied to an altar and Robbie standing beside her along with Thomas. There was also a small child tied up and crying, and a woman's headless body lay on the floor. Then he saw him, Nestor, in the middle of the room, with what could only be described as a look of shock on his face.

And then Ezekiel and Father Connors both stepped inside.

He says, "You are My war-club, My weapon of war;
And with you I shatter nations, And with you I
destroy kingdoms."

—JEREMIAH 51:20 (NASB1995)

CHAPTER FORTY-EIGHT

And One Shall Fall

"Hey, you never know until you try, right?
Besides, he talks too much."

NESTOR LOOKED UP, SURPRISED, ALONG WITH EVERYONE ELSE IN
the room. In this place, which was a separate realm within the alter-
nate dimension inside the house, he alone should have been the
only being able to wield power. Who was this person who had just
crashed his party? Voices began whispering, but he heard nothing
that was coherent. The energy coming off of this being was not
earthly—it was Godly. He felt something he hadn't felt since the
night he had lost his fingers so many years ago, when Michael stole
his intended meal. But why would Michael be here now? It wasn't
time for him to be there, and even if it were, it would be *his* time to
reign he thought, not Michael's.

"Away from her, demon," a voice said from within the light. It rang like thunder, and Nestor felt compelled to obey. Both Robbie and Thomas were swept off their feet and thrown back into the wall away from Vera. Nestor knew this voice and had tasted the steel of this being's blade before. His deformed hand bore the scars of that encounter. But again, it was not Michael's time. He shouldn't even be able to be in this place.

"Why are you here, Michael? Have you come to watch? For even you must know that in my realm, I ams all-powerful. This is not the time of judgment and, as such, you have no claim here."

<< >>

The light around Ezekiel died down, and he was now visible to all. The voices in the room began whispering again, this time loud enough to be understood. "The foretold one—he lives!"

Vera's heart was racing at the sight of him. The last time she had seen him, he was on the ground in the alley, bleeding out, after Robbie had stabbed him. How was he here now? How was he not dead? Robbie, who was now getting back up on his feet, was thinking the same thing. He knew this couldn't be true, and yet here was Ezekiel, in living color.

"The foretold one," Nestor said. "I heard tells you were dead. Apparently, that was not the case." He glared at Robbie. "So whats brings you to this place, 'foretold one'?"

He sarcastically made air quotation marks with his elongated fingers as he spoke.

"Comes closer so I can sees you."

Ezekiel felt strangely compelled to do what he said. As he approached, Nestor's stench became unbearable. His face grimaced with each breath. He could no longer stomach it and stopped. Much to Nestor's surprise, the stench had apparently lifted him out of his fog, and he was no longer compelled to obey. No mortal had ever been able to resist his command or deny him a request. For that matter, Nestor wondered how he had made it up the stairway . . . or even opened the door. This was a supernatural place that had been blessed by his lord's promise and set just out of phase of human reality and perception. "How is this?" he said to himself with a hazy, raspy, hissing voice? This couldn't possibly be the same boy from so many days ago in the building lobby—the one who had cut him across the cheek. He seemed quite changed. And Robbie and Thomas had sworn he was dead. So how could this be?

Then the demons around the room began whispering his name, causing an echolike effect: "Ezzzzzekiel, EEEEEEzekielllll, Ezekiellllll."

"I've come for the girl, and I've come to put an end to you," said Ezekiel confidently.

Nestor looked him up and down. He looked at Vera and then back at him.

"You're God touched; I didn't notice it before. How odd. On any other day, this might haves given me pause, but tonight is the night of the blood moons, which means you chose the wrong time to challenge me, 'foretold one.' Oh, I'm sorry, I meant Ezekiel."

Again, he made air quotes as he spoke and laughed as he did.

"Well, I don't thinks I'lls be letting her goes, but I'lls tells you what I will do though, before I kills you. I'lls lets you lives just long enough to see me takes this girl's life, body and soul. Then I'lls peels the flesh off of your priest over there, and finally, after I'ves had my fun with you, I

will kills you too, and you will welcome it," Nestor said with a smile, drool falling from his mouth as he spoke.

Ezekiel, seemingly unphased by Nestor's threats, addressed him again. "I won't ask you again, Nestor, give me the girl."

At that, Robbie and Thomas both made their way over to Vera and started to undo her restraints, as if in a trance. Nestor immediately struck them down, sending them both back into the wall.

"Weak-minded fools. My orders are the only ones you should heeds, less I be done with you both and releases you from your pitiful lives."

Then he turned around furiously and faced Ezekiel.

"This is my place, and in it, I am everything here. Whoever you think you are or—"

His speech was cut short with a shotgun blast to the head followed by two more to the body and another to the face. Nestor fell over, holding his riddled face. Skin was hanging from his cheekbone, and most of his jawbone was now exposed. He tried to say something but instead spit out a few teeth and shotgun pellets. Ezekiel turned to look over at Father Connors, who was smiling and reloading his still smoking gun. As he pumped the fore-end back on the magazine, readying his weapon, he looked up at Ezekiel, still smiling, and said, "Hey, you never know until you try, right? Besides, he talks too much."

Nestor was still struggling to pull his face back together. He was beyond angry and more than a bit confused. This was an earthly weapon, and yet it had hurt him. How? He didn't care; all he wanted now was the priest. His jaw finally managed to rehinge itself, and he pointed at Father Connors. **"Take him."** One after the other, a stream of demons poured out from all over the room, covering Father Connors like a blanket, while others grabbed hold of him, holding him down. He did manage to get a few rounds off, taking down a few more of them before they were able to hold him down. For a moment, he looked like a living shadow the way they all covered his body. One by one, they began to enter him. Father Connors's was snatched up into the air, feet kicking and arms flailing about. He could smell and taste the foul breath of the things that had him, which caused him to gag and throw up. His entire body felt as if he were on fire. It seemed like hundreds of voices were screaming in his ears. He felt them pushing themselves inside of him one by one. He had lost control of himself, and his body no longer responded to his commands. It was as if he was outside of himself. He opened his mouth to scream, but no words escaped his lips. He felt like he was stuck in a nightmare in which he was falling down a hole or on a descending roller-coaster with no turns. It just kept going down. His heart felt like it might explode as he struggled to regain control of himself.

Ezekiel heard hundreds of evil voices saying, "He's ours now, and soon you will be ours as well." He watched, horrified, as Father Connors's body twisted into some hideous reflection of what he had once been. He could hear bones popping as his body stretched and swelled, trying to accommodate the new entities within him. Visible rips and tears began to appear on his face and hands as he hovered above him. He realized that there would be no coming back from this. The damage to the priest's body was too severe. This was why the vampire had asked him what he would do if it were him. He was overwhelmed with rage; it washed over him in waves, causing goose-bumps to pop up on his forearms. They had been chasing him for most of his life, constantly attacking and plaguing him at every opportunity, and now they had stolen his friend and made him one of them. He'd had enough. He was tired of always being a minute late and a dollar short. He was tired of keeping a low profile and not being able to make friends. They wanted a fight; well now they had one.

Nothing would leave this place tonight.

They would pay for what they had done to Father Connors, and they would pay for what they had done to him as well.

Thou wilt keep him in perfect peace, whose mind is
stayed on thee: because he trusteth in thee. Trust ye
in the LORD *for ever: for in the* LORD JEHOVAH *is*
everlasting strength:

—ISAIAH 26:3–4

CHAPTER FORTY-NINE

Full Circle

Nestor smiled even more broadly now, revealing
hundreds of hideous brown stained teeth all jammed
into an oversized mouth. Then he was gone.

FATHER CONNORS COULD FEEL THE DEMONS INSIDE HIM TRYING
to get into his mind. They had his body, and his mind was all that
remained to take over. Then they would have his soul. He couldn't—
no, he wouldn't let that happen. The question was how. This feeling
was so surreal. He could see and hear everything that was going on
around him, and he could feel everything too, much to his dismay.
The pain from the changes his body was going through was excru-
ciating. He felt himself slipping away a few times, and a voice in his
head would say *Hold on, Father, hold on.* And somehow, he did. But

only his mind and soul were his; his body was theirs. He could hear them inside his head—so many voices, all saying the same thing repeatedly: "Let us in, Father, let us in."

He had formed a bubble around himself in his mind's eye, and he could see them all around him, pushing at the walls and trying to get in. He closed his eyes and began praying. It was all he could do; it was his last vestige of strength. He asked God to forgive him his sins, and for his weaknesses that had allowed him to be taken. And then suddenly, the demon was there in his head with him: Nestor. His eyes were piercing. It seemed like he was looking directly at him within his mind, but he didn't understand this; it was like he was just standing there outside of the bubble he had erected to protect his mind and soul. He was almost invisible in the dimly lit room within his mind's eye—very thin and freakishly tall. His face was long and pointy. But it was his eyes that scared him the most. The pupils were red, and everything else was black. Even with all the demons around him, he could still feel the evilness of his aura pushing through.

"How longs do you thinks you wills be ables to keeps me out, Father? An hour, a half, or maybe just longs enough for your partner to find a way to saves you. I suppose it's possible but highly unlikely. You see Father; you're not special likes Ezekiels, even though he turned out to be a bit underwhelming in persons considering the reputation preceding him. If Robbies over there was ables to get the drops on him, what chance does he haves against me? Even this girl has a gift that I will soon discern and make mine. But you, Fathers, you're just a regular mans—oh, I'm sorry, no you're not. You're less than that; you're a priest who up until very recently was lost. A man of the faith who had lost it, and then found it again. How ironic that circumstances haves brought you heres, to me.

"No, Father, I don't think he'll be ables to saves you this times. I don't think he'll even be able to saves himself at this point. Even now I can see the terror in his face as he witnessed your transformations. It's just a matter of time before he's mines too, as it is with all things, and time is something I haves in abundance."

He smiled his hideous smile and winked at him sarcastically.

"Excuse me, Father, but it seems I have a small matter to attend to. But not to worry, I'lls be back for you in a moment. So make your peace with your God, Father, whiles you cans; this shouldn't takes more than a minute or two."

Nestor smiled even more broadly now, revealing hundreds of hideous brown stained teeth all jammed into an oversized mouth. Then he was gone from his mind. He had turned his attention back to Ezekiel for the moment. Father Connors had never felt anything as evil as this demon before. It was all he could do just to keep from turning away from him. That thing was intent on not just killing him but taking his soul too. He prayed that God would give Ezekiel the strength needed to kill him, or he knew that all was lost.

"So, here you are—finally," Nestor said. "You're him. The angel slayer. I've heard much about you. It is even said that you spoke to the seven judgments and lived to speak of it. Something not even I would welcomes on myself, and yet heres you stand. You must be a half-breed, which would make yous as much of an abomination as I am in his eyes. You should be fighting alongside me rather than against me. You do know you can't wins, right?"

Ezekiel was completely taken aback by these words—angel slayer and half-breed. "Liar! You must think me a fool. You know as well as—"

But before he could finish his sentence, Nestor had crossed the length of the floor in an instant. He grabbed Ezekiel by both wrists and glared at him.

"Makes no mistake, boy, you are an angel killer. A demon is just an angel who has fallen, and for every ones you've slain, somewheres an angel has shed a tear."

"I doubt it. No true angel has ever fallen, and I know you're not trying to compare yourself or any who serve you as such."

Nestor was astonished. He couldn't understand how it was that this man was still awake, even as he was in his grasp, especially in this place. This was his realm. He finally said, "Who are you, boy?"

It was a rhetorical question, but Ezekiel started to answer anyway. However, before he could speak, Nestor opened his enormous mouth, exposing what now seemed like thousands of teeth, and bit him on the neck. His teeth cut deep, passing through flesh and down to the bone. Blood poured freely from his neck and down across his back and chest. He could feel his body being poisoned. But stranger than that, this bite and touch was actually familiar to him. Ezekiel realized that he had crossed paths with Nestor before, in a dream, when he was just a boy. That homeless man he had tried to help in the alley so many years ago turned out to be a demon in waiting. It was him. And he was trying to do the same thing to him now that he did then, only this time it was no dream.

The taste of Ezekiel's blood intoxicated Nestor. His soul was intrinsic, pure, and clean. He had tasted nothing like it before in all his infinite years. He knew this boy. He had come to him many years ago but he somehow escaped, and now fate had delivered him to him once again. But then he made another startling realization. He knew this boy's mother. There was no mistaking it. This was the child of the woman he had raped and would have killed had it not been for the intervention of Michael.

That makes two times that this boy has evaded me, but not now. I have him now. This thought excited Nestor deeply, and he found himself aroused. How fitting it would be to rape the boy of the mother he had raped so long ago. The thought of that alone was so overwhelming that he gagged a bit on his blood.

Ezekiel, still linked to Nestor's mind, knew his thoughts and intentions. But they didn't bother him as much as learning that this thing had violated his mother while she was carrying him inside her womb. A rage began to rise from within him. He started pleading the blood, and as he did, he could feel his body begin purging the poison from inside of him and his strength returning. He began shouting out, "The Blood of Jesus is against you! The Blood of Jesus is against you!" Each time he chanted this phrase, he regained a little strength.

Finally, he had enough strength to break free of Nestor's hold on him and grab his wrist. There was a loud crackling sound, akin to that of meat being dropped into a vat of oil. Nestor cried out, releasing his bite on Ezekiel as he did. Ezekiel instinctively head-butted the demon, breaking a few of Nestor's teeth and causing him to take a few steps backward.

Nestor was momentarily stunned again. That made twice in one night. No one else, save Michael, had managed to hurt him in the thousands of years he'd been alive. But he was an Archangel; this boy was human. His wounds were mortal, and yet he had broken free of him. He looked down; his wrist was raw and blistered. *How has he managed this?* he thought, enraged.

Ezekiel was still very weak; he had lost a great deal of blood. The bite on his neck was extraordinarily painful, and streams of smoke escaped from the puncture wounds where he had been bitten. A brownish substance that looked like blood bubbled up through the puncture wounds, making a hissing sound as it burned away on his skin. He looked over to the table where Vera was tied up and gagged, then back at Nestor. He thought, *If I can just get to her, I know together we'll be able to beat him.* But he knew that would be extremely difficult. He tried to take a step forward but found it was almost impossible to move. He realized that all the demons from downstairs were now in the room. They had joined together and were trying to restrain him until their master could regain his composure. "The Blood of Jesus; the Blood of Jesus," he kept pleading repeatedly until the demons around him cried out in agony and burst into flames. Even Nestor, who seemed to have recovered somewhat from his head-butt, was smoking and sparking at this point. Ezekiel ran toward Vera just as Nestor lunged toward her. They both reached her at the same time, on either side of the table. Nestor went to grab her neck with his right hand, with the intent of breaking it and ending her life. He knew that whatever power she had would be his. But Ezekiel caught his hand just as it reached her chin. His touch sickened her, and she twisted her head back and forth trying to keep from being touched. Nestor cried out again in pain from Ezekiel's touch. His hand began sizzling and crackling and finally simply burst into flames. The smell of rotten flesh burning assaulted his nostrils, but Ezekiel would not release his grip. He was unaffected by the flames. If anything, they seemed to be purifying him and making him stronger. Nestor drove his left hand deep into Ezekiel's chest with his long sharp fingers, hoping they would reach his heart. This time it was Ezekiel who cried out in pain as he grabbed onto Nestor's wrist. Although his left wrist was burning now, he continued to smile that horrible, oversized smile of his.

"I can takes the heat, boy, and I'm no strangers to pain; can you says the sames?" he said, laughing. "After I'm done with yous, the things I'm going to do to your little girlfriend wills makes her longs for death, but it wills not comes. She wills be with me for eternity—or untils I tire of her, whichever comes first—but you'll be long gone by then. Long gone!" he bellowed.

Vera gave a muffled roar through her gag while shaking her head back and forth. Tears were falling from her eyes as she watched helplessly on the table. Her fate was in the hands of someone she had only known for a few months. She started calling out for Jesus over and over, but her words were muffled by the gag. All she wanted was for God to hear her voice as she was now, before this evil thing could defile her and remove her from his sight.

New demons were beginning to appear in the room. It was almost as if they could sense that this battle had gone as far as it could go. They jumped on Ezekiel's back and began pulling at his arms and legs, biting and digging their talons into his flesh. "Father God, help me," he said. His voice was almost a whisper, but it was heard. "Let go of his hand and remove the gag from her face," was what he heard in response inside his head. But Ezekiel thought if he let go of Nestor's hand, he might reach his heart, and then they would both be dead. He guessed that this must be a trick—one of the demons whispering in his ear.

Then the voice spoke again. "Trust in me as I do in you, let go of his hand and remove the gag from her face, and you will know your Father's mercy."

Ezekiel looked down at Vera, who was kicking and thrashing about on the table, and back at Nestor, with his evil grin. He grabbed

Nestor's right hand with both of his. Nestor's left hand slid a little deeper into his chest, trying to reach his heart. It seemed like the demon's arm weighed a ton; he could barely hold on. "Jesus, give me the strength to do this last thing, help me save this girl," Ezekiel pleaded. Very slowly, he managed to pull Nestor's hand away from Vera's face as the pain in his chest grew deeper within him.

Nestor's ever-growing fingers finally reached his heart, and he threw back his head and began cackling as he squeezed.

"Last chance, boy. Let go, and I might let her live!"

The pain was like nothing he had ever dreamed possible, and he could feel his consciousness slipping away. He wanted the pain to stop so badly that for a moment, he thought about agreeing, and at that moment, all eyes in heaven focused on him, literally hanging on his next word. Nestor could tell that he was done, and he smiled, for soon he would be feasting on this boy's soul, and it would be like spitting in the eyes of God himself. This was almost too good to be true.

"OK, I'll do it," he said, and there was a silence in heaven and earth alike. All who could hear were shocked, believing that Ezekiel had agreed to the unthinkable. Then he said, "I trust you, Lord," and he let go of Nestor's hand.

Nestor looked down and saw that the little boy, Hector, had somehow managed to get to Vera, and his hands were on her gag. His eyes bulged and he shouted "Nooooooooo!" but it was too late. Hector pulled the gag from her mouth, and she screamed "JESUSSSSSS!" Her voice was akin to an explosion, full of energy and power that could be seen and felt. The initial word caused Nestor to release his grip on Ezekiel's heart and recoil backward. She yelled out again, "JESUSSSSS!" and all around the room fires began to explode into life. Nestor's whole body burst into flames, and he began squealing like a pig as he tried to find a dark corner or shadow that he could fade away into. She called out Jesus's name again and again. Her voice shook the very foundation of the building. The room lit up and began to glow. No shadows could be found for Nestor to slither into or hide behind. Shock wave after shock wave rattled the building as the melodious thunder that was her voice wreaked havoc in that most unholy place.

All the demons in the structure had long since exploded into flames and perished; it was just Nestor now, and he was not faring well. Without anywhere to hide, he was on his own. He had to silence that bitch before she called down the very heavens upon him. It wasn't until that moment that he truly realized just how powerful a tool she was in God's plan: the voice of God in a mortal. He figured that explained how she could pull him out of his human host and sense his presence, no matter what form he took.

Incredibly, Ezekiel appeared to be fully recovered. In fact, each time Vera spoke, his body seemed to radiate with energy. To Nestor, it almost appeared as if he was feeding off her. Then it dawned on him: they were the "New Kings" on earth to be. The new Adam and Eve, as it were, and the spiritual evolution of man…right under his nose all this time.

Nestor was trying to regain his position as the aggressor, but he was finding it hard just to keep from being knocked off his feet. He reasoned that however it came to be that these two had ascended to this level, they were still but mortal, and as such, they could not possibly possess what was necessary to stop him. After all, he thought, *I transcend time itself, I've fought and killed angels, I was here at man's birth, and I will be here when his time has reached an end. I am outside of any laws of man and will not be bound by truces not authored by God himself. I will not be backed into a corner by the likes of a mere mortal.*

His body began to grow, and his skin cracked and peeled away. It was as if light was ripping itself free from his body and stripping away his flesh as it did. Then an image began to take form and emerge from the cocoon of light. It was unlike anything Ezekiel had ever seen: a huge winged figure, completely devoid of light and growing steadily.

As it lifted its head, Ezekiel could see that while the body had changed, the eyes were the same. Nestor stood up tall, nearly doubled in size and now adorned with huge feathered batlike wings, which he outstretched to mimic his ridiculous smile but also to show Ezekiel the hopelessness of his situation. There were clawlike hands at the mid-joints in the wings, not unlike that of a pterodactyl, but these hands were much more functional. The wings swung forward, stirring up all the dirt and dust in the room and making it impossible for Ezekiel to see much of anything. He was squinting and had his hands up, covering his eyes. Then there was a sharp stinging sensation across his back and arms. He could feel warm wetness flowing from other areas as well, and then, "Whoosh!" fresh stings and more blood followed. This happened over and over, until Ezekiel fell to one knee. He glimpsed what had beaten him to the ground. It was the huge wings. Each feather was like a blade, and every time Nestor flapped them, he was being cut. Then he heard Vera cry out, and he knew that she was being cut too. Nestor wanted to silence her. He felt she was the source of Ezekiel's strength and the reason he was forced to reveal his true self, a form that, until this day, no man had ever seen before, and would never be seen again. He swung his wings down toward the table with the intent of decapitating her and shutting her up. He would devour her soul and her power in one blow. But when he struck the table, it simply shattered; the wings found no body to claim. Nestor stopped waving his wings and folded them behind his back. The unnatural dust and debris settled down and, to his astonishment, he saw that Vera was in Ezekiel's arms.

"Nothing can move that fast. How did you get to her, boy? HOWWWW?" he roared.

Ezekiel didn't answer; it was better to have him upset and guessing. They were still connected, even after his transformation. As soon as he had seen what Nestor was planning to do, he had made his way over to the table and freed her, unseen because of all the dust Nestor had stirred up. His wings had cut her up pretty badly, and she wasn't healing as quickly as he was, if at all. Each gift was unique for each person, he knew, and the thought of losing her after all he had gone through to find and save her was just too much to bear.

"Can you stand?" he whispered in her ear. She nodded. He put her down in the far corner of the room, out of Nestor's reach for the moment.

"Stay here and wait for me," he said, and she held onto him a moment longer and kissed him on the lips.

"You can do this; just continue to trust and believe in God, and in yourself as he does. It's the only way, and you are the only one who can do this."

Ezekiel looked at her and smiled. He said, "Wait here," and turned to face Nestor, who looked even bigger than he had been a few moments ago.

For you will not abandon my soul to Hades, or let
your Holy One see corruption.

—ACTS 2:27 (ESV)

CHAPTER FIFTY

Transcendence

Black wings crisscrossed back and forth around
Ezekiel, separating flesh from bone.

"Let's end this, boy, I grow weary of this game. You and the girl have provens to be quite the surprise, but in this game, there can only be one winner. I'lls ask you one last times, join me and I will spares you and the girl, or don't, and I'lls eat her in fronts of you, just before I takes your soul."

"Really, after all this, we just let bygones be bygones and go our separate ways off into the sunset?" A half-smile made its way across Ezekiel's face and he let out a little laugh. "Nestor, I wouldn't give you five cents to get cheese on a whopper, much less consider anything that comes from your mouth."

"Then die."

Black wings crisscrossed back and forth around Ezekiel, separating flesh from bone. The two tips of the wings pierced both of his shoulders, pinning him to the wall.

Nestor cackled like a hyena, wild-eyed as saliva spilled from his mouth.

"I gots you now, boy. I gots you."

His voice had changed back to its normal condescending tone, which meant he no longer considered Ezekiel a threat. He produced a long silver sword. It almost seemed to glow and, to Ezekiel, it looked strange in Nestor's hands, because it almost seemed to represent purity.

"This is all that I have of my former self, boy. And now I'm going to share it with you."

Ezekiel noticed that Vera and Hector had backed themselves into an open closet in the room. Vera was trying to cover and hide Hector with her body to protect him from Nestor's wings. Nestor followed Ezekiel's glance to where they were trying to hide and saw his concern. No, not concern, *fear* for them. He feared what would happen to them if he failed, and that fear made him weak.

"I see your fear, boy. You stink with it, and you should, because I am going to make them suffer."

Then Nestor began laughing as he drew back his sword. Ezekiel tried to pull himself free, but Nestor had him pinned securely. He would need more time than he had to break free of his grip. Nestor thrust his sword forward for the finishing blow. Ezekiel, unable to move, could do nothing to evade the silver death drawing down on him. He closed his eyes and whispered a silent prayer: "Keep them safe, Lord, and receive my soul. Amen." The sword cut through flesh and into the wall behind Ezekiel, but to his surprise, it was Father Connors who had been pierced by the blade. It felt as if time had slowed down around them, like the time when he had spoken with the seven judgments in front of the church. Everything in the room was in a state of suspended animation except for him and Father Connors.

The priest spoke. "It was the only thing I could think to do. Something happened to me when Vera started shouting earlier and I regained some control of my body. A voice inside my head told me you were going to need me and to go to you. I was able to make it over to you just in time. The voice also told me to tell you that He is keeping them safe, and that's why he sent you." Then he reached into his pocket and pulled out the item Ezekiel had put there just before they entered the house. He placed it in Ezekiel's hand. "Remember, you can do anything through faith if you believe. You taught me that."

He smiled at Ezekiel, lowered his head, and slipped away. Ezekiel saw his soul leave his body and ascend toward the heavens. It appeared that he was the only one who was aware of this or able to perceive it at that moment. He looked at his hand and saw the mustard seeds he had given him earlier. Then he looked back at Father Connors and said, "You rest now, I've got it from here."

Then time returned to normal. It shocked Nestor to see that he had run the priest through instead of Ezekiel. He was not pleased.

"He just delayed the inevitable!" he shouted as he pulled back his sword and prepared to strike again.

Father Connors's body fell to the floor as the blade released him from the wall. Then Nestor thrust it forward once again with murderous intent. But somehow, Ezekiel caught the blade with his hand and was able to stop it. Nestor tried and failed to pull it free from his grasp. Then he snapped the blade and used the broken piece to cut off the wingtips that had him pinned to the wall. Nestor fell back, astonished. It was not possible. He should not have been able to snap that blade. It was just not possible. Vera, overwhelmed with elation as she witnessed Ezekiel break free of Nestor's grip, shouted out, "Thank you, Jesus!"

Her voice was pure energy. It went through Nestor, back to the other end of the room, and flowed into Ezekiel like water in a stream. *There's power in his name.* She had heard this said before but had thought it was just a figure of speech. She'd never actually realized that it was literal. She shouted out again, "Jesus!" and her voice was like a beam of living energy that was absorbed directly into Ezekiel's body. He unsheathed his own blade from his hip and pulled it out. It was glowing and began to transform from a dagger into a sword. It resembled the one Nestor had, but it was much more elaborate in its design. There was some angelic script down the center of the blade that read, *"Behold, the finger of God, Woe unto he who is its intended."*

Nestor recognized the blade instantly. It belonged to Michael. It had destroyed cities and conquered armies. It was the weapon of an Archangel, here in the hands of a mortal boy. Again, this was something that was simply not possible. Vera was now speaking in tongues, and amazingly, so was Hector. The spirit of the Lord filled them and could be felt all around them, even in this unholiest of places. A quote from the book of Acts came to Ezekiel as he witnessed this. "For you will not abandon my soul to Hades, or let your Holy One see corruption."

He then turned to face Nestor, who was struggling to get to his feet. The demon swung his wings with their deadly feathers at Ezekiel's neck, hoping to separate his head from his shoulders, but Ezekiel, now fully restored, easily evaded them and brought his sword up to counter Nestor's attack. As he did, the energy from the sword cut through the entire side of the building in all of its realms, taking Nestor's right wing in the process. He screamed out in pain and disbelief.

"Can you hear them, Nestor, the prayers of all the believers? That's having faith in something bigger than yourself. To be willing to lay down your life because you know that what waits for you on the other side is the glory of the kingdom of God. No, I do not think a being such as yourself can see anything beyond your own selfish desires. Well, tonight all of us who have ever suffered at your hands are going to bring this chapter of your misbegotten life to a close. Tonight, you die. Now, tell me, Nestor, when I take your life as the so-called angel slayer, will any angels shed a tear for you, or will you just be another dead demon that I sent to Sheol?"

Nestor, now back on his feet, dashed forward at a speed that could not be tracked by the human eye. He managed to get behind Ezekiel and grabbed him by the shoulder with his three-fingered hand. His intention was simple: to rip him in half, but Ezekiel moved almost as quickly as he did. Once again, the blade cut through all realms connected to the house, along with Nestor's right arm. The demon dropped to his knees, holding his shoulder where his arm used to be. Black blood oozed through his fingers as he stared at Ezekiel, befuddled, wondering how this could have happened. Then Ezekiel ran him through with his blade, and he fell over onto the floor.

The building's structural integrity had never been much to speak of, but with Nestor down, it seemed that his entire realm was coming apart. The ceiling began to fall, and the floor shifted like waves under their feet. The cracks in the ceiling and fallen debris let light into the room, causing shadows to form. Ezekiel rushed back to the closet and got Vera and Hector, and then they all hurried to the, door, rushed down the stairs, and spilled out the front door. Ezekiel very nearly carried both of them the whole way.

Then he shook his head and swore. "Father Connors. I have to go back for his body. I can't leave him in there, in that place."

Vera didn't want him to go back in, but she knew this was something he had to do.

"Get him and bring him home," was all she could say.

He kissed her on the forehead and was gone before she could open her eyes. He got to the top floor and saw Father Connors's body lying on the floor. He picked him up and started toward the door. Then he stopped just short of the doorway. Where was Nestor? He only saw an arm, but where was his body? It should have been right by the wall as it was before. He walked over, thinking maybe his body had fallen through the floor into a different room below him. But before he could go check, Robbie sprung forward from the shadows in the room, startling him, something he must have picked up from Nestor. He had completely forgotten about Robbie.

Robbie charged at Ezekiel, screaming obscenities and holding the broken piece of Nestor's sword. "You stole her from me! Everything was fine before you showed up. She will never be yours; I'll kill you first before I let that happen!"

Even while holding Father Connors's body amid the falling debris in the room, Ezekiel easily avoided Robbie's attack.

"I don't have time for this, Robbie. This place is coming down all around us. If we don't get out of here now, we'll both end up dead."

Then Thomas appeared from a shadow behind Ezekiel holding a syringe. He had hoped to go unnoticed as Ezekiel fended off Robbie's attack while dodging the fallen debris. But Ezekiel had anticipated that, and he grabbed Thomas by the neck and tossed him over onto Robbie. They both fell back onto the floor just as the rest of the ceiling collapsed, covering them. There was no more time to lose. Ezekiel had to hurry if he was going to make it out alive. Everything was falling apart all around him. He descended the stairs more quickly than he had thought possible, and the entire building came down just seconds after he made it out the front door with the priest's body. Vera and Hector were waiting for him across the street, holding hands. He walked over to them and gently placed Father Connors's body on the ground. Then he hugged both of them tightly. Suddenly, a loud bellowing sound cracked the sky open, and a tornado dropped through the crack and began descending toward them.

Happy is he who reads aloud and those who hear the words of this prophecy and who observe the things written in it for the appointed time is near.

—REVELATION 1:3 (NWT)

EPILOGUE

Tribulation Song

Behold, the day of revelations is now upon mankind, and soon the seven judgments shall be poured out upon the earth.

A GREAT HORN BLEW, AND THUNDER AND LIGHTNING CRACKED the sky. They watched as it grew dark all around them. Vera, still holding on to Ezekiel's and Hector's hands, looked on in awe as a cloud formed in the sky and began spiraling down toward them like a tornado, ripping into the earth and devouring everything in its path. The ground was shaking beneath their feet, and the wind picked up speed and strength as the whirlwind cloud stopped, ripping up the ground in front of them. If she had not been holding onto Ezekiel, she might very well have been swept up by the wind and into the spinning cloud. Ezekiel, however, was ever steady. She couldn't be sure, but it was as if he had transcended, or evolved into, something more than human. She had always felt that he was, but now it was so much more evident. The horn blew again, and the sound was deafening as lightning cracked the sky once more. A figure took form within the cloud, and as it did, the air seemed to get thicker and harder to breathe. A grand angel appeared holding a golden horn in one hand and a long silver sword with a golden hilt in the other. His wings moved ever so slightly back and forth, which allowed him to hover, keeping his feet from touching the ground. The wings also seemed to be the source of all the wind.

"Come forth so that I might look upon you better, young one, for you are truly deserving of my gaze."

His voice was like living energy, much like Vera's. It washed over Ezekiel and almost seemed to lift him off the ground. It was physically warm and almost deafening, but not hurtful to the ear, and when he spoke, no other sound could be heard except his voice.

"I am Gabriel, and I have blown the great horn so that all will know the appointed time has finally come. Woe unto all who have walked by the water but not gotten wet, for the sea of tears is now dry, and all who try to fill their bowls will know thirst. But not you, Ezekiel, you have done well, and I, like Joshua, always believed that your path would lead you here. Behold, the day of revelations is now upon mankind, and soon the seven judgments shall be poured out upon the earth. There is still much to do in the coming days, and your journey has only just begun. You have mortally injured the dark one, but I fear he may still live, and if so, your paths may yet cross again. The outcome of that encounter is yet unclear to me. If this is true, it will not be as easy to defeat Nestor when next you meet. Also, there are others like him that will come for you when they learn of what happened here.

I do not know how this can be, but a part of Joshua lives within you now, along with Michael. All that is good with them is now in you, along with their power. You are in a place where no man has been. I pray it does not overwhelm thee."

Ezekiel, confused and unsure of exactly what Gabriel was trying to say, dropped to his knees, still holding Vera's hand, and addressed him directly.

"Gabriel, I have many questions I would ask of you. Please speak plainly so that I might understand what you're trying to tell me and what I need to do."

"All praise to God that one such as you, newly blessed and endowed with the power of a god, still humbles himself when seeking guidance. Rise, young one, for we are brothers, you and I. Though you are mortal, you now have all the attributes and power of an angel. You are a prince in the spirit, a beacon of hope for humanity, as well as signs of things to come for the fallen. All praises to God, for only he could have truly seen how wonderful you could be. Man still mystifies me, but alas, none save you have reached this point. Hold fast to the female with you now, for she is your mate, chosen by he who is most high. In the coming days of tribulation, there will be many who will test you, who will test your faith. Do not let them deceive you; do not let them break you. Your strength comes from your faith, and with it, you can do wonderful things. I must go now, but I will never be far from you. Should you need me, call, and if it is possible, I will come."

He sounded the great horn again and cracked the very heavens above. The sky turned red, and the ground began to shake and shift beneath their feet.

"It begins, Ezekiel. Soon the father shall be with us, and all shall know his mercy. We shall all be weighed and measured on the blessed day of atonement. Until that time, it will be on you to go forth and find the Twelve. They, too, are like you, but they are unawakened as yet. They will need someone to lead them into the light and protect them from the dark ones, and there is none more suited to the task than you."

He placed his hand on Ezekiel's forehead, and flashes of people and places etched themselves into his mind's eye. They were the ones he spoke of: *the Twelve.*

"There, young one. I have given you what you need to find them. Now I must take my leave of you. Go and find shelter, for now is the time of the Horse Men, and they give no quarter."

Gabriel ascended and disappeared into the clouds. As he did, the mini-tornado dissipated. The air was a little easier to breathe, but the sky was still dark, and the ground was still shaking, but not as much as it had been a moment ago. Vera, finally able to stand without needing Ezekiel's support, still found it hard to let go of his hand. She felt like it was meant to be there, and she never wanted to let go. Somehow, through all of this, she had fallen in love with him. She guessed she knew it all along, but she had never played into it. Ezekiel felt the same way. Even if Gabriel had said nothing about her being his mate, he still would have known. She was one of the few things that he had always been sure of, and whatever challenges the Tribulations song would have them face, he knew that they would face them together.

CPSIA information can be obtained
at www.ICGtesting.com
Printed in the USA
BVHW041337080322
630895BV00014B/739